DATE DUE

DEMCO 38-296

ECCO
Travels

PROVENCE

PROVENCE

FROM MINSTRELS TO
THE MACHINE

BY

FORD MADOX FORD

ILLUSTRATIONS BY BIALA

THE ECCO PRESS

Published in 1979 by The Ecco Press
100 West Broad Street, Hopewell, NJ 08525
Published simultaneously in Canada by
Penguin Books Canada Limited
Printed in the United States of America

Fourth printing, 1991

LIBRARY OF CONGRESS CATALOGING-IN-PUBLICATION DATA
Ford, Ford Madox, 1873-1939.
Provence, from minstrels to the machine / by Ford Madox Ford;
p.   cm. — (Ecco travels)
Reprint. Previously published: New York; Ecco Press, 1979.
Includes index.
1. Provence (France)—Description and travel.
I. Title.   II. Series.
DC611.P958F55   1991
944'.9—dc20   91-3692 CIP
ISBN 0-88001-316-8

TO
CAROLINE GORDON
WHO CHRONICLES ANOTHER SOUTH
AND TO
ALLEN TATE
WHO CAME TO PROVENCE AND
THERE WROTE TO "THAT SWEET
LAND" THE POEM CALLED
"THE MEDITERRANEAN" AND
WHERE WE WENT IN THE BOAT
WAS A LONG BAY

F. M. F. AND B.

CONTENTS

PART I

THE GREAT TRADE ROUTES

PART II

PROVENCE SEEN FROM THE NORTH

CONTENTS

PART III

MISE A MORT

ILLUSTRATIONS

ILLUSTRATIONS

Part One

THE GREAT TRADE ROUTES

Avenue at Tarascon

CHAPTER I

ON THE LATEST ROUTE

THIS is to be a book of travel and moralising—on the Great Trade Route which, thousands of years before our day, ran from Cathay to the Cassiterides. Along the Mediterranean shores it went and up through Provence. It bore civilisation backwards and forwards along its tides. . . . And this may turn out to be in part a book of prophecies—as to what may and mayn't happen to us according as we re-adopt, or go ever farther from, the frame of mind that is Provence and the civilising influences that were carried backwards and forwards in those days.

I have told somewhere else the story of the honest merchant who came to Tarascon which is at the heart of Provence on the Greatest of all the Routes—driven there by an elephant. But the book in which I told that story is long out of print and I do not think it is to treat a reader dishonestly if one repeats in a new book some story or piece of morality that is contained in an old and unobtainable work by the author.

For if the reader wants to read that piece he must buy this book—or obtain it from his library—since he cannot get the other without going to more trouble than any sane or normal person would take over a mere book. If on the other hand he should buy this one whilst already possessing the other, one may, as an honest vendor, assume either that he is so mad as not to be considered or that he so likes the writer that he will pardon in him the very slight dishonesty of obtaining—for a new book should be new all through—the fraction of cent or penny that will be represented by that repetition. . . . I indulge in that speculation to show that considerations of commercial morality are not completely alien to this writer. . . . I may or may not repeat the story of the elephant: if I do I shall now consider the repetition to be justified.

Long ago, then, I was sitting in the Café de Paris which is the most fashionable café in the city of the Good King René and of St Martha. That is not to say that it is very fashionable but that it is the resort of the ex-officers of the famous but disbanded Fourth Lancers, the officers of the brown-skinned, scarlet-fezzed troops that now occupy the casernes of the regiment of Ney, of the notaire, the avoué, the avocat, the justice of the peace, of the ex-picture dealer who still possesses Gauguins and Van Goghs that he bought from those artists when they were in Arles at twenty francs a time; and the honest—and indeed never to be sufficiently belauded—merchant who still prints and purveys beautiful bandannas. They have been made in Tarascon for hundreds of years and still shine in and beautify, not only the darkest forests of darkest Africa, but the brightest suns of the most coralline of far Eastern strands. Officers, lawyers, judges, honest merchants, professors, surgeons, land-owners . . . twice a day all that Tarascon has of the professional and not too newly-wedded classes meets under those awnings, basks beneath the shade of the planes or shivers beneath the blasts of the immense, life-giving and iced *mistral.*

And, careful as this writer is of commercial morality he is not less careful of the company that he keeps, for twice a year, twice a day, he will be found amongst those impeccables taking his *vermouth-cassis* before lunch and before dinner his *mandarin-citron.* Twice a year, twice a day for five or six days at a time. For wherever I may be going in the round-and-round of the great beaten track, begin it where you will, stepping on the eternal merry-go-round at the Place de la Concorde, the

Promenade des Anglais, Fifth Avenue or Piccadilly—wherever I may be going on that latest of the Greatest Trade Routes I contrive to fetch up both going and coming for my four or five days in the little city that looks across the Rhone at Beaucaire. Beautiful Beaucaire of the ivorine castle of Nicolette "au clair visage," whose feet were so white that they made the very daisies look dim!

Beaucaire from across the Rhone

I am bound to say that Beaucaire, one of the stations of the great pre-historic Trade Route that ran from Cathay up the Rhone to the Cassiterides and then sighed for more worlds to conquer. . . . Beaucaire that still has her fair that has existed every year on the old merchants' tabu ground since before history began. . . . Beaucairè, then, looks far the best, when seen across the Rhone, with her white façade and her white tower. And I am equally bound to say that when, the other day, I asked the young lady who presides over the bookshop at Tarascon for a copy of "Aucassin and Nicolette" . . . "*Voulez vous entendre l'histoire de deux beaux enfants, Aucassin et Nicolette?*" . . . she replied:

"Monsieur desires the book of M. Francis Carco? We are not allowed to stock such works."

[15]

I do not know what book of M. Carco's she may have meant but I know that none of the inhabitants of the city of the Good King René had ever heard of the shining figures that are, at least for Anglo-Saxondom, the chief glories of the town in which the great Napoleon first saw service. To be sure that city is as unaware of the latter fact as of the former. And I am consolingly reminded that when in June 1916 I asked in Rouen —another of the stations of the prehistoric trade route—for a copy of Flaubert's "Bouvard et Pécuchet" not one of the book-shops of the city that saw the burning of Joan of Arc could yield one up. . . . Yes consolingly, when I remember that the Reading Room of the British Museum cannot provide for you nearly all the books of the writer whose lines you are now reading! . . . *Nous autres pauvres prophètes!* . . . Still, Rouen has this in revenge. The captain of the transport that was bearing us, reinforcements, to the first battle of the Somme pointed excitedly to the banks when we were passing Croisset and exclaimed to the astonished British officers who were on his bridge:

"Voilà. . . . There. . . . It is in that pavilion that 'Bouvard et Pécuchet' was written!" . . . And all the population of the Rouennais country were there to cheer our passing and great streamers bearing words of welcome covered all the headlands. . . . Alas!

At any rate I have spent hours and hours in the Café de Paris at Tarascon. . . . And on one of those occasions I saw, depressedly in a corner, drinking gaseous lemonade, the honest merchant who was chased—by an elephant—from Ottery St Mary's to the city opposite Beaucaire. He was complaining bitterly of his drink and when I asked him why in the country of the vine, the olive tree—and the lemon—he should be drinking highly diluted sulphuric acid, for it is of that that artificial lemonade consists, he answered with agitation:

"You wouldn't have me drink their wines or eat their messy foods!"

Alarm grew and grew in his wild eyes and he exclaimed:
"Why, I might get to like them and then what would become of me?" . . . I think that, at his brilliant exposition of that theory that is at the root of our uncivilisedness, I had my first impulse—it must have been eleven years ago!—to write this book.

He was an honest merchant, retired. . . . To Ottery St Mary's which, though he did not know it, had been the home of a great poet. He would have been horrified at the idea of writing verses; he had passed an honest life as a cutler at Sheffield where they supply, to the ignorant heathens that trick themselves amidst forests and on coral strands with the bandannas that are the glory of Tarascon, knives that will not cut.

He had, he said, been all his life aware that merchants did not receive the social respect that should be due them. The most honest of Sheffield merchants retired will not be received by the County. That seemed to me odd in a cosmogony whose chief claim to call itself civilised lay in the successes of its merchants. But he, presumably, knew what he was talking about. He continued, however: All his life he had dreamed of visiting and travelling along the Great Trade Route—the one and only Great one. It ran, he said, from China across all Asia to Asia Minor; then along the shores of the Mediterranean as far as Marseilles. There, up the Rhone, it ran inland, by way of Beaucaire and Lyons to Paris; then down the Seine past Rouen to the English Channel which it crossed at its narrowest and so away along the South Coast of England past Ottery St Mary's to the Scilly Isles where it ended abruptly. . . . And for ever backwards and forwards along that beaten track had gone the honest merchants bearing the merchandise of China to Cornwall and the products of Cornwall to Pekin. And they were regarded as sacred messengers, the protégés of the gods.

To that honest merchant it had seemed all his life that that track must be a paradise. Bearing your goods, regarded as sacred and so protected by kings and priests, you moved from tabu ground to tabu ground—at Nijni Novgorod, at Stambul, at Athens, Marseilles, Beaucaire, Lyons, Paris, Dover, Salisbury, Ottery St Mary's. On the tabu ground, as in the great shaded fair-ground at Beaucaire, today, you laid down such goods as you were minded to sell and retired. The inhabitants came, inspected your offerings, laid down such goods as they were minded to give in exchange for yours and in turn retired. You advanced again; inspected their goods and if they seemed sufficient took them and went off with them. . . . And you were sacred. Druids with their sickles, priests of Moloch with their tridents, of Mithras with their arrows, of Baal with their serpents, all kings and princes with their myrmidons and, more dreadful still, all gods, hidden in mountains and seas, with their appalling thunderbolts, their dread pestilences and famines, protected you. You were tabu. Sacred!

That honest merchant sighed when he thought of that splendid vision, the image of a great beaten track extending across the world, like a broad swathe cut through vast plains of very tall grasses. All his life, till the elephant aided him; . . . who is a symbol of a very high Trade Route God indeed . . . he had had dreams of moving one day along that track. And for me it caused the realisation that in all my always migratory life no place outside Provence has ever seemed really a home to me though all my life I have been moving along parts of that same track, resting for five days, or a month, or six, and then moving on and on again. For me—as for most of humanity—the Route has today become the Grand Tour. At Monte Carlo or Mentone or possibly even Genoa, it suddenly takes a turn to the right, across the Mediterranean and through the Straits of Gibraltar and so to the west. . . . And indeed it occurs oddly to me that the only place in which I ever spent eight solid months, never sleeping outside its city walls—the only place in all my life must have been New York which is usually accounted unrestful enough. . . . But still, from Genoa to Sandy Hook and Sandy Hook to Tilbury Dock and thence to Calais

Pier and so, by the Overland Route to Marseilles and the Quai
de Cronstadt at Toulon the gyratory journey continues and
continues. . . .

It is my thoughts upon those journeys and the projections
of the places that form the beads of that string of voyages that
I am setting down. . . . My thoughts on faiths and destinies and
chances and cuisines and digestions and the Stage and music and
the fine arts and the neglect of writers and love and honest
merchanting and treason and death and strategies . . . and the
Parish of St Marylebone and the harbour of Chichester and
the Sixth Arrondissement and the semi-circular Place in front
of the palace of the Dukes of Burgundy at Dijon and the Roman
city of Vaison where Provence begins and was begun and the
theatre of Orange and disasters at Tarascon and so onwards. . . .

If I write of Provence a little as if it were an earthly Paradise the reader must amiably condone what, not being fully in
the know, he will consider as a weakness. I shall dwell on
Provence far, far more than on Piccadilly or the Place de la
Concorde. But let him again pardon the writer whose whole
motive is to get him into that "know" as fully as lies within
the power of his pen. The well-advertised motive of the sainted
of many centuries has been to leave the world a little better
than they found it. To such haloes it is not for me to aspire. It
has however become more and more manifest to me as the years
went by me that the safest road to fame and fortune is that of
the Moralist, whether he be Marcus Aurelius or St Paul or the
late Robert Louis Stevenson or my friend Miss Katherine Anne
Porter's life's hero, Cotton Mather. And, if I do not set about
soon to procure myself those desiderata, fame, fortune and the
consequent esteem of my fellows will be for ever strangers to
me. So I here make that bid. . . . I shall point out recurrently
to my reader—recurrently and apparently without relevance in
the middle of paragraphs otherwise devoted to the climate of
the parishes of St Marylebone and Greenwich or to the lost

and gone speak-easies round and about West Forty-eighth Street—that Provence is the only region on the Great Route fit for the habitation of a proper man. I run thus, I am aware, the risk of being styled prolix or of having lost control of my pen or faculties. But it is proper that the good should be defamed by people like reviewers and my strength is indeed as the strength of ten because of the purity of my purpose. That purpose is none other than to induce my readers—that goodly and attractive band—either to settle in the land of Clémence Isaure, St Martha, the Tarasque, Marius and Olive of Marseilles, MM. Gambetta, Thiers and M. Bonhoure, the winner of the Five Millions, and other fabulous monsters, or at least to model their lives along the lines of the good Provençal and his Eden-garlic-garden. So in the end, like the jongleur who juggled before Our Lady and was rewarded by a smile from the Bambino in her arms, I may be pardoned my sins of inclusion. And if I may not receive the reward of those who have left the world better than they found it I may have led my readers to a world better than any they yet knew. And the rest of the world may, for all I care, go on living in its former abomination. . . .

In the middle of some reflections on the meeting, on East Forty-second Street, of the spheres of influence of Mrs Patrick Campbell coming from Her Majesty's Theatre and Mrs Aimée Macpherson coming from California, I may introduce some directions as to the real, right and only best way to make bouillabaisse. . . . That will be because I am capable of anything in the furtherance of a just cause and not because I suffer from a senile impotence to marshal my thoughts. Moreover I may desire to suggest to my reader how much better engaged those two electrifying ladies would have been had they been seated one on each side of a bowl of that amazing fish stew, at Martigues on the Etang de Berre, in the sunlight, than the one in the pulpit of an East Side Temple and the other, not of course with a baby in her arms, but at least lost in the snowdrifts outside that fane. . . . For where better and more fittingly could Beauty and Righteousness kiss and clasp hands than over one of the great steaming bowls of M. Pascal? And indeed if Beauty and Righteousness cannot be induced soon to be reconciled what is to become of this poor world? That at least is the moral of this book. For, in the end, it is about the Courts of Love that the Troubadours held in the little castle of Roumanille in the Alpilles above St Rémy de Provence five miles or so from Tarascon. Since the last of those Courts was holden our Western World under, or awaiting, the leadership of Mr Mather, gave up the attempt to reconcile those necessary concomitants of the existence of a civilisation—and slid towards the Pit. And still slides.

I do not mean to say that even in Provence it is all perfection. A really perfect Garden would not be one in which the dog had none of the little irritants that a dog's life calls for. Provence will always have its three flails . . . *Le Parlement, le Mistral et la Durance sont les trois fléaux de la Provence* . . . Parliament, the North Wind and the dire river that with sudden and utterly unforeseeable disaster floods the whole valley of the Rhone. . . .

And Providence there too is apt to be inscrutably lavish of her gifts. Of the first six great *Lots* of the new French lottery five have gone to the inhabitants of the Midi as against all the rest of France. The cold Northerner will point out that that is because the Provençal, being a gambler, has bought exactly five times as many tickets as all the rest of France together. . . . But the Northern world is dying because of the disappearance of that very gambler's spirit; Provence alone continues on her tranquil way beneath the sun . . . and mops up the *Gros Lots* in addition.

CHAPTER II

LONDON FROM PROVENCE

FORTUNE and ruin strike you each alike without reason, as a gift from the High Gods in Provence. On the face of it, there is no relationship or similarity between Tarascon and London except perhaps that neither St Martha of Tarascon whose marble feet are all but kissed away by the lips of suppliants nor all the preachers and minor catechists of London Town can save a fool from the consequences of his folly.

My honest merchant of the Ottery St Mary's elephant whilst lamenting in the shades of the Café de Paris at Tarascon the hardship of travel on the Great Trade Route had frequent recourse to a little box labelled: "Bile" . . . Something. He resembled in that the snuff-takers of the eighteenth century: there was nothing else of the eighteenth century about him. He persisted in sitting in the deepest shades of that place of rest and refection although, as I pointed out to him, Provence is the country of the sun-god and that health-bringing flail, the mistral—and the deeper recesses of the cafés of Provence are neither very sanitary nor anything but malodorous.

He replied that he in his turn had conquered that country that, since the beginning of time, has lain at the feet of ten thousand succeeding devastators. By persisting that every place in which he dined should give him the tepid pink india rubber that in his home he called underdone roast beef and potatoes boiled in water without so much as a tiny piece of *gros-sel*, he had succeeded in maintaining himself, with the aid of the specific in the little box, at his usual level of home-health. He was disagreeable at breakfast and the whites of his eyes were yellowish, his pepper and salt hair was ruffled and without shine and he sat in those shades that smelt slightly of urine. A proper conqueror of Provence he was. Did you expect him to sit in the sun and mistral at the little white marble-topped tables of that café front? And let any passer-by from Ottery St Mary see him? And be suspected of ogling the Bad Girls? And lose his church-wardenship and his membership of the Junior Imperial League? He would be damned if he would. . . .

He would of course be damned if he did. . . .

It is a curious coincidence that it should be dusk when with precaution—and afterwards with quickly vanished triumph—I introduced the artist who has decorated these pages to what I consider to be the only Great View in London or the British Empire. And the only thing that Biala could see were the pink, shuddering, illuminated letters of publicity for the anti-bilious specific that that honest merchant had drawn from his vest pocket in the shades of Tarascon. The View itself was invisible behind them.

It is to be seen from the third step of the left-hand entrance-staircase of the National Gallery. You look from there across Trafalgar Square, down Whitehall, that wide historic street that has seen the fall of our kings and the making of the histories of worlds, to the dreaming spires of the Abbey in which Nelson expected to be buried and was not and the other, taller-mounting spires of that Mother of Parliaments who too has played her not always inglorious part in the story of our planet. In certain weathers and most usually at dusk these things are lifted up; Whitehall becomes a majestic canyon, the spires tower and tower, filling the skies, and if the Londoner ever wants to be inspired with thought of his Imperial destinies there is the place where he may be proud. That View cannot show you the Parthenon, or the Forum of Rome, or the Place de la

Concorde or even the Maison Carrée at Nîmes. But in its way it is enough!

The Londoner, however, practically never wants to remember that or anything else—except the cup-tie results. I doubt if, now, he even wants to be bothered with the late scores of that game that supplies us at once with our morals and the iron bonds that bind together our far-flung realms. At any rate we stood side by side on those steps and those livid, shuddering and blazing portents chased themselves across the dusk. We were recommended to purge one organ; we were warned that we should not sleep unless we wore ONE WAY PANTS; that we were starved and should lie awake all night unless we CRAMMED OURSELVES with CRAM'S MALTO or washed out another organ with SOMEONE ELSE'S SOMETHING ELSE. It gave irresistibly the impression that someone having murdered London's sleep all the witch-doctors of Macbeth were dancing in a *Walpurgisnacht* across the London skies.

My artist said hesitantly beside me:

"It *may* be a Great View. . . . But isn't it extraordinarily like New York?" I expressed my sense of outrage and Biala timidly changed the subject to:

"Let's go quickly to a café so that I may get down my impressions while they are new. . . ." It was that artist's first dusk in London.

A new sound almost drowned my voice as I exclaimed:

"A CAFE!!! Don't you know that there are no *cafés* in London? Besides, I'll be damned if I let you be seen in a *café* if there was one. . . . Don't you realise that you are supposed to be illustrating a serious book? . . . A moral one. . . ."

Biala said:

"But if London does not provide *cafés* for her artists how can she expect to have any art? . . . Or any letters? Or any civilisation? Or any anything?"

I was considering the new sound. It is very difficult to explain the fine shades of London to the alien and it was twenty-

odd years since I had been there for anything like keeps. . . .
This is a book of travel.

The new sound was made by starlings. . . . Their evening
chorus drowned our voices, the dull roar of the traffic and
seemed to obliterate the very dithering of the tumultuous sky-
signs. Every cornice of the National Gallery, of St Martin's, of
the whitish buildings that give Trafalgar Square the aspect of
any Capitol in any Middle Western Capital—every high-line
round the square was blacked in by the line of heads of those
birds singing their evensong of thanks to the not unkindly city
of my birth. I saw nothing else in particular that was new to
make me love the great careless, sinful, brown, sooty place. But
that at least was new and extremely lovable. Even Biala had to
remark that in that at least London was one up on New
York. . . . Even on Paris! Perhaps only Tarascon, where in the
heart of the town you cannot sleep for the nightingales, can
equal for that the city where the pale ghost of Hudson, who in
life was so appalled in her streets, can at last there take pleasure.

I have never known such a place for nightingales. . . . Alphonse Daudet, who was born in Nîmes in 1837, has, to serve
his private ends, represented the inhabitants of Tarascon as
being so avid of targets to blaze away off the surface of the
earth that no living thing is to be seen or heard on the rocks
and groves around it. But Daudet was not a true Provençal;
for, with all its charms and the *mises à mort* and the Maison
Carrée and one memorable eating place, Nîmes is not true
Provence, is *Royaume*, not *Empire*—as you shall later read. And
the author of "Tartarin de Tarascon" treasured up numerous
grudges and avenged them as he saw fit. So his making fun of
the Tarasconnais is at times bitter enough and has done no
great good to Provence—has done more harm than his "Lettres
de Mon Moulin" can ever atone for. Perhaps that is because he
never really lived in any mill in Fontvieille near les Baux where
the letters pretend to have been written. But he certainly was
in Tarascon where something disagreeable happened to him—

even if it was nothing worse than being rather painfully worsted in an argument by the great Frédéric Mistral. . . .

My good friend M. Devin who for many years owned the India-print works which he had inherited from his father, used to declare that that was what was the matter with Daudet. He claimed to have been present—in that very Café de Paris—at a frightful argument at which Mistral, who was seven years older, brought tears to the eyes of the young Daudet. I do not know how that may be. My old friend was a Tarasconnais of the Tarasconnais and may be excused if he wished to avenge his city on the author of "Jack." As against it I remember sitting as a young and by no means too unargumentative man, with Mistral in the café at Arles in the Place du Forum and being treated with extreme gentleness and tolerance by the great poet. . . . At any rate Daudet was too hard on Tarascon and does not refrain from poking fun at Mistral himself—however gently and skilfully, *aceto*, as you might say, *infuso*—in the "Lettres" . . . Or again I do not remember Daudet as being too kindly or tolerant to me when as a still younger and then quite unargumentative, shy boy, I was detailed to shew him the Elgin marbles in the British Museum. But at that time Daudet was suffering terribly from the disease of the spine that rendered his life a martyrdom. It was however no fault of mine that Lord Elgin should have taken those statues from the Parthenon. . . .

It is curious that the two French men of letters on the great scale to whom as a boy I was privileged to shew bits of London were each suffering from painful diseases, each not of but connected intimately with Provence and each—and Zola almost more than Daudet—inclined to take the very gloomiest views of the habits, tastes and climate of the city of my birth.

At any rate there have always seemed to me to be more nightingales in and around Tarascon than in any other spot on the earth and it was in Tarascon that I acquired the habit of writing to that bird's strains. How that was I have already recounted [1] but I intend to go on writing about the nightingales at Tarascon for a minute or two in order to clear the inhabitants of that little town from one at least of the hits below the belt of M. Daudet.

There is, then, round the city a high wall which serves not so much to keep away Northern invaders as to keep out the waters of the Durance at such times as that flail-stream chooses to try to devastate the lowlands of the neighbourhood. This wall prolongs itself for some miles in the direction of Avignon. On the one side it shuts in, between itself and the miniature mountains that are called indifferently the Alpilles and the Alpines, a little territory of an extreme fertility where the Tarasconnais garden in the evenings and erect the little huts that serve them for week-end cottages. For the Tarasconnais, like the Parisian and like myself, is an inveterate kitchen gardener. Be he never so much a *fonctionnaire* or ever so honest a merchant, the moment the shades of evening begin to fall he is up and away from desk or counter and wading amongst the profusions of his melon-patch, his pumpkins, his gourds, pimenti and his tomatoes. On the outer side of the wall is the high-road to Barbentane and then some flats that—for purposes of their own cultivations of osiers, flax, hemp and certain kinds of vine— the proprietors like to see inundated from time to time and covered with the thick layers of alluvial soil that the Rhone there deposits.

Shutting in road and wall on themselves runs as stately a grove of planes and chestnuts as you will see anywhere—an avenue running, not to any palace, but just out into the open country. It is in these shade-trees and in the thickets upon the flats that there are nightingales. Nightingales! . . . I have never imagined that so many nightingales could be got together for, like the robin to which it is related, the nightingale is a solitary bird and does not like the propinquity of neighbours of its own species.

[1] In "It Was the Nightingale," Lippincott.

But upon that wall—and at noon—I have known the nightingale voices to be as loud and extended as were those of the starlings on the cornices of the National Gallery, the other evening.

I am accustomed to twit myself with exaggeration and, when I can, I like to check up on my statements. So, the other day, I took a long-suffering New Yorker—who is accustomed to twit me with exaggeration even more than I do myself and whom,

King René's Bastide

in consequence, when I can afford it, I take on gastronomical and other tours—I took the long-suffering pilgrim from Gotham, where there are sky-signs but neither nightingales nor starlings, towards that grove beside the Rhone. I say "towards" advisedly because we had hardly got out of the shadow of King René's *bastide* where by the force of the *mistral* and at the hand of God the worst disaster of my life had formerly overtaken me, than it became evident that, since there was no *mistral*, we should never reach the grove towards which our rash footsteps had set out. For, in the latter end of May, when there is no *mistral,* you do not go on pedestrian expeditions. You sit in your dim room watching in the arrow shafts of light that the sun hurls through the cracks in your jalousies the slow dance of motes that are brighter than the flashes from an electric drill at midnight. . . . We looked questioningly the one at the other and took a step or two. The tar-fixings of the road scorched the soles of our espadrilles. We took two slow steps more. That New Yorker said:

"I'll accept your statement as to the number of those singing tit-bits!"

I cried: No! no! My veracity had been impugned. Better be carbonado'd than live in an ice-box where no honour is.

We plodded on. When, eschewing the temptation of the deep shadows of the little park, we stood at the foot of the long slope that blazed up towards the wall-top, I could already raise my finger and cry listen. That New Yorker expressed the conviction that a thousand nightingales were singing from on top of that wall. But, no, no, I said, we must be exact. Today was the day of the empire of the Scientist. Besides, nightingales do not sing on walls. . . .

Finally, on top of the town-wall, with its view of the blazing convent-front, the red-hot castle wall, the streak of flame of Beaucaire castle tower across the boiling Rhone, we heard nightingales. . . . In the pitiless stare of the white sun I counted seven—a hundred yards away from the beginnings of the grove. One was on the top of a lime-tree; three in cypresses in the convent garden; two in thickets between the wall and the river and one sang from a wild olive tree above a white hut in the allotments. . . . Seven . . . at broad noon. . . . What would there not be in the dusk?

My American friend wanted to make it twenty-two and get away into the shadows of the park.

But: No, no, I fulminated. This thing must be settled—and without exaggeration! I pointed to the lime-tree "One!" I said. . . . America is a vast continent but it contains no nightingales;

no New Yorker could know how polyphonic and how ventriloquial a bird that is. . . . I turned my back on my friend to point out one by one the three black cypresses in the convent garden. . . .

"There are three there," I said, "but only three. They produce the illusion of being nine which in your characteristic locution, *à la* Tom Sawyer, you would call 'mornamillion.' " . . .

But I was addressing the empty, scorching air. My friend was already seated on a bench, amongst green shadows and dust, beside the green bust of the félibrist poet, above the little pond where the goldfish were asleep, amongst the dead stalks of the asphodels.

Yet, often as I have eaten in the town of the Good King—I may as well interpolate that he was called the Good because, being short of money, he substituted for the executions, drawings and quarterings, tortures and other penalties for crimes that were the delight of most mediaeval potentates, an intricate and weighty system of fines so that crime disappeared and peace brooded through all his realms. For a man will face the thumbscrew for murdering his grandmother but will not even contemplate that atrocity if it is going to cost him more than the old lady's meagre savings. Upon that fact I shall dwell more at length when I come to my chapter of moralising on the incidence of penal laws. . . . But I will depose before a notary that never in Tarascon have I partaken of bird smaller than a chicken. I have never so much as been offered one.

Whereas in Nîmes! . . . Aha, M. Alphonse Daudet!

For shall I, or anyone who was with me, ever forget the exquisite—the *exquisite*—flavour of the huge platter of little birds, with their little claws in the air, with their little eyes disproportionately enormous in their tiny skulls, lying on the tiniest of croûtons of an incredible deliciousness, that we ate in the wine-vault behind the Protestant temple at Nî. . . .

But no! . . . See to what turpitudes local patriotism will lead one! . . . I have enrolled myself under the banners of Frédéric

Mistral and of Tarascon against the mendacious hosts of Alphonse Daudet and of Nîmes. At once I find myself about to perjure myself. It is true that in Tarascon I never ate robin, wren, tomtit or nightingale but neither did I in Nîmes. It was in Arles, the capital of the true kingdom of Provence and the very seat of Mistral and of *félibrisme*, in a wildly clamorous farmers' ordinary that we ate that miraculous platterful of microscopic songsters.

I may formally discuss the cruelty or the reverse of eating tiny creatures when I arrive at my chapter on bull-fighting, football, stage-tumbling, the humane slaughtering of cattle and the slaughter of men in war and my meeting with Mr Ernest Hemingway on the bridge between Tarascon and Beaucaire when I was coming back from seeing six bulls disposed of by Chicuelo, Maera and some matador from Mexico whose name I have forgotten and he hastening to see the same heroes function at his first tauromachic fiesta at Pampeluna.

For the moment I will content myself with giving you a menu, some receipts and, since we are about to set out on a journey, some hints as to how to find good restaurants in the country of Provence where as a whole the cooking is very indifferent.

The South of France—the Midi—divides itself into three zones. In Provence proper—from Mentone to Marseilles—they cook with oil and the products are discouraging. In the territory from the Rhone to Spain which is only by courtesy called Provence you begin to find traces of butter introducing itself into the *cuisine à l'huile*. There are two good restaurants in Marseilles and one in Carcassonne—in a little street in the Basse Ville. But if you want to eat really well there you must order your meal beforehand. By Carcassonne they have already begun to use a little pork-fat. Twenty-one years ago I ate there some *côtelettes de veau à la Maréchal* that were really good.

But it is not until you get to Castelnaudary—of the *cassoulets*—that cooking with goose-fat begins, and *foie gras* and truffles and the real *haute cuisine* of the Toulousain district and the real, high wines of the Bordelais. There too I remember eating. . . . But to say what would be unkind. We have to do the best we can with Provençal food. A shadow fell across my memories of the Toulousain the other day. I was in the train between Avignon and Tarascon with opposite me a masterly lady from Toulouse who had only one working arm and an infinitude of parcels. I helped her with these and we fell into conversation—about cooking. She expressed the deepest contempt for the cooking of Provence. She said that there the peasants were too miserly to cook properly or to do anything else with dignity or generously. . . . *"Parce qu'ils vont trop souvent à la messe!"* . . . "Because they go to Mass too often!"

Guessing that she was a Huguenot, I avoided the subject and fell to complimenting the *cuisine à graisse d'oie* of Toulouse. She said:

"Of course you only find cooking with goose-fat in private houses, now."

Consternation fell upon me. Was it possible that Toulouse—and Castelnaudary itself—had become Anglo-Saxonised and that there, even as in the regions of the Palaces of the Côte d'Azur and Paris, and as in London and New York, unless you ate in private houses you had to content yourself with tepid, pink, india-rubber beef, wet potatoes and wetter greens or string beans all cooked in water without salt? Was it possible that one more invasion of Northern barbarism had taken by storm an apparently untakeable fortress?

The lady however comforted me. She said that in the eating-places of her district the methods of preparation and purging by fire were the same as they always had been. Only, since the crisis, the proprietors of restaurants had determined to use ordinary butter in place of the specialty of Périgord and Alsace. Even at that such Toulousains as had no homes in which to eat had gone on strike and there was some hope that the restaurateurs would be brought to their knees. For herself it did not matter very much because she cooked at home and every winter laid down several half-hundred weight jars of goose-fat. . . .

Indeed, *à quelquechose malheur est bon* and I have eaten lately a decent meal in Tarascon where for twenty years since quarrelling over prices with a Basque chef who used to make Tarascon eating bearable, I have fared very indifferently indeed. But now I have eaten several quite passable meals. This astonished me for, as a Papist, I am forbidden to be a perfectibilist and seldom expect to see things improve. And indeed I had thought to see public cooking in all France as lost a battle as it was in the Strand or in Forty-second Street. But, for ever blessed be the Crisis! the proprietor of the place where in Tarascon I eat tells me, that that world phenomenon having stopped the flow of Anglo-Saxon tourists, he has been forced to take another chef and cook French again for the sake of the Parisians and commercial travellers who are now his mainstay and till lately had abandoned him. So that there is hope.

In spite of that ray of sunshine the traveller in Provence will never, I feel sure, be able to enter an unknown town and go into any restaurant with any certainty of good food. That used to be the case in almost every district in France and may well again be so if the Crisis continues and the Anglo-Saxon tourist keeps away. But except along the sea-shore where the indigenous populations have several ways of producing savory— usually garlic-saffron-flavoured fish stews, fish-soups, sauces or stuffings, Provence has no regional dishes and the true Provençal has neither the gift, nor the patience nor yet the materials that are necessary for the serious cook.[1]

[1] Here is the recipe for bouillabaisse as it was written by A. Caillat, chef of the Grand Hôtel du Louvre et de la Paix at Marseilles in 1891–the year in which I first ate bouillabaisse in that city. It should be premised that there exist three schools of bouillabaisse–those who sanction langouste, those who sanction potatoes and those who sanction neither–though very occasionally you will find both together in the bouillabaisse of quite famous practitioners. Personally I favour potatoes and no langouste.

Take then large quantities of the fish called *rascasse*–for which my dictionary gives no translation; of the *grondin*–the red gurnet of the North Sea; of the *boudroie*, for which again I have no translation; of the conger eel; of

Nevertheless every Provençal town harbours a number of French officials, officers, federal policemen and a certain number of real Provençaux who are careful of what they eat. So you may be certain that every town of any size at all will contain one restaurant where food at least eatable may be had without ordering it beforehand.

To find it you must adopt one of two courses: Walk the streets with your eyes open until you see a comfortable, good-humoured-looking man and then ask him where to eat. The only way in which good humour can be secured for humanity is by habitual good eating and even though your good-humoured-looking man—he should be of a certain age and embonpoint—even though he eat usually at home there will certainly be occasions enough in his life in which he will need to give dinners to acquaintances at restaurants. So he will have the necessary knowledge.

Or, going about your town you will see a *café* that must be clean but not too American in aspect. . . . The *café*-keeper who has Americanised—or Lyons-Corner-House-ised—the ap-

the *roucaou*; of the *merlan*, or whiting; of the *Saint Pierre*, otherwise the *zée* which my dictionary calls the *zeus-fish*, which Larousse states to be a genus of Australian(!) though you see it caught every day in the Mediterranean, I believing it to be a species of haddock. And last of all you take the *loup du rocher*, the most radiant, the most delicate and the most costly of all the fishes of all the seas and rivers that God has made, its flesh having the firmness of the finest trout, a consistency and whiteness of its own and a complete absence of the slight suspicion of aftertaste of mud that mars the finest of Scottish brook trout.

Having chosen very fresh specimens of these fish, scale and clean them and cut them in vertical slices; set aside the whiting, the *loup*, the *zée* and the *roucaou*, which being more delicate call for less cooking.

Place in a saucepan a minced onion, two tomatoes and three or four cloves of garlic, some fennel, bay, and peel of bitter orange all equally minced fine, a sprig of thyme; add the fish that you did not set aside, a quarter of a pint of olive oil, pepper, salt and saffron; just cover with boiling water and place on a quick fire so that it may come quickly to the boil. Five minutes later add the remaining fish; keep boiling five minutes longer, always very quickly so that the mixing may be thorough.

Have ready on a soup plate or tureen slices of bread one-third of an inch in thickness; pour the bouillon over this whilst straining it; arrange the fish on another dish, removing the pot-herbs, sprinkle with parsley and serve.

pearance of his establishment will imagine that he has done enough for the world. He will spend the rest of his life raising his prices, debasing the quality of what he supplies, employing cheap waiters and quarrelling with his lavatory attendant over the proportion of her tips that he should get. . . . But look for a clean, old-fashioned *café* with the bowls for napkins shining like the glass spheres in a Dutch garden and a good-humoured-looking waiter. Take your apéritifs at one of the tables of that waiter. Get into conversation with him if you can. Tell him that he is better off where he is than in London or New York—or in Paris. Before leaving give him a good—but not an extravagant—tip. If you under-tip him he will think you a miser, if you over-tip, a fool. He *might* tell you the name of his good, secret restaurant if he thought you close; he would never do so if you presented to him the aspect of a squandering Anglo-Saxon, because he would despise you. And he will not want the prices and tips of his restaurant put up. He will want to dine there himself—and tip.

A *café* waiter should be given a slightly higher tip than one in a restaurant, ten per cent on the bill being the established wage. If in a restaurant you have·an expensive wine you do not tip ten per cent on that, nor, in restaurants where ten per cent is charged for the service, has the proprietor a right to ten per cent on his wine. The theory of the tip or the ten per cent is that they are gauged on the amount of service the attendant puts in. As it gives no more trouble to bring a hundred franc bottle of wine to the table than one costing five or fifteen francs it would be absurd to give the waiter who brings it ten francs. But of course if the wine calls for special care in carrying from the cellar, basketing, *chambrer*-ing, uncorking and pouring, you give the *sommelier* a tip all for himself—supposing the results to be satisfactory. But watch his every movement, test the heat of the wine against your cheek and inspect your cork with minute attention so as to be sure that it is newly drawn. I will tell you why later on. . . .

The tip in the restaurant should be ten per cent. At the *café* it should be a little more if you are a reasonable user of *cafés* . . . if, I mean, you limit yourself to a single apéritif before dinner, a cup of coffee with a possible *fine*, afterwards, or a *bock* at odd moments . . . and if while consuming them you ask the waiter for the time-table, the telephone book, the local directory, writing-materials, postage-stamps. You can do all that for the price of a cup of coffee as far as the management is concerned. But it would be absurd to give the waiter only twelve and a half centimes as being ten per cent of the Frs. 1.25 that the coffee has cost. . . . And above all, give your tip with the air that you are the one that accepts favours. Remember that he has as much right as you to be there—and more. Remember that he is as honest a man as you, with as engaging a family to support and that, the human cosmogony being what it is, he has as much right to his tip as you to the emoluments that by force or guile you extract from the universe—and then more. And remember above all that whilst you are a mere transitory nuisance he is carrying on, for his town, the great work of civilisation since for you, and how many others, he can and, if decently treated, will, infinitely soothe your way through life and his town.

Remember, I say, all these things. And having given a tip of a franc on your four franc apéritif, ask with proper deference of your good-humoured-looking waiter:

"*Où est-ce qu'on peut bien manger ici. . . . Et modestement, bien entendu?*" . . . "Where can one eat well here. . . . And, of course, reasonably?"

The waiter will then address himself seriously to the task of guiding you and the chances are about nine to one that you will fetch up in some unpromising-looking place where you will eat real cooking. Of course he *might* have an aunt who kept an atrocious hotel. But that is very rare; waiters are adventurous souls and loving travel seldom ply their trade in their home towns until they have made savings enough to let them open their own establishments.

Yes, those two systems work very well. I owe to a fattish, cheerish-looking gentleman with a grey silk waistcoat whom I accosted in the market at Arles the wonderful meal in the farmer's ordinary—the one at which we ate the *petits oiseaux* as well as an inimitable *soupe de poissons;* and to a waiter at the café near the arena at Nîmes I owe the direction to the heavenly wine-vault behind the Protestant temple at Nîmes. There such *pieds de mouton à la ravigote* were consumed by us that one at least of our party of good and true diners has never ceased to rave about them. . . . Personally I prefer my sheep's trotters *à la sauce poulette*. It is the more classical mode. *Sauce poulette* is made according to the old formula by. . . . But maybe I have given receipts enough!

At any rate the first thing you should do when you get to Provence is to achieve some intimacy with a waiter and then to ask him endless questions, for the more advice you ask of him the more he will respect you. Then, in an astonishingly short space of time, you will become *un homme connu* in that town. And to be a 'known man' in a Provençal township is very worth while. . . . When you go to get your *carte d'identité* a smiling functionary will tell you that it is a quite unnecessary formality; you will be able to commit with impunity all sorts of minor irregularities with your car; you will be met with smiles in places where indifference is the lot of all other foreigners and when, purposing a longer stay than you had expected, you come to bargain with your hotel keeper you will find that he will reduce your rates with an alacrity that will astonish you, supposing you to be any sort of a bargainer at all. . . . And all that because one townsman asking your address of another will be answered:

"Nay, I do not know that monsieur's address. . . . But his *café*, it is the Café du Commerce." You will have achieved a local standing and the reputation of being 'serious.' Nothing more is needed to make of your life in these regions a bed of roses.

Something of the same sort is observable in London or New York—or even in Paris, but the incidence is slightly different. I went the other day—there are no *cafés* in London—to get my hair cut by a barber who lives underground in Charing Cross Station. The tonsorial artist put his sheet round my neck without any visible emotion, flourished his scissors, made a few passes and then with a fine casualness remarked:

"Forty years ago it was that I first cut your 'air, sir. . . . Cup Tie day, 189–, it was." . . . He had indeed cut my hair most times when it had been cut during the twenty years which preceded the 4th of August 1914—when German troops at six in the morning crossed the Belgian frontier near a place called Gemmenich—and then never again! . . . I mean that he had never since that date cut my hair again. I don't know about Gemmenich. . . .

I had been used to go there because, living down in Kent, it had been convenient to have my hair cut in Charing Cross Station when I contrived to be a little early for a down train. But, during all those twenty years, no particular sort of relationship seemed to establish itself between that man and myself. He had cut my hair, had taken my tip and I had gone away. . . .

He remembered now that I liked my hair cut: "that way"; that I never had anything "on it" and disliked powder after a shave. Also that I had given him "Pirate" for the Doncaster Autumn Meeting of nineteen hundred odd and hadn't fancied "Bread and Cheese" for Redcar, next year so that on both occasions he had made a bit of money—Marwood of course had given me those North Country tips.—Also I had recommended him to buy somebody's special sweet peas twenty-two years before and they had done proper in his Purley garden where he still grew the same strain. . . .

When he had done with me he accepted my tip, brushed my hair and I went away without his making any comment.

But the next time I went there and was fumbling for my money to pay, the cashier said: "Next time will do very well" and there was that rarest of conferrings of a citizenship—a barber's offering credit. And the same phenomenon occurs every time I go back to New York . . . I dealt with the same tradesmen for many months, on Sixth Avenue between twelfth and eighth, on the first protracted visit I made to that city. Now, whenever I make another visit and enter one of those shops I get offered unlimited credit and all the bootleggers of that precinct would till lately call on me and offer to supply me with liquor on unprecedentedly easy terms!

In Anglo-Saxondom prolonged residence and settled behaviour are not in themselves sufficient to gain you marks of a neighbourhood's esteem. But go away—settling of course your accounts—and return again and you are sure of being radiantly treated and reminded of virtues you have long forgotten. . . .

I used the words "tonsorial artist" just now because I was thinking of M. Bonhoure—of M. Bonhoure of Tarascon, the most famous man of all France who must one day, surely, be the patron saint of all barbers the world over.

CHAPTER III

DESTINY ON THE GREAT ROUTE

Sings Mr Belloc:

"When I am in the Midlands and the day is left behind,
The Great Hills of the South Country rise up into my mind."

. . . or something like it.

So, when I am down on my luck for a short period and think the time has come to make my effort, I go and have my hair cut. But when the period of depression has been long and anxieties seem to be becoming too much for me, I make a bolt for Provence. And, if after passing Montélimar where Provence begins, I do not at once feel that the cloud has passed, I jump off the train at Tarascon and hurry to the studio of M. Bonhoure.

It has been my fate in life to be brought constantly into contact with the great, to which fact I attribute at once my modesty and what I have of a sense of humour. But there is about M. Bonhoure—today the best known man in France—nothing to smile at: he is an artist not only with his scissors and neckshears but also before the face of Destiny—and he may be regarded as the redeemer of the fair fame of his city.

For the moment when every man, woman, and child in France learned simultaneously that Destiny had willed that the *Gros Lot*—five whole millions: five *millions*, you understand—should fall to Tarascon, all those French mouths exclaimed:

"Aha! Tartarin! Now we shall see Tartarinades!" And you

will say that thirty-nine million, two hundred and ten thousand Frenchmen could not be wrong. . . . Those at least are the latest figures for the population of France that I can come by. But can't they? Can't thirty-nine million, two hundred and ten thousand Frenchmen be wrong—when they are misled by Alphonse Daudet?

Everyone of them, including myself, my household, my friends and the friends of my friends' friends—who are not of course all Frenchmen—had been trembling at the thought of how indecently they would certainly behave when that five millions fell at last into their hands. . . . What orgies wouldn't there be of wine, automobiles, women, country houses, charity, political candidatures! There had been no one whose conscience had not troubled him or who had not feared that he would end in a roadside ditch, starving and in rags, because of the excesses into which he would be driven by that ironic smile of fortune. The heart knoweth its own weaknesses.

. . . And then suddenly . . . Tarascon! . . . Did you say Tarascon? Yes, Tarascon. . . . All France rolled on its carpets in irresistible merriment. . . .

But what happened? Did the Café du Commerce know him no more? The relatively humble, but from now on glorified Café du Commerce, whose dignified clients sit, less fashionably, looking up the avenue, at right angles to the professionals and officers of the Café de Paris! No, sir!

The Provençal day-labourer, who is usually an Italian, prefers to talk in his native language about the latest miracle of St Onésime, the latest disaster wrought by the *mal'occhio* of the patron of the *Mas St Gilles*, the latest assassination contrived by the fascists of Nizza or the havoc caused by hailstorms on the vines of Draguignan. The fisherman's chief pleasure is to hear of split canes, bate-dopes, drag-nets, sudden floods, drownings, stickles, eddies and the behaviour of nine-day corpses in those stickles and eddies. So that fisherman or that non-French speaking day labourer will avoid *cafés* filled with lawyers who discuss the niceties of the French used in the law-courts, or officers whose talk is of women and horses—or even of commercial travellers whose talk is as to what kind of half-shoe is temporarily appealing to the shoe-sellers of the Arles circuit; or again the barbers' assistants whose conversation is all about the behaviour of the bulls at St Rémy last Sunday.

I do not mean to say that class-feeling, in the state of an organ that is rapidly becoming atrophied owing to disuse, is quite unknown in France outside Provence or even in Provence itself. The thirty-nine million two hundred and ten thousand who heard of M. Bonhoure's miraculous good-fortune fully expected that he would at least buy a seigniorial château, a thousand bottles of champagne, six Rolls Royces and spend in Monte Carlo such of his days as should precede his final beggarment. He might even assume a title, since there is nothing to prevent your calling yourself Prince de Rohan-Penthièvre in France as long as you do not use it as part of the paraphernalia of the confidence-trick.

At the very least he might be expected to change his *café* and, for the rest of his life, sitting amongst *rentiers* as a *rentier*— an 'independent gentleman' amongst independent gentlemen, survey the plane trees of the Cours Aristide Briand from the side instead of having of it the view with which Biala has presented us. . . .

But did M. Bonhoure do any of these things that would have been in character in M. Daudet's Tartarin? No, *sir!* The Provençal character is the most many-sided that can be found— a character founded on shrewdness, frugality and infinite pawky knowledge of the vicissitudes that beset human lives and so branching out into infinite manifestations of passions that he has nevertheless always extraordinarily—pawkily!—well in hand. In the convent schools of this district—as of some others—on the festival of the Boy Bishop the pupils after class hours are permitted, are even encouraged, to perform every kind of excess from dancing on the desks to smashing inexpensive articles of

The Café de Paris, Tarascon

furniture. A regular pandemonium will at times ensue. But, at the ringing of the Mother Superior's bell, suddenly absolute silence and order must at once obtain. That is supposed to be good disciplining.

Well, the Provençal, apparently drunk with the reflection of the sun from the white walls and orange rocks and with the perfume of rosemary, lavender, thyme and orange blossoms that float in his bone-dry air—the Provençal has his passions, apparently clamorous and inclining to pandemonium, as well in control as that Mother Superior with her bell. . . . You should see the audience at a Nîmes *mise à mort.* . . . At one moment the walls of the arena will seem to totter at the groans, catcalls, shouts of rage, objurgations of the sun-drenched crowd. It will be protesting with all the passion of its being against the clumsiness, indifference, laziness or cowardice of a picador. You would swear that in an instant all the seats of the arena would be torn up and flying at the head of the obese and slow-moving being. But by that instant a delicate titter of appreciation for the placing of banderillas will run all round the immense space with the noise of wind amongst wheat. Or a great roar of laughter will go up at the side-slipping of the bull as he turns too swiftly after the scarlet cape of his desire and fury. Or the birds flying in the air will drop from overhead at the unanimous roar that will greet the appearance of the trainer of the perfect, wonderful bull just after it has been slain with incomparable art by the great and for ever impassive Lalanda. . . .

All those passions are awake and ready in that immense multitude—but each passion is completely under the control of the event that is passing, as are the children by the bell. Your usual crowd is so made up that once an impulsion is given it, it will march on, stampeding like the bulls of the Camargue before the *mistral* until all is lost—to the destruction of the Bastille or to the all-but smothering of a Lindbergh arriving from across the Atlantic to the flying-fields of le Bourget. But that Provençal crowd at Nîmes, roaring like maniacs for music to salute an

The great and for ever impassive Lalanda

unsurpassed *faena*, has yet its eyes so open and so observant of the next movement of bull or matador, that in the minutest fragment of time suddenly that apparent mad, fool fury has become such a passion of reprobation and resentment as, at a cup-tie game would lead to the storming of the field, the destruction of grand-stands and the assassination of the referee. Or it may similarly yield before an equally passionate, critical appreciation of the finest shade in the flirting of a cape above the dreadful horns. . . .

It is the quick, disciplined habit of emotion of a people that for thousands of years has been accustomed to see at the one moment its vines shining beneath the sun with their burden of perfect grapes and, in the next, shot unrecognisably to ruin by hailstones from sudden clouds or trampled beneath the feet of pagan Aryan or Saracen hordes. . . . And with an equal discipline it will see, dropping from the sky into a world of full Crisis, the Five Millions of the *Gros Lot* itself.

So M. Bonhoure's first, seigniorial reaction to the news of his fortune was, standing amongst the cheering crowds of the Café du Commerce, to promise his city free bullfights during Christmas Week for the rest of his life—and the next to make over to his chief assistant his studio and all that decorated it. So, truly, M. Bonhoure manifested the spirit of the ancient Romans, his ancestors. For their governors and ediles built the great arenas in which still those gladiatorial contests take place and there on every occasion of public gladness provided the *panem et circenses*—the bread and circuses—that for generation to generation kept tranquil the Roman populace and their colonial dependants. It was a fine, instant manifestation that of M. Bonhoure. Innumerable indeed have been the conquerors and devastators that, since the Roman day have desecrated the soil of Provence. But beneath all the veneers of Saracen, Gaul, Rhenish Aryan, Anglo-Saxon and Visigoth occupation and in spite of Parliament, the *mistral* and Durance, the first unconscious manifestation of the Provençal soul goes to prove that

that territory beside the swift Rhone is still indeed that *Provincia Romana*, that province *par excellence* Roman, from which it still draws its name. . . . So M. Bonhoure's gesture may stand beside the proud words of President Wilson or, as a demonstration of the unchangeability of race characteristics— beside the memorable assertion of an August day: "When it is a matter of the fulfilment of treaties the British Government is not accustomed to count the cost." . . . Alas!

In any case that first seigniorial gesture in the Café du Commerce was, for M. Bonhoure, his last. . . . It is indeed characteristic of the innate shrewdness of the Provençal that his next should be to decree that the famous *courses de taureaux* should, the rates levied on entertainments being there very high, be held not in the city of Tarascon but in a convenient rural locality where generosity is less inconsiderately mulcted. But after that no gesture of prodigality. Not a single Tartarinade. . . . If you question the helpful waiter of the Café du Commerce as to the habits of that hero he points triumphantly down to the ground that forms his territory of the tray and napkin and exclaims: *"Non, non, c'est ici le café de M. Bonhoure. . . . C'est ici qu'il a entendu sa bonne nouvelle."* It was at the Café du Commerce that he heard his good news and to the Café du Commerce he would be faithful. Though, being a *rentier*, he might well move to the Café de Paris and sit amongst *rentiers*, Lancers, pharmacists and the literati, he will never make that quite modest gesture. For it might well cause a smile to rise on the faces of the thirty-nine million two hundred and ten thousand profane. . . . It would nevertheless be, for reasons that I shall tell in a minute, a gesture perfectly fitting. But M. Bonhoure has never by one hair's breadth deviated from his task of redeeming Tarascon from the sneers that the man of Nîmes cast upon that fair city. It is true that, mindful of her own laws and the precedent set in the case of Gyges, Destiny has not failed to put a few flies in the amber of that otherwise perfect felicity and, ever since the arrival of the Five Million, M.

Bonhoure has been afflicted by a disease of minor automobile accidents. It is not that he has acquired the habits of a road hog. I read in today's number of the *Petit Var* that M. Bonhoure has had the misfortune to run into a half-blind, nearly deaf, eighty-year-old crone who coming with a bundle of wood on her shoulder suddenly out of a by-path near Arles ran right under M. Bonhoure's wheels. . . . That sort of pestilential accident no man can avoid! And M. Bonhoure cannot have been speeding or the old woman would have been killed and, anxious to prove that millionaires cannot with impunity commit outrages on the high-road, the Court would have mulcted him in hundreds' of thousands of francs fines instead of a mere fifty with a thousand francs to the old lady as plasters for her scratches. . . .

But in addition to its admirable *apéritifs*, its coffee which is indeed black as night, hot as hell and sweet as love; its admirable view up the vista of the Cours Aristide Briand and the lively and instructive society of its commercial travellers, the Café du Commerce possesses a *Dancing* whose violins and hautboys may be heard offering up sweet music until far into the night. Thus a multi-millionaire who is also *bon père de famille* might well find a pretext for changing his *café*.

Until the disaster overcame me in the shadow of the Good King's Bastide and being unable to go further I staggered into the open door of that admirable place of refection, I had never been in the café where good fortune later awaited M. Bonhoure. . . . But indeed, being ruined, I might well have decided to patronise for the future only the cheaper kinds of *cafés*. . . . Nevertheless, except for the occasion when Biala was making the drawing of the Cours, I do not think I have ever been in that particular *café*. I did not want to be seen coming away at night from a *café* where there was a *Dancing!* This is not because I do not like dancing. I love it. The secret ambition of Lord Palmerston at sixty was to become a ballet-dancer and I can parallel that ideal of the great and virtuous minister by say-

ing that, years ago when I met Miss Adeline Genée one of the
first things I asked her was whether with her lessons she could
not turn me into a clog-dancer. I did not ask very seriously but
I was expressing a certain longing. For my frivolity she gave it
to me; as the saying used to be, in the neck, by answering un-
compromisingly: "You're too old. . . . And too fat!" . . .
And that must have been in 1909. . . . *Eheu fugaces!*

Memorial Tablet, Antibes

But at least I cannot be accused of disliking dancing or of
having any contempt for the most lovely as it is the most fugitive of all the Arts. And indeed of all the beautiful and mysterious motives and emotions that go to make up the frame of
mind that is Provence the most beautiful, moving and mysterious
is that of the Northern Boy of Antibes. The boy danced and
gave pleasure, died two thousand years ago and his memorial
tablet set into the walls of Antibes which is Antipolis of the
Greeks sets forth those salient facts of his life and portrays in

the lasting stone the little bag in which he used to make his collections. . . . He indeed along with Herod's daughter who came after and King David who preceded him must be amongst the earliest dancers upon whom Destiny has conferred the immortality of stone, papyrus or wax. . . . The most mysterious and the most beautiful.

And that is the note of the frame of mind that is Provence—that and the sculptured tablets of the cloister of St Trophime at Arles, of the façade of the church at St Gilles, of the Maison Carrée at Nîmes, of the triangular white tower of Beaucaire and the legends of the Good King René, the Good Queen Joan, the ruined city of les Baux and the wine called *Sanh del Trobador*, the blood of Guillem de Cabestanh.

Years ago, when I was a little, little boy in London, before my father died, we had a great and mysterious garden. It was, I suppose, not much larger than a pocket handkerchief, but it had gloom, romance, immense trees with sticky leaves, an end wall a hundred and twenty feet high and a topography that today is as clear in my mind as is the topography of, say, Gramercy Park. There was a discouraged lawn in the centre of which we dug a pond for the duck who liked claret better than water. The water never stayed in the pond for longer than to let the jackdaw take a bath, but on the mound made by the earth displaced from the pond we caused to grow, using for seed only their dejected peelings, enough Jerusalem artichokes to make, year in year out a forest as black and mysterious as the one in which Nicolette met the woodcutters. And there was the ventilating hole which led beneath the boards of the playroom which was behind the glamourous kitchen we were never allowed to enter and the coal-hole. Into that last I used to retire in order unknown to my father to read the adventures of Jack Harkaway, of Turpin the Highwayman, of Sitting Bull and of a thousand heroes. Into the ventilating hole Jack the Jackdaw would retire when soaked with his bath and before it Ike the Duck would collapse when it had succeeded in coaxing my father into giving it enough—and more than enough—of his claret. . . .

And indeed, when I think of the *Sanh del Trobador*—the Provence wine called Troubadour's Blood—I see it shining in its chalice in the hand of Bérangère des Baux across the shadows and mysteries of that garden. . . . But sometimes the Blood of the Troubadour will be dark purple in the scarlet glass with the emerald green stem from which my father drank—and Micky, the great, savage, white buck rabbit, will be sitting on the immense pent-roof of the dusthole drumming with its fore-paws before an audience of hungry cats below. Choosing its moment it will spring down, and in its descent kick with its enormous hind paws the eye out of one of the cats who will disperse howling with fright. . . . A wicked old devil, Micky the rabbit. . . . A true Voodoo apparition. . . .

Guillem de Cabestanh, the Troubadour, however, appears to me over in the far shadows, leaning with one hand against the largest of the trees, behind the artichokes and the duck and the rabbit and the jackdaw and the phosphorescent bust of the Venus of Milo that used to gleam through the dusk. Guillem is a little stout, in dark green, almost black, velveteen gaberdine and trunkhose with a belt set with enormous stage jewels constricting his waist rather tightly and a stage coronet round his puffed up hair. . . . And he stretches out his hand towards the chalice that is offered him by Bérengère des Baux whose dress, except for the fact that it had a long white satin train I do not—how like the infant male novelist!—much make out. . . .

It was of course wrong historically for the lady to offer the chalice to the troubadour because it was really she who drank the poet's blood from the chalice. . . . But that is how it comes back to me—the chalice and blood shining against the end-wall for all the world like the Sangréal of Parsifal. . . . Indeed I may well have mixed up the two legends, for my father, besides being the greatest Parsifal-fan in the London of his day, was a great champion of English music and had written for music of Sir A. C. Mackenzie the libretto for an opera called "The Troubadour." This at our tender ages my brother and I were duly taken to see, and the opera centred round the loves of Cabestanh and the lady and the blood and the cup. So that, in that London scenario, my mind recalls Provence!

Why, behind that hundred foot black wall, was a glamourous wicked district called The Mews where, we were given to understand, lived a blasphemous and dishonest crew called hansom cabmen. And, if we could climb up that ebon expanse and, hanging on to the trellis-work that topped it, peer down into that Gehenna we should see, throwing buckets of water at their cab-wheels, polishing bits and doing other devilish things—the pirate who was the foe of Jack Harkaway; the sleuth who finally brought down Dick Turpin; Sir Hudson Lowe who tormented Napoleon; General Custer who was the sworn foe of the gallant Sitting Bull—and the execrable husband of Bérengère, the unspeakable villain who slew Guillem de Cabestanh and made his wife drink her lover's blood and eat his heart, no doubt prepared as you prepare *rouelle de veau Mistral*, with plenty of garlic, olives, tomatoes and spices.

I don't know how my father did it. He was far too much of an English gentleman to suggest that we should read his books—the famous one on the Troubadours, the other about the Music of the Future and the rest. But somehow there got through to me the impression that one of the poems of Guillem de Cabestanh, who was my father's favourite hero and poet, though Mr Pound prefers Arnaut Daniel and I later developed a leaning towards Peire Vidal and Bertran de Born—that one of the poems of Guillem de Cabestanh was the most beautiful poem in the world. And across the projection of the dark garden that my memory gives me there seems to depend, in letters of light, that poem and the translation of it that I made. I cannot have been more than eleven at that date—certainly I was not more than twelve, because by that time my father was dead and I have never looked at his book or the poem of

Cabestanh again. But the poem remains fresh in my mind and innumerable times in wakeful nights or walking amongst sun-baked rocks, quite unexpectedly, I find myself going in memory over and over again through my translation.

Li dous cossire and *That pleasant fever*, they began—though *cossire* docs not mean 'fever' . . . and that bothers me a good deal at night. . . . But rhymes that are so frequent in Provence are so scarce in the Northern World that is ours!

Li dous cossire	That pleasant fever
Quem don amors soven	That love doth often bring
Domnam fan dire	Lady, doth ever
De vos mas vers plaszen	Attune the songs I sing
Pessan remire	Where I endeavor
Vostre cors car é gen	To catch again your chaste
Cui eu desire	Sweet body's savour
E cui non fasz perven	I crave but may not taste.

I don't know where at that tender age I got my philosophy any more than I know where I got my knowledge of Provençal, which must have been as great then as it is now—that is to say that if peasants speak not too fast and in the dialect of Maillane I can understand the drift of the conversation and I can still read Mistral with some ease. . . . But certainly at that age I had the conviction for all the world like that of Boccaccio or the Courts of Love—that husbands were ignoble beings when they were not villainous. Their function was, in the Mews beyond the hundred foot wall, to throw buckets of water over cab wheels whilst their ladies in white satin trains handed chalices to Troubadours in black velveteen. . . . And then to be condemned by the Courts of Love and for ever to stink in the memory. . . .

Ah, the Courts of Love of Provence and the Troubadours! . . . I imagined them shining in the sun before a castle keep. The ladies, all awave with their hennins and steeple-crowned hats, and their knights in rose-garlanded tilting helmets sat about in red plush armchairs, manicuring—I can't imagine why—their finger-nails and discoursing of *le gaie sçavoir*—the gentle Science. . . .

Alas, I must make a confession. . . . When we went away for our summer holidays Ikey the duck, Micky the rabbit, and his friend Jack the daw, used to be confided to the father of a boy from another—a very superior—Mews. . . . The Mews of gentlemen's coachmen who washed down the wheels not of hansom cabs but of shining broughams and majestic landaus . . . for Lord Mayors and Common Councillors of the City of London! A very superior Mews indeed.

There it was always sunshine. . . . The brightest sunshine my eyes have ever seen. . . . I suppose that was because the Mews faced on the great open space that was the Great Western Railway's shunting ground. . . . At any rate that Mews comes back to me as always white and shining, with Ikey the duck swimming rapturously in the horse-trough. And I suppose that Ikey the duck and my friend, the gentleman's coachman's son were, along with Guillem de Cabestanh, Sitting Bull and Napoleon Bonaparte, the most important and glamorous figures of my horizon.

And alas, oh shame! In the fore-court of the Mews, the coachman's white house being the Castle Keep, there sat . . . the Courts of Love. And they still sit there. . . . Later I was to sit myself—and catch my scorpion—in the courtyard of the castle of Roumanille where one of the very many Courts of Love used to be held. On the little range of the Alpilles near St Rémy de Provence it was at convenient distance from Les Baux, Arles, Tarascon, Châteaurenard and a great many other places from which could come the troubadours and their ladies. . . . Nevertheless for me *the* Court of Love, the great court of all, still, when I have not my thoughts under control, sits in the fore-court of that gentleman's coachman's Mews. . . . I knew, you see, that those Courts were held—'holden' I should then have said—in great, open, stony, sunlit spaces, before the white tower of some great celebrity and that fore-court was the only place I knew of as supplying all those necessary features. . . . And after all a Lord Mayor's coachman is surely a great enough celebrity and that was what the father of my friend was. I do not believe that I have ever again beheld such another Great Man. Not even Colonel Cody or Mistral who so much resembled him was greater. . . . Why I have been privileged to hold the silver wig of that pursy little, bowlegged man whilst, with the air of the supreme connoisseur he brushed his three-cornered, cockaded hat. . . . And even today when Le Lor' Maire visits Paris in state and there are pictures in all the papers my heart beats rapturously when I see his coachman sitting high on the box of the State Coach, his cocked hat and silver periwig silhouetted against the Palace of the Chambre des Députés across the Place de la Concorde. . . . There are I know poets and novelists who delight in the fact that they have for backgrounds of their youthful remembrances the boundless prairies of their boyhood—the cornfields stretching from horizon to horizon in which they stalked the tremendous buffalo, scotched the repugnant rattlesnake, rode for their lives before the fell tornado on the back of their unbroken mustang. . . . Yes, my friends I have heard your boasts. But who among you has for your background a Lord Mayor's coachman . . . with the Courts of Love thrown in as make-weight? . . . None, I think.

At any rate, now you can understand why I so much love Provence.

CHAPTER IV

FIN DE SECTION

A WRITER in a Manchester paper accused me the other day of having indefatigably pursued the Great throughout my life. For myself I should have thought the process rather resembled that of falling beneath the wheels of successive cars of Juggernaut and emerging crushed, to be scarified with knives and flailed with scorpions. For I have never paid my tribute to greatness without being subsequently massacred—by the disciples of the Great Men. . . . But at any rate in the case of M. Bonhoure I may hope to escape. Since he became great, I have never seen him again.

In the old days, as I have said, after periods of trial and disaster I used to get my hair cut; if the disasters were prolonged I would bolt to Tarascon. But if the disasters seemed so prolonged as to appear to have no end I would not only bolt to Tarascon but immediately I was arrived there I would go with such speed to the studio of M. Bonhoure and remain for so long subject to his art that the friends with whom I travelled would think that I had disappeared for good. . . . Before, indeed, he received his Five Million bolt from heaven, I must have sat under him I do not know how many hundred hours. So I might be said to have had his acquaintance.

Nevertheless I have never presumed on the fact and I presume that I shall never see him again since I shall never again see him in his *atelier;* and he will sit obstinately in the Café du Commerce whilst I, as obstinately, shall patronise the Café de

Paris where the clients are professional—and more *rangés*. Great changes occur during lives—in tastes, habits, circumstances, views, ambitions. But that change I imagine that neither M. Bonhoure nor I will ever make. Neither of us shall be unfaithful to the *cafés* that are ours.

When one travels on the Great Trade Routes and fetches up in smaller localities one should be circumspect—at any rate if one plans to return. And I am hardly exaggerating when I say that all my travelling has always been one long planning to return. One should skim through a place and if one likes it establish little contacts, with a waiter, a marketwoman, an honest merchant, an eating-place, or merely those contacts that are part of memory. Then, when one returns to stay a little, one has already made some sort of preparation for digging in. So it was not snobbishness that made me avoid being seen coming away late at night from a *café* that boasted a *Dancing*.

In such places you should be circumspect. You should give the impression that you are what the French call *sérieux*—at any rate if you are a novelist or an honest man. If you are a moralist it is different; you will want to distort truths so you do not need to see them. But the moment that you present to the world an aspect that is not "serious," the world will change its attitude towards you and the class of men who present themselves to you will also be "unserious." The novelist and the honest man on their travels need to see the world and the Great Trade Routes under their normal aspects. They have serious missions; they desire to make acquaintance with the truth, whereas for poets, conquerors, bankers, moralists or street singers that is unnecessary. A State Senator from the Middle West can—and not unusually does—make a hog of himself in a Paris night resort and no great harm will be done. He does not come there to learn and he will find himself amongst his kind. He will offend no prejudices.

But the novelist is an ambassador and the honest man with his voice and his vote will influence the policy of his home-country towards the country that he is visiting. It is their duty to see straight and in order to see straight they must attract to them and form their transitory society of normal and honest men like themselves. So they must appear neither frivolous nor fanatical, neither mean nor over-generous, though it is less harmful to be close than to be prodigal; and they must seem neither puritan nor loose in manners. Otherwise they will give unfavourable aspects to their own country and see the country that they are visiting in disagreeable lights.

I do not care who sees me coming out of what sort of resort in London or New York; I shall in those cities be seen in a number of places, my conduct will be averaged out and I am indifferent to the impression that I there produce. But in Tarascon I will not be seen coming out of a *café* to which a *Dancing* is attached so that M. Bonhoure and I will never meet again. . . .

I had for the moment forgotten that I have fallen from my high ambassadorial estate and, in pursuit of advancement, have announced myself a Moralist—and the Moralist will never be seen leaving whatever sort of *café* because he will never visit one. He will acquire his knowledge of life lying on his bed behind the closed jalousies of his hotel room, reading salacious gossip about Montparnasse—that will have been written for him specially. But a *café* is a serious place where serious people discussing serious subjects mould civilisations—and if the Moralist frequented such places his occupation would be gone.

But though I may change my condition it is extremely hard to change of set purpose one's habit of mind or even of body. So, though I try to break myself of it, my habit still remains that of one always out and about seeking for human instances where humane men congregate or go about their normal occupations. . . . And I doubt if, even though I repeat again and again: "Every day and in every way I get more ethical and more ethical and more ethical" I shall now much change. . . .

Still, inward change does occur in men without any consciousness on their parts, so that there may yet be hope.

I have, as you may be aware, lately been thinking about the Troubadours. . . . Talk of changes! I began in my young days and under the serious and rather awful auspices of my father by regarding the troubadour as occupying an enormously important part in the poetic cosmogony and as being a man, serious, subtle and heroic upon whom one should model oneself. Then, shortly after my father's death, I became possessed of a piano of my own.

I came then upon a popular song that I strummed unceasingly in our playroom. It ran:

> "Gaily the troubadour touched his guitar
> As he was hastening home from the war,
> Singing: 'From Palestine homewards I come;
> Lady-love, lady-love welcome me home!'"

Alas, the vapidity of the tune and of the occupation of its subject—for I was by then of an age when it began to appear to me to be unmanly to be overmuch concerned, or to be concerned at all, with ladies and it seemed to me that that fellow would have been much better employed getting on with the Crusades. So I put my father's books on a back shelf and, as it were, subscribed to the Northern reaction. Ibsen and Sudermann and Hauptmann and Tolstoi were coming.

I did not go altogether to those lengths. I do not think that I ever went mad about Ibsen and Sudermann. Tolstoi I always disliked, though I actually printed a long, long poem in German, by Herr Hauptmann, in the *English Review* at a time when I was looking for world figures and paid enormous sums for articles by President Taft, for unpublished poems by D. G. Rossetti and sketches by Anatole France. . . .

But towards the age of fourteen I substituted, as my life's hero and Greatest Poem in the World, for Guillem de Cabestanh, that is to say, and *Li Dous Cossire* the Minnesinger,

Walther von der Vogelweide and his poem "Tandaradei." My
translation of that latter poem begins:

Under diu Linde	Under the lime-tree
Uf der Heide	On the heather
Da unser zweie Bette was	There was our two-fold resting-place
Ir muoget vinden	You might have found there
Sckoene beide	Close together
Gebrokken Bluomen unde Gras	Broken flowers crushed i' the grass
Bei ein Wald in einem Thal	Near a shaw in such a vale
"Tandaradei,"	"Tandaradei,"
Suose sanh diu Nachgingal	Sweetly sang the Nightingale . . .

It afterwards achieved its little celebrity and was belauded
by Mr Pound. It must have been made when I was just over
fourteen though, as is the case with the poem of Cabestanh.
I have gone on mentally polishing it ever since. Indeed it is only
ten minutes ago—for a reason which will be apparent to those
whose memory goes back for twenty years—that I substituted
in the first line the word "lime-tree" for the word "lindens"
which for forty years odd must have given that translation a
Potsdamish aspect.

I am about to make a confession.

There can have been few literary figures that I more disliked—or who more disliked me—and few poets for whom I can
have had more, if kindly, contempt than respectively Mr—afterwards Sir—Edmund Gosse and Henry Wadsworth Longfellow.
Yet it is to a poem of Longfellow's and a book, "Northern
Studies," by Sir Edmund Gosse that I owe the beginnings of
my knowledge of Walther von der Vogelweide—a knowledge
that became almost a passion and that has lasted all my life.

Longfellow's poem began:

"Vogelweid the Minnesinger when he left this world of ours
  Laid his body in the cloisters underneath yon abbey towers;
  And he gave the monks his treasure, left them all with this behest,

They should feed the birds at noontide, daily on his place of rest. . . ."

That poem too was set to voluptuous music and over and over again I used to play it on my piano in the basement play-room and, with my *voix de compositeur* I used to chant those words. . . .

I will add as a digression that, on the same piano and with the same voice—I was then intending to be a composer of music—I used to chant the words of a song called "By The Waters of Babylon" which, to music suited to a throaty contralto, began:

> "The harp is now silent; unstrung is the lute;
> The voice of the minstrel for ever is mute;
> Each day bringeth trial, each night bringeth woe
> Whilst o'er Judah's children exulteth the foe.
> Oh, fatherland dear, once happy and free,
> We ne'er shall return from our bondage to thee!"

And when, as I subsequently did, I used all my powers of persuasion to impress on Masterman and through him on the Asquith Cabinet the desirability of making the return of Zion to the Jews one of the items of our return to peace, I used to hear myself—putting the loud pedal down meanwhile—play-ing, *rallentando* and exceedingly *portamento*, in those basement shadows, the resolution, adding b flat to the common chord of C. major—the resolution from the dominant into the tonic, which preceded my bellowing the words . . . "Oh, fatherland dear! . . ."

And don't I, too, when sitting beneath my olive-trees above the Mediterranean, thinking of bouquets to present to the night-ingale that, from above my head, is with his little throat shaking the whole world. . . . Don't I—not always, but every now and then—see the red binding with gilt letters of "Northern Studies by Edmund Gosse" . . . and the Middle High Ger-man words of "Tandaradei" that Mr. Gosse printed in his ap-pendix? I must have read at any rate that part of the book over and over again in my shadows and certainly I set "Tandaradei" to music, chanting that, in turn, over and over again . . . for months.

I make these confessions for a set purpose of moralisation.

Down below my house resides a distinguished American scholar, and along the coast an almost more distinguished American poet. When they condescend to visit me the main burden of either's conversation is reproaches to me for having praised writers whose prosperity annoys them or may be taken to interfere with the careers of their friends. I remain however Damas, or it may have been Daimas, the unrepentant thief of the Crucifixion. . . . I never, I think . . . or never but once, wrote a contemptuous word of another living writer and I have praised, along with one or two who subsequently became swans, an almost infinite number of goslings.

I have said that dog shouldn't eat dog so many times that I won't any more dilate on the text that *noblesse oblige*. But merely as a matter of expediency one writer should never abuse another. The reason for the abuse is as a rule that A thinks that if B is praised and so sells his books A's sales will be diminished—or, as Conrad used to put it: "*Le bien est l'ennemi du mieux*"—The pretty good is the enemy of what is best.

Nothing is more fallacious. The real obstacle to any writer's fame and wealth is not the sale of books by others but the extreme distaste that the Public—and particularly the Anglo-Saxon public, though under infection from the North the Northern French are taking too to football, though not, thank God, the Provençal who is faithful to his bullfights and his *Escolo de Targuen*—the real obstacle is that the Public has an extreme distaste for reading books. If, then, the layman can be induced to acquire the habit of reading, the writer—any writer—will have a proportionately increased chance of making money. When the first troubadour with harp, lute and attendant jongleur first went pricking across the plains below les Baux and sought by his *sirventes* and *albades* to obtain hospitality from the Les Baux family, he was roughly chased away from the rocky slopes. "What," said the Vicomte-King, "do we want with this gut-scraping and caterwauling?" But when, taking his wife's advice, Raymond Bérenger of Barcelona got some troubadours to attend him on a visit that he was making to the Emperor Frederick at Milan, Bérenger got from the Emperor all the boons that he desired. . . . Without question, because the Emperor was so delighted with the musical knights that he himself straightway became a troubadour and incontinently wrote the canzone beginning: "*Plasz mi cavalier Francez. . . .*"

Immediately the boom was on. Raymond Bérenger was granted not only the investiture of the fief of Provence but its ratification. And "Hearing thereof," as Mistral sings, "the lords of Baux"—those Philistines who had repelled the troubadours—"came down in wrath with a great clangour of armed men. But music had already gained the day and where the Phoebus of Provence had shone the Æolus of storm-shaken les Baux was powerless."

The great Sordello sang the triumph of the Provençal lute and rhyme; every lord of Christendom hastened to write verse to be sung and to attract troubadours to his Court. Henry II of England was worsted by Bertran de Born of Altaforte who carried off later the mistress of the Lion Heart. So he shook the world, even as did Orpheus or Philomela. It was the golden age of writers!

Now supposing that some scholar of the day had written against the unnamed bards of Bérenger and had persuaded the Emperor that those poets were unworthy to be listened to. Or supposing the great Sordello had persuaded the Emperor that your only poetry came from the Province of Genoa. . . . I do not mean to hammer on the moral; but it must be obvious that many troubadours would have lacked hospitality and many more would have had to put up with the fate of Guillem de Cabestanh at the hands of a lord of les Baux. . . . Whereas, is it not well known, that when la Louve, wife of the lord of the twin castles of the Black Mountain up behind Carcassonne—

when la Louve treated with disdain the advances of the great
singer Peire Vidal who was the son of a furrier, her husband
not only remonstrated with her but even fitted out an expedition to bring back the troubadour when he had got himself
into trouble on the way to the Crusades? He did that so that the
bard should write more and always more odes to the charms
of his—the lord's—wife. Such advantages must be seldom enjoyed by the scholars and poets of Anglo-Saxondom today—
or such publicity! Only think! . . . Yet it all came, in the end,
from what we may well call the team-spirit! Nor did even
patriotism interfere with that boom, for it is odd to think that
few indeed of those writers and contrivers of the Provençal
tongue came from true Provence—and a great many Northern
French poets took in those days to writing the Langue-d'Oc. . . .
Much as if American writers in a sudden period of Eastern
boom in books should take to writing in English-English. . . .
Or of course, the reverse! . . .

Scholarship is a quality for which I have always had a great
contempt and of which I have always felt the most supreme
distrust. . . . The best scholar of his day would have interrupted
and destroyed the flow of the Sermon on the Mount by cavil-
ling at the Preacher's use of the enclitic *de* and if in Bloomsbury I should chance today to say that I consider Frédéric
Mistral a greater poet than Homer the most prominent critic of
that district would wince and exclaim: "Oh, but surely, Mr F.
Not *Homer!*"

That is what I mean when I say that Provence is not a
country nor the home of a race, but a frame of mind. To find
yourself in harmony with the soul of Provence you have to be
of a type that will not be pained when someone says that
Mistral was a greater poet than Goethe—or that the Maries,
after the Crucifixion, came to and settled in the country round
Tarascon. Indulgent Provence has no vested interests and there
illusions do not matter.

I don't know whether Mistral was a greater poet than Virgil

and I don't care. . . . Where I went to school in London, amidst
the dreaming spires, we used to have a mathematics master. His
name was Thompson and he had waxed moustaches. I did not
see as much of him as I ought to because his classes were held
in the afternoon and, most afternoons, in furtherance of my
musical education I used to go to concerts. But when I did
attend his courses I would hear him setting problems of which
I only remember one and that dimly. It was this: If you had
for lever a straw of sufficient length and, for fulcrum the planet
Mars, how much force, the weight of Mars and of the Earth
being ascertained, must an elephant, standing on the end of
that straw exert in order to move the Earth 1.065 millimetres?
. . . He would then add: "The weight of the elephant may be
neglected."

So I don't know whether Mistral was a greater poet than
Tennyson. . . . What I do care about is that if, for the purpose
of an argument or to hear what it may sound like or in furtherance of a train of thought, I choose to say and, intoxicated by
the sun, momentarily to believe, that Mistral so was, I don't
want to be interrupted in my sermon or my train of thought
by someone who will be pained. The question of what is 'greatness' may be neglected.

And in the frame of mind that is Provence I shan't be interrupted. Almost anywhere else along the Great Trade Route I
shall. Certainly in London; almost certainly in Paris, where too
there are mental vested interests. . . . As to the territory behind
the Statue of Liberty I am not so sure. In New York, for
instance, you may declare any number of goslings to be birds
of paradise. No one will be pained; some few, or a large crowd,
will believe you; and you yourself will not grieve when your
cygnet begins to waddle and hiss. That, I fancy is why, on my
journeys, I am content to stay in that city for longer periods
than anywhere else—except the sea-shore of the Roman Province. What I—and civilisation—most need is a place where,
Truth having no divine right to glamour, experiments in

thought abound. And that, neglecting the weight of the elephant, may open for the mind the road to regions of conjecture that could not otherwise be explored. That place will be found on the left bank, not of the Seine, but the Rhone.

In that country there is room to think. For, though there is little there is a little of everything. . . . It would be absurd to say that there are as many vital pictures in Provence as in the galleries of London or that in the whole Roman Province you could get as bad a gallery headache as you can in any fourth-rate town in an Italy that is one long gallery headache. But with the matchless picture in the convent at Villeneuve-lès-Avignon—the picture that the popular mind ascribes to the good King or the slightly more learned to Clouet and the positively learned to Quarton or some other painter of the Avignon Group—with that and the miraculously beautiful ivory virgin of the church of the same place, with the Avignon primitives of the museum in that city and scattered here and there in churches and monasteries; with the primitives of the Nice *atelier;* with the thought of Cézanne at Aix-en-Provence; Renoir at Cagnes; Monticelli at Marseilles; Gauguin and Van Gogh at Arles and the votive paintings at Notre Dame de Laghet in the hinterland between Cannes and Nice—with all those there is in this territory enough to last a proper man for his lifetime. And he can live a fine life without the agonising wildernesses of worthless Old Masters that make the searching for living painting in the Louvre, the Vatican, the Pitti or even the Metropolitan Museum one long calvary! And as with painting so with poetry, prose, music, myth, religion, history, science—remember Henri Fabre of Avignon!—economics, handicrafts, gardens, seafaring, bulls, crime, and above all architecture, there is in this territory enough. And there is neither mass-production nor the worship of mass-production and Provence is at once the cradle and the conduit of that humane, Romance Latinity that alone can preserve from putridity our staggering civilisation and world. . . .

The perspicacious Reader will by now have perceived what I am here getting at in the way of Form. The Novel, as Mr Wells long ago told me, can very well be based on the structure of the Sonata! FIRST SUBJECT Hero; SECOND SUBJECT Heroine; RE-STATEMENT of Case of Hero; ditto of Heroine; the FREE FANTASIA or mix-up of the affairs of Hero and Heroine; the RECAPITULATION or Marriage in which the themes of Hero and Heroine are re-stated in one and the same key. . . . Well, for this book I have chosen the larger form of the Opera. We approach now the limits of this section—the *fin de section* that the careful bus-conductor in Paris announces when, if you have not already done it, you must pay a supplementary fare. . . . And the perspicacious Reader will have perceived that this section is in fact the Overture of the Opera—the division in which the composer adumbrates, without dwelling on, the themes that he will later work out. He has, that is to say, put in and registered, his *leit-motiven* . . . his main-subjects. In what follows they shall be worked out in as you might say two keys, the dominant and the tonic. . . . With that statement I seem to have drifted into a thing I never thought to find myself perpetrating. . . . But, pun and all, it is illustrative enough. For in music the 'tonic' is the normal, or first and last, key of a piece, the 'dominant' being the key whose scale begins with, and is named after, the fifth note. . . . In *this* piece you may say that the dominant theme is that of our great, noisy and indigestion-sick Anglo-Saxondom which can only be touched by inspiration from the spirit of Provençal Latinity, frugality and tolerance. That consideration begins and ends and is the tonic or normal key of this piece of writing.

Or you might, if you liked, say that, its Hero being Septentrionalism, its Heroine is the warm South. That image of yours would be pretty good too. For it is the Great Truth of the South that those households prosper most and work most smoothly where the till and the accounts are kept by Madame, Monsieur meanwhile galloping from Vaison to Palestine on his outrageous errands. So our Northern civilisation—if you can call it that—set prancing out from humanity's warm home towards Lyons, which you would say had the worst climate in the world, to places like Paris, London, Dublin or Detroit, in search of adventure, of pioneering, winning numbers in lotteries, empire. . . . What is it that we live for? . . . And he found, poor Hero, nothing but always worse and worse climates, worse and worse food, worse and worse Crises, worse and worse wars, pestilences, indigestions and despairs; heresies, inquisitions; worse music, dances, fears for his soul.

And all the while in the territory south of Montélimar Dame Provence sits at home, forsaken but reading in her little account books with, in her apron pocket, the one bulb and the sole herbs that cure all indigestions, crises, impulses to massacre. . . .

I have been told that, before he sent his telegram to President Kruger of which you may have heard but which finally put an end to all chances of friendship between Anglo-Saxondom and the more pink Nordic branch of our Northern barbarism, the German Emperor had partaken of a surfeit of underdone roast beef prepared by Mrs Kennard's cook from the famous *White Heather*. . . . At any rate the Emperor used to hire the *White Heather* and go cruising in the Mediterranean. And he mightily embarrassed Mrs Kennard by sending to her from places like Corfu and Valetta and Jerusalem, telegrams signed only "William." . . . And Heaven Knows, Mrs Kennard used to say, what her village post-office people might think! . . . Innumerable telegrams saying what a good time William was having and how he blessed her and what perfect heaven it was to eat day after day the cooking of a real English *chef* like hers. . . . I actually saw some of those telegrams. . . . And eventually the Emperor bribed the *White Heather chef* to desert Mrs Kennard and go to Potsdam. Heaven knows what became of him after, on the night of a third of August he cooked the over-greasy *homard à l'Américaine*. For it caused the eventual despatch, at four in the morning, to Gemmenich, and so ended our makeshift for a civilisation. . . . And delightful old Mrs Kennard used to say that she was only too glad to get rid of her cook. The amount of grease that he used to manage to get into his *plats* and his complete refusal to use herbs or other seasonings had been till then her despair on the great waters. . . . The cook indeed was only a promoted deckhand from Wapping, the real *chef* who came from Clamart having fallen sick of Malta fever. . . . However that may be, and I will vouch for the hiring of the *White Heather*, the telegrams and the bribing of the cook to desert, the moral seems to be that there is no hope for us unless we reform the cooking at least of our rulers. In our over- gas-, steam-, or oil-heated apartments, fighting in our climates that are unfitted for human life, the endless chills on the liver, nights without sleep and four-in-the-morning horrors, we shall go on getting grosser and ever more gross, further and further away from Latinity and plunging deeper and deeper into mass-production, ruin, reaction and massacre. . . . When we have finished burning all Jewish books we shall burn all 'foreign' books, each in his own nation. And then we shall burn *all* books. It shall be night from Pole to Pole. . . .

Only, in one sunlit triangle of the earth to the right of the Rhone looking North, the frame of mind which is Provence shall sit keeping her sheep on the sun-baked rocks, amidst the unnumbered tufts of pot-herbs. She shall spin to the drone of the false-wasps that Fabre wrote about. In her apron pocket a clove of that plant that is sovran against not only true-wasp stings but against most of the ills of the flesh. She shall sit and spin and spin, awaiting the return from the North of her Gentleman spouse. And when we shall have succeeded in slaying or in starving through over-production the one the other until no more is left of the peoples of the earth than shall comfortably populate the Roman Province and its kin triangle of the Narbonnais, the Good King shall come again and civilisation begin once more its upward climb. . . . And who knows that we shall not by then have learned the wisdom of the Good King's lesson?

For it is related of that King of Sicily and Naples, Duke of Anjou, Bar and Lorraine, and Count of Provence that, after he had lost all his dominions save Provence and was retired to Tarascon, certain ambassadors came to him from Catalan Spain. They talked of the glories of his old, lost wars and offered, he aiding, to avenge him on his nephew, Louis of Anjou, and his other enemies and to restore to him his lost dominions. But he, answering nothing, pointed from the battlements of his *bastide*, at his lands as they lay beneath the sun. . . . May we, one day, learn to do the same, and in contentment live obscurely the inner life. . . .

For the glories of Provence are obscure and inner glories. There were no doubt Homer and the famous men before him; there were the Augustans and their glories and a tiny sheaf of poetry; there were the troubadours who shed glories over Provence but were aliens. . . . Then after centuries came the *félibriste* poets whom Mistral drew, like Cadmus with his dragon's teeth, from his native soil round Maillanne. That poetry, largely because of the Troubadour-Tartarin legend, has for years in the outside world been taken to be rumbustious and of the hyper-Romantic order. That again is largely because French with its minced and worn spelling is familiar to us and not Provençal with its greater approximation to Latin.

Mounte soun la clarour de l'aubo e l'abrivado has a barbarous aspect to eyes accustomed to reading: *Où sont la clarté de l'aube et la galopade*. . . . But actually, if "où" be more agreeable in sound than "mounte," "clarour" is much more agreeable than "clarté," "aubo," a little more sonorous than "aube" and "abrivado" infinitely more beautiful than "galopade." And Provençal being nearer that Latin that is the fountain of all cultured speech of today it is difficult to say which is the nearer to being a dialect, French or Provençal. . . . That apart, the extreme simplicity and the domestic imagery of the

Provençal poets seems to set them, in the realm of pure poetry, infinitely above any group of poets of their age. . . . Listen to "*Rêverie d'un gardian*" of Joseph d'Arbaud . . . the reverie of one, grown old, of those who, on their white horses, year in, year out, until they can no longer ride, head the wild gallops of the bulls along the vast, solitary, salt stretches of the Camargue. . . .

Mounte soun la clarour de l'aubo e l'abrivado	Where are the clear light of the dawn and the gallop
Di chivau s'esbroufant dins lou vent matinié?	Of horses neighing in the wind of the morning?
Li fougau mando i plat lusènt de l'estanié	The fire throws onto the shining pewter of the dresser
Sa michour douço e lou rebat de la flamado.	Its soft warmth and the reflection of the flame.

Lou cat dor sus mi cambo e roundino

Lou cat dor sus mi cambo e roundino;	The cat, asleep on my knees, is purring;
En escoutant lou vènt que despampo li souco;	Listening to the flutter of the wind amongst the brands,
Iéu sounje à tant de grun qu'ai quicha sus mi bouco;	I think of all the fruits that I have crushed in my mouth,
Sounje à tant de draoù mounte me siéu perdu.	I sit thinking of all the paths on which I have gone astray.
Ma jouinesso s'en vai coume li dindouleto	My youth has gone as went the swallows
Quand veson s'avança li nèblo sus la mar,	When they saw the mists come towards them above the sea

E lou coupo es asclado e lou vin es amar	And the bowl is cracked and the wine is bitter
E dins lou cors malaut l'amo se sènt soulèto.	And in the failing body the soul sits solitary.
Pamens, per li carriero, e li muraio blanco,	There was a time when in the little streets with white walls
Cavalié, m'abrivave au soulèu de miejour	Proudly I galloped in the mid-day heat,
Eme lou ferre au poung a la taiolo is anco	Lance in hand the belt above the haunches.
Quand partian do sansouiro à la primo dou jour	There was a time when we left the corrals at the break of day.
Li chato amoulounado i porto di cabano,	The girls clustering round the doors of the cabins
Emé soun rire fres nous cri-davon: bonjour.	With their clear laughter wished us their good-days.
Mai serious, plega dins li bernous di lano	But, grave, rolled in our woollen burnouses,
A l'auro dou matin butavian nosti tau	In the breath of the dawn we pressed the bulls along,
E lou souléou levant fasié lusi li bano.	The rising sun shining on their horns.
Ourguianço di fort, cresçenço di catau,	Pride of the strong, swelling pride of the chieftains,
Ruscle di conquistaire abriva dins li vilo	Thirst of the conqueror swoop-ing down on conquered towns. . . .
Erias nostro quand passavian sout li porto.	All these were ours when we galloped before the door.
Solides augalop, imbrandable, intravian dins l'areno	A-gallop, invincible, we swept into the arena
E li chato, is autin, nous picavon di man.	And the girls from the balconies clapped their hands for us.
Pièi quand l'errour venié davans la niue sereno	Then when came evening be-fore the calm of the night
Quiha sus lis estrieu se tiravian dou rond	Erect in our stirrups we drove out of that oval

FIN DE SECTION

En butant nosti tau prim com   Pressing before us the panting
   l'alabreno   bulls

E lou sang di chevau bagnavo   And the blood of the horses
   l'esperon.   bathed our spurs.

You understand that these men every Sunday, armed with trident-headed lances, drive their wild bulls from the Camargue through the crowded feast-day streets into the bull-rings of a hundred Provençal villages—the bulls not being killed but having rosettes planted, in the open rings, on their shoulders or between their horns by the village youths. . . . It is of course not a glorious sport like the rodeo performances of international fame. The bulls are mere savage wild bulls, not tamed steers. . . . But it goes on week in, week out, without any fuss, obscurely, like the poetry of the *félibre* poets, the pastorales at Christmas, the water-joustings in the seaboard harbours, the pilgrimages to the shrines on the nearly inaccessible mountains—and the Rhone which, though not a glorious stream like the Rhine or the Hudson or even the Seine, yet keeps on rolling and, as Till said to Tweed, for every one that all three together can drown . . . drowns two.

But isn't there a certain universality expressed in that poem of Arbaud the *félibriste*? Can't you imagine the rodeo rider retired on his fortune, thinking like that? Or the banker retired without his fortune? Or the king in exile? Or any old poet? Or I, and, one day, you? . . . The quality of quiet universality may not make for greatness. . . . Who can tell what does? But it is indispensable to poetry . . . which is life eternal.

And you may observe that I have got along without having to tell that story of the elephant. So that I retain my commercial integrity and may style myself an honest merchant.

Part Two

PROVENCE FROM THE NORTH

CHAPTER I

PROVENCE FROM LONDON

SOMEWHERE between Vienne and Valence the South begins; somewhere between Valence and Montélimar . . . Eden! The Rhone, having those towns on her banks runs due South from Lyons to the Mediterranean. And nothing will persuade me to believe that when Man in contagious madness left those regions for the North that was not the real Fall and that what Eve ate sinfully was, not an apple, but a dish of Brussels sprouts boiled in water that lacked the salt of the Mediterranean. Let that at least serve for a symbol.

The Arts, Creeds, High Finance and the rush for Lottery Tickets of one kind or another are no doubt important factors in human happiness, virtue or despair. But the most important of all are climate and the nature of the soil. You will say I say that because ageing arteries convey less and less the warm blood to my extremities.

That is not so.

I am sitting writing in the garret of a gloomy, fog-filled, undignifiedly old, London house. I have no fire, having lost in Provence the very habit of fires. A purplish phantom of sunlight filters, on the most depressed day of the London year, beneath the black-purple pall of the upper sky across the view from my elevated casements. It is Good Friday and this is a cavern of drafts.

Nevertheless it is only if I feel with my left the back of my writing hand that I have any sensation of coldness. To live in

Provence is to forget how to be cold and within me all is warm. . . .

The brilliant notes of a brand-new barrel-organ rise from the pavement far below. Even they have no power to make me shiver. Yet, next to the pailful of little fishes that the Princess poured into her bridegroom's bed, the *Intermezzo* from *Cavalleria Rusticana*, rising in hard, silvery notes from a London Good Friday street should most drive the warmth of the vital fluid from the superficies of the body. . . . And imagine a city where the *Intermezzo* may still draw alms from the charitable!

But somewhere between Vienne and Valence, below Lyons on the Rhone the sun is shining and, south of Valence, *Provincia Romana*, the Roman Province lies beneath the sun. There there is no more any evil for there the apple will not flourish and the Brussels sprout will not grow at all.

Do not believe that I am indulging in a reverie of green sickness. I can pick up my traps and away to the South whenever I want to. No, what I am about is preaching salvation to my City and to Humanity which can only be saved by achieving for itself and within itself the frame of mind that can exist only south of Montélimar.

I hear you say: "An apple a day keeps the doctor away."

Yes, but south of Valence you pay the starveling doctor only twenty francs a visit. Except for the hypochondriac there is there no need for doctors and hypochondria itself dies amongst the vines, in the shadow of the olive trees.

"A grape-fruit in the morning will keep your brows from horning," they sing in New York, which is perhaps a little nearer Eden than is London. At any rate it is in the same latitude as Valence or so near as makes no difference.

If in the caravanserais called Palaces on the Côte d'Azur, of a morning, in the accent of old New England, you ask for a Grape-Fruit you will be given one. On your bill you will find it charged for at seventeen francs and seventy-five centimes. But in the shouting, sun-shot market that is just round the

corner, you will obtain a *pamplemousse* for fifty centimes . . .
or for ten. Or you will have a couple thrown in as make-weight
with a pound of haricots, according as the market-wife likes
your face or has breakfasted well or ill. The *pamplemousse*
grows in Provence like a weed and is accounted one, a little
'zest' of its rind being used to give flavour to certain dishes of
fish and the rest being thrown to the pigs.

The *Pamplemousse* is the Grape-Fruit—and pamplemousse
and grape-fruit alike are the shaddock of the Old Testament.
The apple will not grow in Palestine nor will the shaddock in
England. So, in James I's day the Translators of the Author-
ised Version finding in Genesis the Hebrew for "shaddock" as
the Forbidden Fruit just set it down an apple. . . . That was
the fruit that Eve ate and since no-one eats the pamplemousse
in Provence there is there no more any evil.

Why should there be? The olive there gives its oil; the vine
lets down the grape and its juices; the hills are alive with hares,
boars and, in thousands, with the *grive*, the partridge, and the
ortolan. Garlic there grows wild amongst all the other potherbs
—and in such profusion that the foam the Mediterranean churns
out on those shores is nothing less than *aioli* so that the strongest
swimmers from the unperfumed North in those waves turn pale
and sink to the halls of the syrens.

Yes, why should anyone there sin? It would be superfluous.
Life there is so pleasant, that if, as the Pilgrim Fathers, their
Nordic ancestors and descendants held, to enjoy is to sin all
life is there one long breaking of commandments. . . . Which
is absurd—or Nordic-sublime which is the same thing.

The sublimities of the North become, amongst the orange-
coloured, sun-baked rocks south of Montélimar, pleasant ab-
surdities, the South making for ever of our Nordic virtues a
continual *reductio ad absurdum*. Fafnir, the spouting Eddic
dragon is there translated into the Tarasque, a spiked, moon-
calf monster of osier and tarpaulin, gambolling around the footsteps of St Martha as she walks the cobbles of Tarascon.

Grettir the strong is there Tartarin, and Brünnhilde, Nicolette whose feet were so white that the daisies they brushed look like coal. Nay, Calvinism itself was there ante-dated by the gently sceptical heresy of the Albigenses whom it took an English reformer at the behest of a king of Nordic France to root out. And the very Divorce Courts that, grimly in Fleet Street and in Reno to the sound of jazz, render our Nordic domesticities one long and grinning cacophony—the very divorce courts were there preceded by the tribunals that once sat at Roumanille and enquired into the nature of Love. . . .

From the battlements of that joyous castle in the Alpilles the knights and other knights' consorts, presided over by the beauteous Clémence Isaure, could see in the plain of Orgon below them the raging tempestuous battle in which Caius Marius defeated the Imbrogenes and saved civilisation. Later they could see the vast assemblage of wedding guests that filled the whole landscape. They were attending the ceremony by which, amongst the tufts of lavender, thyme and rosemary, that same hero made an honest woman of St Mary the Magdalene and became the ancestor of the infinite tribe of Mariuses that populates the Roman Province.

In the interval that Court sat in judgment on the following cases: ONE: A lady, convinced that her lover is perfection's self, has taken other lovers in the effort to assure herself by the test of comparison that her conviction is not a mistaken one. Is she guilty of infidelity? . . . Answer: No. She has paid her lover the highest of tributes.

TWO: The wife of a gentleman dies. Immediately after her soul has left the still warm body the soul of another lady enters it and there takes abode. The husband continues to live maritally with the compound: is he guilty of incontinence? Answer: *De minimis non curat Lex.* . . . The Law does not take account of trifles.

It is thus, you see, difficult to sin in Provence and the climate and perfumed vegetation are there such as to make men avoid

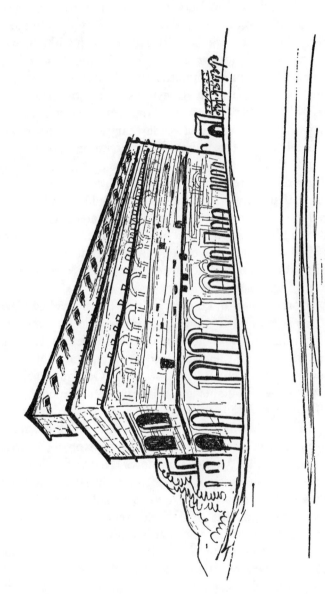

The Roman Theatre at Orange

difficulties. The husband of Bérangère des Baux made no bones about taking the easiest way, slaying Guillem de Cabestanh and giving his wife the poet's heart to eat and his blood, with perhaps a zest of *pamplemousse*, to drink. Bérangère was faced with a difficult problem in etiquette. . . . What should you do when you discover that you have unwittingly become philochthonous? She took the easy way out and declaring that so sweet were that meat and that wine that none others should ever pass her lips, she threw herself from the highest point of Les Baux into the Camargue. And the wine that grows on that spot is to this day called Sanh Del Trobador.

It is true that others sing the fate of Guillem differently, declaring that she gave him a love-potion "whereof he sickened and grew mad." But that does not detract from the moral which is that in Provence you circumvent rather than overcome difficulties, since love obtained by a philtre can never be much else than an *ersatz*—a synthetic—passion.

Stern effort is not unknown in the Rhone valley. The Romans there assembled several characteristically immense masses of masonry. The Pont du Gard supplied Arles with water—and water-rates; they built also the arenas of Nîmes and Arles, the triumphal arch and the theatre at Orange which are now handy for the bull-fights and classical performances by the Comédie Française of today. But these hugenesses were put together whilst they had Nordic captives in plenty. The smaller Augustan monuments—the little triumphal arch on the *Plateau des Antiquités* on the Alpilles outside St Rémy de Provence and the rest—were the work of Greek slaves and, if delicate and, in that solitary place, emotional, are yet so small that you would hardly notice them if they had been erected at the base of the Statue of Liberty or inside the Albert Hall.

And when it came to the treatment of at least one sin did not the Romans, coarse as they were, under the suns of Provence achieve a certain delicate humour and even fineness of appreciation? For, in disposing of Pontius Pilate who as well as being an unsatisfactory governor of Palestine must be accounted the greatest sinner of all, since he not only failed to appreciate the necessity for Truth but actually made a jest of that indispensable arcanum of the Nordic just—the Romans, then, simply condemned that miserable fellow to pass the rest of his shivering days in Vienne, of all places of the world. That city is north of Valence and so outside not only the Roman Province but outside the South itself. And it must have been all the more bitter for that perfumed and indifferent hedonist that the Holy Maries and others of those who had attended at the Sacrifice he had done nothing to prevent should be permitted to finish their quiet lives in the sunlight and olive-shadows round Tarascon of the Tarasque and Arles of the Aliscamps. . . . Almost under his poor eyes. . . . Indeed, with a good glass, he could almost have seen arising the little church that you may still see in those Elysian fields—the Champs Elysées, Aliscamps, outside Arles. For that basilica was built by St Trophime himself during the lifetime of the Virgin and, in Her presence, dedicated to Her.

In the Aliscamps, truly, having traversed the sunlit and rocky expanses of the Roman Province, you may best in the shadow of the black cypresses consider how innocent lives may most fittingly find their close. Along the avenue goes the austere double line of the austere tombs of the pagan Romans. And, the legend avers, so holy was that place rightly esteemed even in the days of St Trophime that, when that Saint proposed to consecrate that old burial ground, Christ in person appeared and, kneeling on a stone that you may still see, extended His Hands over the avenue so that it is for ever suited to Christian burial.

And the Aliscamps remained seeming so holy right down the Middle Ages that it was the desire of every man of pious mind to be there buried. Thousands so were laid to rest and if your coffin was set afloat on the Rhone anywhere above Arles with, in it, sufficient money to pay for the burial, it would, if it got caught on a bank or in a backwater, be pushed by the pious into mid-stream until at last the watchers at Arles took it and buried it in the shadow of the cypresses. . . . A holy place!

In the name of progress it was however decreed that the Paris-Lyon-Méditerranée railway should be driven right through the sacred fields so that very little of it remains.

So, one night you shall take the 9.40 from the Gare de Lyon.

The Aliscamps, Arles

Rumbling through the vineyards of Burgundy beneath a trail of sparks you shall fall asleep somewhere before Dijon where magic cookery begins. You shall sleep through the long halt at Lyons that has the worst climate on all God's earth and where Industrialism, the Commercial Spirit and Puritanism all together reach at once their apogee and find their earthly close.

But at Vienne you will find yourself turning over on your

couchette; by Valence a new feeling will invade you. An unrest! Before Montélimar you will be in the swaying corridor looking for your first olive tree through the dark plate glass. Then you will find all sorts of Beings peeping, leering, ironically smiling, miching and mowing at you on the banks that fly by.

No doubt every region of the at all habitable globe is overlaid by dust on dust and shard on shard of successive, dead civilisations. But in Provence, which by that time you will have entered, those civilisations are familiar and easily recognisable. If you talk of Mayas or Goidels no images arise in your minds. But say: "Phoceans, Greeks, Romans, Saracens, Troubadours, North French and the Félibrists of Mistral!" and at once, across the dull, liver-coloured brick of the house-walls of the parish of St Marylebone or whatever other dullnesses you may be momentarily contemplating, your mind will see a procession of typified objects—the horse-hair-plumed helmets of Ulysses and his wanderers, the hennins and silks of the Courts of Love, the chain-mail of Saladin, the Phrygian cap of Liberty of the Marseillaises and all the black sombreros—of the poet of Maillane, of Gambetta who begat Tartarin in the mind of Daudet.

And behind all those images your mind will connote their hardly-visible or just-glimpsed deity-molochs and goblin-goddesses—Baal and Mithras and Diana and Allah and the Holy Maries and the Apostles and the angry Gods who fought the one against the other in the terrible wars of religion that devastated all Provence—the God of St Dominic and the other Gods of the Albigenses and the Huguenots. . . . And then all the attendant demi-gods and goblins of all that cloud of witnesses to the fugitive nature of mortal grandeur.

In our immense, flying, weighted meteor that hurls itself through the shadows between the olive and cypress trunks that were old when Zeus was new-born we seek to persuade ourselves that we and our civilisation signify something before the face of the Eternal. But the smiles of all those Beings Who

have existed since before Eternity began and Whom, in the
dawn, the mind figures irresistibly as standing watching us
amongst the tufts of rosemary, lavender and thyme . . . those
smiles may well awaken in us the deeper knowledge that we
have—that our thunderous approach and passing signify no
more than the shadow of a swallow flying between the cypress-
groves of the Aliscamps at Arles.

That is a sense that we—our civilisation if it is a civilisation—
lost when our fathers left the Roman Province and adventured
into these North parts. I don't know what has brought me here,
now, to London. I daresay it was more than anything sheer
curiosity as to prices. For the whole world now talks daily for
hours of nothing but the cost of living and, each person talking
always from the depth of momentary passions, the result is a
confusion that there is no deciphering at all. One must go and
see for oneself. The unscrupulous New Yorker will tell you
that clothes cost nothing in New York and that meat and cinema
tickets are given away for nothing on Sixth Avenue; the
unscrupulous Londoner tells you that prime fillet beef costs
threepence a pound everywhere within sound of Bowbells; the
advocate of the Quartier Latin will tell you that in the open-air
market of the Rue de Seine food costs exactly one quarter what
it costs in Montparnasse; the hardened Montparnassian will declare that not only is food cheaper on the Boulevard Port Royal
but that everything that you buy on the Rue de Seine was
beginning to be rotten before it was sent to that market. The
Londoner is however at the moment the most clamorous. So
that, no doubt, is why I am here.

And what strikes me first about the city of my birth is the
return of a sense that I used to have when years ago I wandered
about its streets—the sense of the permanence of London. One
can imagine an earthquake destroying the underlying rock that
is Manhattan and the tall buildings falling down and folding
together like a four-story house of cards; one can imagine Paris
razed by the Germans from the face of the earth. . . . But

London so spreads out; it is so broad-based that it could not overturn; it is so without features that one can credit it with neither human soul nor mortality. . . . And, here, the very immutability of human occupations conveys to your own self a sense of immortality. The barber who shaves you shaved you first forty years ago and has in no way changed; the waiter who waited on you as many years ago in your once favourite Soho restaurant has in no way aged; you would say that the same rabbits, ducks and puppies decorate today the naturalist's shop at which at the age of eleven you bought your first jackdaw; the urn above the door of your grandfather's house in Fitzroy Square has in the carvings of its rams' heads exactly the same soot as when first, trembling at the idea of its falling on your head, as a child of eight you went up the steps of No. 37! And if all these things are so immortal and unchanging why, why should you alone put on mortality or become, as reason tells you you must become, such a mere little heap of dust as would not fill a cup?

I shall be here—even if I were to be here for the rest of my life—for such a short time; the milk shop at the corner will be here for ten times as long a space. . . . Nevertheless I sit here writing in my dim garret on a Good Friday. From the street below, in compliment no doubt to the day, rises the sound of a man's voice that sings:

"There is a green hill far away without a city wall. . . ."

. . . And I don't mind saying that at that sound something like tears made themselves felt in my eyes . . . for if London is nothing else. London is the city and last stronghold of Christ. So I up with my shaky guillotine-casement, let in more fog and throw out twopence and hear it jangle on the pavement. . . .

But, as I sit down again and begin once more to write, I have the feeling that I shall sit here for ever, with the drafts seeping through the ancient casements, the water dripping in the cistern, writing whilst the man's voice rises from the street that is invisible because of the fog. . . . A very old, a very familiar feeling; and, as far as I am concerned, one that I have only in London.

It is no doubt that illusion that made my first sight of Provence the most memorable sensation of my life and that makes my every renewal of contact with those hills where grows the first olive tree of the South almost as memorable. It is as if one wakened from a dream of immortality to the realisation of what is earthly permanence.

And, ever since I first had that sensation in a train hastening through the dawn I have had two existences—a Provence life that was persistent and a life of other regions on the Great Route that were for ever changing. . . . I will not depress myself by reckoning out how long ago that was. It was a long time.

I sit with equanimity in a Nordic attic of a grey city; but the equanimity exists because I am composedly sure that I shall again see Provence. The purplish wash of sunlight has been replaced by an uncertain downfall of depressed rain and hesitating smuts. The man in the street has changed his song. He is now the man who broke the bank at Monte Carlo. . . . Provence, you see, has to come creeping in.

> "Has I walk erlong the Bor de Berlong with an independent air,
> You should 'ear the girls declare: "He must be a millionaire."
> You should 'ear them sigh and wish to die
> And see them wink the other eye
> At the Man who broke the bank at Monte Carlo."

What a permanence, if only in taste, and how truly they speak when they say that London is faithful to her old favourites! For presumably street singers and the manufacturers of brand-new barrel-organ cylinders must know what tunes will most surely elicit the twopences from the closed windows of the street-fronts—and I must have first heard those words at about the same date as that of my first sight of that landscape of shelving rooks, rosemary fronds, olive branches and imagined, primæval deities.

The poor singer has now been replaced by a brass band. What an unimaginable multitude of the indigent immense London must somewhere hide. . . . The band begins to play "The Girl I Left Behind Me." That tune was originally called "Brighton Camp" and was the quickstep of the London militia who were arrayed on the cliffs against the foe in 1780. . . . Did you say: 'Old favourites!' "

So my feeling for Provence is a loving equanimity. Provence shall always be there and, if not with the eyes of the flesh, then at least with those of the spirit I shall always see it as I see it here in spite of the fog and the tumult.

And yet that is not the state of mind of the Teuton who is always filled with *Sehnsucht* and sighing for the land *wo die Citronen bluehen*. That state of mind is probably unhealthy and certainly it is a misfortune for the rest of the world, if most particularly for France which stands between Germany and the lemon trees. But one may attain to a firm and quiet resolution to go to, to finish one's days in that home and cradle of one's kind without either loss of dignity nor yet sword and torch in hand.

To understand what that means it is necessary at least once to have seen the Roman Province. Having once seen it you may, like a lover who is convinced that his young woman still desires him beyond the mountains and across the seas, draw strength from the knowledge that that land exists and is unchanging. There will be no actual need to visit it again.

Obviously the ball we inhabit and whose surface we scratch will, after million-wise gyrations, one day fall back into the sun, and nothing earthly is in the absolute sense immutable. But, for all working purposes, Provence is. In forgotten and pre-historic days, before even the Great Trade Routes had been trodden through her valleys, her grey stone hills may have been scratched and scored by the glaciers and moraines of an un-remembered ice age. But, standing on a rock above les Baux and looking inwards, we see astonishingly exactly what was seen in turn by any individual of the cohorts, legions, phalanxes, hordes and chevauchées that, since thousands of years ago have poured in uninterrupted succession through the Rhone valley. You could not say the same for the valleys of the Danube or the Rhine, for Palestine or Greece, for old England or for New or for any lands fashioned of clay or chalk or loam or sand or alluvial soil. They and their contours and surfaces will have been ploughed, or flooded or blown away. Above all, man with his next most dangerous competitors, the goats, will have deforested whole regions and there is no saying how in any given hundred years their aspects and very climates will not have altered. Palestine, like Greece, was once a very garden of Eden, to become a bitter desert and now again to be in process of being made to bloom. The Sahara was once a sea-bottom; and consider the climate of the Mississippi valley today! . . . But the sun-hardened rocks of Provence, fretted by neither rain nor frost, have in the meanwhile changed hardly at all. You may go back to les Baux after forty years and find no changes either in the most distant landscape or the objects nearest you.

Nor do sudden, devastating changes much affect the old cities of Provence. M. Bonhoure may re-face his old shop-front with marble and a *café* here and there may have some scagliola stuck on to its inner walls but, except on the littoral, the aspects of these ancient places remain almost unchanged. That is partly because the Provençal being a fatalist is by nature conservative. But it is still more because there are no remarkable deposits of precious minerals or mineral oils and the Rhone is for the most part hardly navigable. So neither gold-rushes nor sudden crowd-ings of populations have there taken place. Provence itself has been continually "rushed" by every known type of barbarian. There can be no part of the earth's surface to have been as consistently taken by the sword. But the tides of men making those incursions have, like other rivers, spread themselves out in places they found attractive or unoccupied and the only pocket into which they have at all crowded has been Marseilles. And

even as to that great city one can say that the more it changes
the more it remains the same, its chief features being its climate
and the waters of its port, the rest being very unmemorable.
They have lately pulled down there a whole rat-and-scorpion-
nest of ancient, dirty and picturesque buildings. But one goes to
Marseilles, which is the second city of France and one of the
first in Europe, for every other reason in the world than to
study ancient domestic architecture, so that no-one need miss
those antiques. And the sun will always shine down on the
Cannebière with such vividness that it is all one whether the
windows before which you pass in that famous boulevard are
made of broad plate-glass or bottle-end lozenges; the cafés
beneath their awnings will always buzz with rich, garlic gossip
and shouted confidences whether the roadways be filled with
Roman chariots or aeroplanes. The rich tang of the boastings
of Marius and Olive will issue from whatever windows; the
Spaniards will loll on the sunlit steps of the churches, the Cata-
lans mend their nets on the cobbles beside the Old Port and the
unending babel of sailors of whatever Mediterranean, Negroid,
Levantine, Visigothic or even Scandinavian descent will for ever
flow about the vast quays. For whatever Marseilles is she is not
Provence. She remains perpetually a Levantine, Negroid-Semitic
colony, pullulating on the edge of a scarcely habitable marsh.

Toulon again has also lost most of her picturesquenesses and
will no doubt soon lose the rest of them. But that too does not
much matter. Toulon is a port and arsenal of the Nordic rulers
of those climes. She arose suddenly in the eighteenth century
as a base for galleys and was built by galley-slaves at the orders
of the King of France, who was no Provençal. The poor
wretches were used in the endless struggle to check the incursions of the Sallee Rovers and the marauders of the Dey of
Algiers. So that Toulon is almost more alien to real Provence
than is Marseilles.

Or once more, there are the parasitic bathing towns of the
Côte d'Azur, the French Riviera, which both historically and

geographically are in Provence. They stretch to just this side of Nice where the territory of the Grimaldis, Princes of Monaco, once began. They have arisen where the Alps begin to crowd in on the Mediterranean and they have arisen there because the light foam of that sea frets their expanses of sand whilst the mountains shelter them from the *mistral*. To say that these little cities of rather mechanical and monotonous pleasure are not true Provence would be as unjust to them as it would be unjust to Provence to include them.

CHAPTER II

NATURE

PROVENCE came into conscious existence in the year B.C. 125 whilst Rome was still a Republic. London, then a suburb of Kingston-on-Thames, was still lost in the mists outside civilisation. In the Thames valley, as had for long been the case in the valleys of the Rhone and the Loire, Teutons were aimlessly fighting Celts in what was no doubt the reign of Arthur who has yet to come again.

You have to imagine the Roman Province as being occupied by Gallic, possibly Celtic, possibly Teutonic, tribes generically known as Cimbri, the name possibly coming from the word *chempho*, meaning warrior. Greek, African, Ligurian, Semitic and other settlements were already scattered all about her triangular surface when Rome occupied true Provence in 125 B.C. By 121 she had extended her rule across the Rhone towards the foothills of the Pyrenees. So Provence on the East of the Rhone became *Provincia Romana* and the Roman Province, joined to what was Roman on the right bank, towards Spain, became the home-territory of the whole region that the Romans called *Gallia Narbonensis*. If you wrote a capital V upside down and divided the space between its arms by a descending straight line which would be the Rhone, the triangle on the right of the dividing line would be the true Provence with which we are concerned. That on the left of the line would be the sort of quasi-Provence that contains Montpellier, Béziers, Carcassonne and Perpignan and that finally merges into a sort of Catalan-

Spanish territory. The whole would be *Gallia Narbonensis* called after Narbonne of the honey. The V would be enclosed as to its two arms by mountains and as to its open space by the Mediterranean.

At the apex of your V you must set the city of Lyons; above that Burgundy, the *Ile de France* and territories with climates gradually deteriorating until you reach the mist-

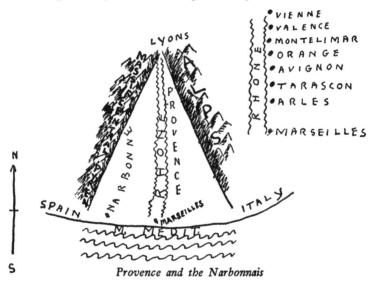

Provence and the Narbonnais

drenched Teutoburger Forest and the territory of sempiternal fog in which these words are being written.

It might have been better for civilisation had the Romans never penetrated Provence but remained at home cultivating the sterner and more frugal Republican virtues so as in perpetuity to be a shining light to outer darknesses. But the Gods saw otherwise. In B.C. 125 Rome was temporarily in the hands of the Patrician political wing and those heroes, like Imperialists of all ages and all climes, alleged that the existence of ignorant hordes near their borders and elsewhere in the world not only caused them to have sleepless nights but seemed during the day to be contrary to their sense of the fitness of things. Besides, the climate and soil of the Rhone valley and the littoral, that mildness and that fertility, offered infinite promise for incomparable summer villas and pleasure settlements.

And the Romans had not very long taken those lands from the Cimbri before the fiery cross went through all the North Lands. Germanic or Celtic, as you will, the Cimbri had already achieved that yearning for the land where blooms the lemonflower that has never since left us and warlike and probably Teutonic savages poured in immense, disorderly hordes from all the North and more particularly from Switzerland all across Narbonnic Gaul and down both banks of the Rhone. They annihilated the armies of grossly inefficient Roman Patrician generals in Carinthia, on the Rhine and on the Garonne. Finally they defeated two great Roman armies under Quintus Servilius Coepio and Cneius Mallius Maximus at Orange on the Rhone where the Roman theatre is. That was in B.C. 107, eighteen years after the Roman annexation.

Rome, as is the case when civilised cities learn that the Barbarian is at the gates, at once went off into the throes of general elections, impeachments, executions and civil disturbances. Coepio, Maximus, Carbo and Silanus being what we used to call Patricians but are now more fashionably styled Optimates, were executed for their defeats by the Cimbri; the Patricians were discredited and from the turmoil there emerged Caius Marius, the beloved of the Provençaux of today, the putative husband of Mary Magdalen and the actual son of a day labourer of Arpinum. The faithful Romans five times elected him consul—from B.C. 104-100.

The Cimbri meanwhile had wandered aimlessly through the Roman Province, through Gallia Narbonensis into Spain where they got into serious trouble with their reputed kinsmen, the Celtiberians. From Spain they were driven out into Gallia Narbonensis once more and happened on Caius Marius who, having reorganised the Roman War Office on a basis of conscription instead of military tenure of property, was ready and waiting for them. They passed Marius on their way down the Rhone. Marius, following, defeated them at the great battle of Aquae Sextiae—which is Aix-en-Provence—in B.C. 102, taking prisoner their king who bore the suggestive name of Teutobod. By the local inhabitants of the country round Tarascon, this battle, as I have suggested, is said to have taken place in the plains of Orgon, near St Rémy, for, they ask, if the victory did not there take place why was the triumphal arch erected on the Plateau des Antiquités to celebrate the victory of Marius? To which, if you are accurately minded, you will reply that there is no evidence to the fact that the arch was set up to the glory of Caius Marius since it was obviously erected during the reign of Augustus, fifty odd years after the death of Marius. Marius died in 86 B.C., which presumably was about ninety years before the birth of St Mary Magdalen.

One may presume that Provence enjoyed whatever measure of Roman Peace the Romans themselves from that day on enjoyed. Marius completed the wiping out of the Cimbri at the battle of Vercellae in 101 B.C. and exactly fifty years afterwards Cæsar, who was to redeem Kingston-on-Thames from complete obscurity, finished the task of rendering Provence fit for heroes by finally subjugating Gaul North of Lyons. This took place in 51 B.C. after the defeat of Vercingetorix in the neighbourhood of Dijon. It was in B.C. 54 during his second expedition to Britain that Cæsar made his week-end visit to Kingston, Cassivelaunus meanwhile attacking his ships in the rear. So, at about the time when Provence became safe for the arenas, theatres, triumphal arches and aqueducts that we may still see, London for the first time emerged from the mists of time.

You may ask what evidence there is that the *arc de triomphe* at St Rémy is the product of the Augustan Age and the answer is that there is none. There is none except that the sculpture on the arch and on the tomb beside it is obviously the work of

Greek hands and that it was during the reign of Augustus that Greek slaves most lavishly supplied the Roman semi-civilisation with works of Art. . . . As if, in the interests of peace, France having been given by England and the United States to Mr Hitler, that leader should have deported to Warsaw makers of *articles de Paris* so that, to the greater glory of the swastika, the captured Polish capital should be adorned with works of art.

For it is queer how the Arts follow in the footsteps of conquerors and, in the end, remain their only traces in subjected territories. . . . You imagine M. Brancusi being suddenly captured in his studio near the rue de Sèvres and led, manacled, and protesting that he is not a Frenchman, between files of field-grey troops, up the Boulevard Sébastopol to end in Warsaw. There, in the great Place that the Poles have made by the destruction of the Russian Cathedral, he shall spend the rest of his days in chains but eternally polishing gigantic replicas of his Golden Bird and the Egg. . . . In years to come the field-grey troops will be driven from the Polish capital by some Bolshevik Poniatowski or some Turkish Marius and the very name of Mr Hitler will have been forgotten. . . . But still the Golden Bird and the Egg shall shine through the centuries across that open Place and be convincing evidence of the capture of Warsaw by Napoleon I. For obviously Bird and Egg will be French work of the XIX to XX centuries. . . . So the Greek-sculptured arch of St Rémy was erected by Augustus. . . .

And indeed Provence with its rare, but sufficient and exquisite monuments of the past, has peculiar evidence of this odd internationalism of the Arts impelled by War. I do not mean that War, any more than Religion, is necessary to the Arts. But conducive it is.

There are many things that most strike the wanderer returning to London after prolonged absence. But I think that what has, as it were, most-most struck me in this city without form is the extraordinary profusion and availableness of its pictures. Let us at once set down that Paris is the art centre of the world.

There is no gainsaying that any more than in the Euclidean sense you can contradict the statement that a straight line is the shortest distance between two points. It has become an axiom.

Nevertheless, if you want to see pictures, to go to the Louvre is to undertake, with a bad headache, a desert journey in which you lose your way amongst hostile tribes and never, never find the oasis of colour whose glamour drew you there. To go on the other hand to the National Gallery is like stepping into a smooth lift in the most obsequious of department stores, to be led as straight as an arrow in its flight to the article that you require. . . . Uccello? you say. At once you stand before the Battle. . . .

For, if the most-most memorable feature of London is her pictures the most-most-most memorable picture of all that are hers is that Uccello. I don't know what victory it celebrates; but it celebrates a victory I don't know whether it came there by the force of arms or fraud: it is there which once belonged elsewhere. I don't even really feel sure that it is by Uccello though it well may be. But there, rendering London loveable, a place to visit, a centre radiating the loveliness that in the end civilisation should be, is a picture that was painted somewhere in Italy to celebrate the issue of some obscure pot-lidded brawl of horsemen. I have said that I don't quite know why I am here in this garret shaken by sounds produced by pauper musicians with frost-bitten fingers. But if I ever come here again and you should ask why I am here I know what I shall answer. It will be to see again that miracle that celebrates a scuffle of Bolognese or Ferrarese against Sienese or Milanese. . . .

In that Provence much resembles London. . . .

After the Marius-Cimbri affair she passed the remainder of her Roman days *tant bien que mal*—much as London may have done after the successors of Caius Julius Caesar founded the Tower, the Port of London seeming to offer advantages over the week-end joys of Kingston. I do not suppose that Provence's mixture of Celts-Carthaginians-Volscians-Ligurians-Iberians that must have made up her populations can have been very enthusiastically Roman any more than London today has much enthusiasm for her Scotch-Welsh-Irish-Jewish-Nonconformist-administered Parliament. But Provence long ago learnt the lesson that she must for ever lie at the proud foot of one conqueror

Playing Boules in the dust

or another. So, as long as she can go on pruning her vines and playing *boules* in the dust beneath the shadows of her plane trees in the little *places*, she does not care much whether it is the Holy-Roman-German Kaiserliks or the French-elected popes of Avignon or the Franks from the *Ile de France* or even the Visigoths that nominally own her soil. She will go on leading her under-life with the bulls on a Sunday and the provision of innumerable *ex voto* pictures to her obscure romanesque church-walls. It will be very much all one to her whether it be President

Lebrun or President Stalin or Louis le Tant-Attendu who sits in a throne up in Paris. . . .

Even before the Romans, races and civilisations that have left only legendary or very slight traces colonised the Rhone valley and its deltas. They had come from further North than the *Ile de France*, further West than Perpignan, further East than Stamboul or even from Africa, further South than Carthage herself. You will find Greek traces as far North as Lyons, a city which at least according to official historiographers was founded by Greek exiles in 590 B.C. Ten years before that a ship from Greek Phocea blundering along the shores of the Mediterranean had come upon a mud-bank belonging to a Gaelic tribe called the Segrobiges under a king called Nann. According to legend Nann's daughter came upon the Greek captain sitting in a body of suitors who had assembled by chance on that day. She chose him incontinently for her mate and thus there had arisen the great Greek city of Massilia, afterwards Marseilles.

Just across the sea, however, was the still greater Semitic empire of Carthage with its warlike and proud civilisation. The Carthaginians like their successors the Saracens continually raided and, during the centuries, as continually occupied the sparsely Greek-dominated territories surrounding Marseilles in its marshy security. The city held out against them valiantly for several centuries and at last joined with the Romans and against the Gauls in wiping Carthage off the map and in securing for Rome dominion over the whole of Liguria. Then Caesar, under the pretext that the Massilian Republic had sided with Pompey, laid waste and occupied the city, confiscated its colonies and extended to it the benefits of the *Pax Romana*.

Marseilles indeed along with the other cities of that territory deserves the love of Provence—and perhaps predominantly. It was the cities of the Roman Province that above all kept alive the tradition of the countryside. Strong-walled, on backbones of rock, peopled by tough, enduring citizens, the country districts might be swept again and again clear of crops, of people, of beasts, of furnishings. But, shut in behind their walls, Arles, Avignon, Nîmes, Aix and Marseilles saw those legions thunder past, and when they were gone townsmen and refugees issued out again and once more took up the eternal and eternally prevailing tale of craftsmanships, cultures, netting the seas, tending the bulls of the Camargue, pruning the vines, crushing the olives—the career of countrymen wringing from a hard if not hopeless soil a sufficient if sufficiently laborious existence. It was no doubt the Romans, who, in the five centuries of their rule and of the gradual penetration of their subjects, established this tradition of life from which Provence has never swerved and which it will probably never abandon. They built the immensely strongly fortified positions at Arles, Saint-Rémy, Aix, Orange, Carpentras, Cavaillon, Riez, Vaison, Nîmes and the tremendous naval base at Fréjus and, just as there is in Provence today a greater profusion than in Italy itself of the immense public buildings that are the trademark of Rome so the continual influx of Romans into Provence has left in that province the frugal, temperate and infinitely industrious strain of mind that was the mark of the Roman people before the advent of the Emperors. And it was to the frame of mind that was Provence far more than to Italy itself that is due the Latinity that today alone redeems our northern civilisations from barbarism. If we speak of the North French of today as a Latin race it is far more because of the proximity of France to Provence than of any immixture of Roman blood in the inhabitants of the *Ile de France*, of Burgundy, of *La Vendée*, of the Bordelais. Provence has been called the great commercial and administrative highway between Rome and the Northern World, but in the long run it was a highway along which travelled continuously the stream of the arts, of thought, of the traditions of life—for literal ages after Romulus Augustulus, the last Roman Emperor fell before Odovaker and the last Roman legion travelled any road at all. That was in A.D. 476, the

Roman dominion in the triangle east of the Rhone having lasted 601 years.

In the meanwhile Christianity had penetrated amongst those sunlit peacefulnesses. Whether the Holy Maries and the disciples with Lazarus, Martha, the servant Sarah, Saints Trophime, Eutropius, and Maximin actually set sail for the ports called *Les Saintes Maries* and *Fréjus* after the Crucifixion is a matter that you may disbelieve or believe at will. The College of Propaganda have never made the belief an article of Faith but neither will you be burned if you express that belief. If you come, say to Tarascon in May. . . . But I had better leave that until I do reach Tarascon in the month of the Virgin. . . .

For the moment I am in the frame of mind to say that any belief that can be celebrated in charming, vivid and naïf pictures the world over is a belief that we may as well grasp to us with both hands—and the voyage of the Maries has been so celebrated from the shrine of Notre Dame de Laghet above Nice to Tiefenbronn. And that we may regard as evidence enough of the spread into barbarian territories of the frame of mind that is Provence.

In any case the legend may be taken as symbolical of the fact that Christianity came from Asia, by way of the sea. And, if it had chosen, the Church of Provence might well have claimed that it was Christianised before Rome and not by way of Rome and another schism would have been added to those that torture and break up Christendom. Fortunately Provence never did anything. of the sort, contenting herself when the time came with inventing a cheerful heresy of interpretation, called that of the Albigenses, a heresy sufficient for the foundation of a relatively cheerful war of religion in which, one side having extirpated the other, the question was settled once for all.

According to history the first martyrdom of Christians took place in Provence under Marcus Aurelius who reigned from 161 to 180. That altruistic emperor is '*célèbre par sa sagesse toute stoïcienne, sa modération et son goût passionné pour la philosophie et les lettres,*' thus proving that, however much you may approve of virtue the putting into practice of even such virtues as you most approve is inherently repulsive even to the most humane of men. . . . I remember discoursing in some such vein with a Monsignor whom I met in the train between Cahors and Montpellier. His Eminence expressed an almost vindictive dislike for the Emperor, finishing up with:

"And see how surely, if we will read the signs, Providence will lead us to the truth. That pagan emperor has often enough been a stumbling block to humanity since it has been continuously asserted that he, though a pagan, had all the virtues that are enjoined by Christianity alone. But mark the omen of his son. For Commodus who succeeded him was a fiend in human shape who died strangled on account of vices and crimes such as have never distinguished any other human being. . . . Yet who but a devil can beget a devil? Even your arch-deceiver Darwin will tell you that that can not be otherwise."

. . . "An extra day of the show having been given to the people on our account," write the Christians of those days, "Maturis and Sanctus again underwent various tortures in the amphitheatre as if they had suffered nothing before. They sustained again, as they were led to the amphitheatre, the blows usually inflicted on those condemned to wild animals; they were exposed to be dragged and torn by the beasts and to all the barbarities which the savage populace demanded, above all to the iron chair in which their bodies were roasted. . . . But not a word could be extracted from Sanctus except that of the confession of the Christian faith which he had at first uttered and, after lingering for a long time, they at length expired, having presented a spectacle to the world equal in variety to that which is usual in gladiatorial fights."

I do not think that that piece of journalism, extracted from the *Epistle of the Churches of Vienne and Lyon to the brethren in Phrygia and Asia Minor,* can ever much have been surpassed in the annals of a partisan newspaper world. . . . Imagine a reporter of, say, communist tendencies who should have the genius to write that his friends, being beaten to death by the

[103]

night-sticks of the cops, put up at least as good a show as is usually to be seen in the Bowl when Yale confronts Brown. . . . The rest of that special report contains more vivid details of the martyrdom, during the same Bank Holiday, of Pothinus, Bishop of Lyons, and Saint Blandina. . . .

"Having endured scourging, the tearing of beasts, and the iron chair" . . . for the ritual of these occasions was as rigid as that of the *mise à mort* in the arena of Nîmes today . . . "she was enclosed in a net and thrown to a bull when, after having been long tossed by the animal, raised beyond pain through the power of hope and realization of her fellowship with Christ, she expired. . . ."

And you may imagine the respectable Roman matron of the day commenting that her sympathies are really always with the bull.

Such admirable propaganda having converted Constantine who, though he finally settled the seat of the Roman Empire in Byzantium had long hesitated over the claims of Arles, the bishoprics that had sprung up all over Provence—at Lyons, Marseilles, Vaison, and Arles itself—were sanctioned as part of the official church of the Roman Empire—in 313 A.D.

The hundred and fifty odd years that supervened between that day and the fall of the Empire were no doubt the happiest that the Roman Province was to know. At any rate during that period were laid the foundations of the great religious buildings that have carried on for Provence the tradition of the great secular edifices of the Roman pagan days. For if, in a sort of mental bird's eye view you think of Provence stretching out beneath the white sunlight in its beneficent aridities you see mainly, dominating its cypresses with the clumps of potherbs at their feet, the long lines of the arenas, the high masses of the theatres and triumphal arches, the long perspectives of the aligned tombs. . . . But also, dominating backbones of rock there will be the great abbeys like Montmajour, the exquisitely fronted cathedrals like St Trophime at Arles or St Gilles over the Camargue, and nestling under their towers the wonderful cloisters with their capitals carved as if by the painters who have left us in dark aisles and lady-chapels the innumerable and touching ex-votos, the little, intimate representations of quiet humanity going upon its daily avocations.

You are expected when you go to London for the first time most—oh, but most-most-most-most—to admire the Parks. And indeed even if you merely return to London after twenty years you will find the Parks almost unbelievable for their immensities, their greenswards, their freedom and the liberty they give to Nature to demonstrate its vitality in surroundings infinitely creditable. They stand for sturdy insistence on rights; their conferring of health on denizens of small streets and slums; their giving to the town-dweller a chance to dream of the green solitudes his ancestors deserted and they are the inalienable landed domains of those for ever without land. . . . You may not keep the People from walking on those swards; from meeting in those open spaces; from sleeping almost shoulder to shoulder in the parched grasses beneath the windows of Palaces. . . . Inalienable rights! I never pass Hyde Park Corner without remembering the London legend. One of the Georges, or it may have been William IV, requested Lord Melbourne to have an estimate prepared as to the cost of enclosing one of the royal parks. Possibly it was Regent's Park which was the darling of George IV; but the story always comes back to me in Hyde Park. And Lord Melbourne answered that it would not cost very much in all probability. . . . Most likely a crown.

The story is perhaps not true, or it may be attributed to the wrong king or the wrong Home Secretary. But it is in any case your true London story.

The foreigner, however, battling across one of those immense spaces against the North-Easter sighs:—I have heard it:

"Ah, but give me the Luxembourg Gardens, with the clipped and orderly trees, the aligned statues of the Queens of France and the sunlight where the palace of Marie de Medici shelters you from the North!" . . . The foreigner if not of Latin blood then will at least be one impregnated with the Latin tradition to such an extent that he sees in open tracts of green land only what the Latinised eighteenth century called 'desarts.' . . .

It was indeed only with the Cockney School of Poetry that the Englishman became de-Latinised, a lover of 'Nature,' a compendium of the names and habits of the few birds or of the extremely limited fauna of his country. For it is one thing to love birds and another mentally to pin them down on the entomologists' cork board or so to anthropomorphise them with anecdote that they become all but little men wearing red flannel pants, a shako and a musket with fixed bayonet as you may see them in the window of old fashioned taxidermists. . . .

And that is really what differentiates Latin from Septentrional Earth worship. . . . I remember being most forcibly struck with that characteristic of the Anglo-Saxon mind the other day. I was walking towards a bathing-hole over what had once been a ploughed field. The exact name of the locality does not come back to me: it was somewhere in New Jersey from fifty to seventy miles from the Palisades. We had, that is to say, motored there from the Palisades in about an hour and a half. . . .

Well, that field that had once been plough-land was a drear desert of sumach and poison ivy and one was warned to watch one's step because of the copperhead snakes. One of them had quite lately thereabouts killed a Professor of Columbia University about to go bathing. I shuddered a little, not so much because of the copperheads as because I love land that has been loved—of which every clod has been turned sedulously and every branch carefully pruned until you have come to love your bit of land as you love a child whose every mental change you have followed. And it seemed to be horrible and depressing to see a stretch of the beloved earth that had once been tended—if only *tant bien que mal*—now given over to dust and weeds and brambles and to snakes whose particular horror comes mostly from their sluggishness. For compared with a copperhead even a rattlesnake is a lively and amusing beast. I communicated my feelings to the American, though not Anglo-Saxon, who was walking beside me.

"Huh!" he ejaculated scornfully, "isn't that like you jaded Europeans! . . . *We* love the great open spaces of a world that has never been bridled and bitted. . . ." And he went on talking as if he had been galloping his mustang across the great virgin forests instead of cautiously watching his step over derelict farm-lands that but for the crisis would have become city-lots years ago. That was all right; it was the national spirit coming out in difficult circumstances. Keats the Londoner found rural heavens on Hampstead Heath.

And, to contemplate the reverse of the medal: Only this afternoon an English poet of the Sussex Cyder School came all the way from Bloomsbury to the Parish of St Marylebone to see me in this garret. I must confess that I find all poets difficult to talk to. A poet speaking to a mere *prosateur* has always—and no doubt rightly—the air of a Bourbon Prince talking to an Orleanist Sovereign, as if we had usurped the land that he should have inherited. Yes, no doubt rightly. Prose is infinitely more difficult to write and vastly the more agreeable to read but it does not confer any divine right upon its advocates.

Well, I had that morning been turning out some drawers and had come upon an article that I had written for a Paris paper—about France. . . . When you write about France for a Paris paper you first pull yourself together mentally, have your hair cut, have your suit pressed, set a gardenia in your buttonhole and then cause to echo through your head great prose passages of all the great French *prosateurs* from Flaubert and Maupassant to Mérimée, Proust, Pascal, and Stendhal. Then you sit down and write:

"J'ai en tête des images—des simulacres—de paysages innombrables et infiniment aimés, des coins de terre infiniment chers, des bois, des étangs, des prairies, des fleuves, des rivières, des champs d'oliviers, des montagnes péniblement ciselées jusqu'aux cimes, de vastes plaines labourées avec le soin que l'on prodigue seulement aux êtres qui nous sont particulièrement chers. . . . Ce sol a été tant soigné—tant aimé—que ce pays est devenu bénin comme quelqu'un qui, se sachant à l'abri de tout mal, peut se montrer toujours généreux, toujours souriant. . . ."

At any rate that was what I had written and, for lack of a better topic I gave my poet that paper to read and went to make the tea in a kitchen the size of a packing-case whose windows looked out on that wilderness of slate roofs, dissipated tin chimney pots and sooty, liver coloured brick that London provides as a landscape for us who are the masters of half the world and keep ourselves going by the ceaseless degurgitations of a black, astringent fluid one teaspoonful of which would kill the largest copperhead snake. When I came back that poet had put down my paper and was looking at the reproductions of the photographs of cinema stars that some unthinking member of my family had left lying about in my garret. . . . He spun round on me and said with pawky reproof:

"Well, what of it? What a fuss to make! Haven't we got—in Sussex—meadows and streams and woods and ponds? . . . Yes, and duck-decoys and hop-oasts and cyder-presses and morris-dances and the South Downs. . . ."

I said how foolish I was to have forgotten that they had all those things in Sussex—and in Wessex and Bucks and Notts and Hants and Staffs and Yorks and Westmoreland. Until at last he told me not to be too down-hearted because a week of reading the poems of the Sussex Cyder School might yet make a man of me and qualify me for a ticket at the London Library.

Alas. . . . I was thinking how in Sussex at every turning of the plough there is a triangular waste piece for the flourishing of docks and darnels and that hedges and bullfinches are yards wide so that in the county the amount of land wasted must be formidable indeed. . . . That is no doubt all right and makes for a sense of freedom and generous waste and provides homes for birds and wild-flowers and stoats and badgers and bottle-tits

and yellow ammers which are first cousins of the ortolan. . . .
And next to Kent I can imagine myself loving Silly Sussex,
whose emblem is a hog, better than any tract of country in the
world except, say, the Ile de la Barthelasse in the Rhone under
Avignon or my piece of land that lies open to the sun, sloping
down to the Mediterranean. That now, because I am in this
befogged garret, is deserted, untended and a prey to a wild
horde of incredible weeds. The oranges must be dropping to rot
and the lemon branches running wild and thorny for want of
the secators, and the mint strangling the cactuses and the little
plant of absinthe become as large as a tree and stifling the royal
malaga grape flowers. . . . Oh dear, oh dear. . . .

Dahin, dahin, mit Dir, o mein' Geliebte. . . .

Anyhow I can understand how one could love Sussex. . . .

But the difference between the Provençal, Latin, love of the
Land and that of the Septentrional is exactly this: For the
Englishman Nature is something generous and relatively untidy
and green and cyder-and-brown-ale-ish; for the Western Anglo-
Saxon she is something to be pioneered in and brutalised and
galloped over and left to ground ivy and sumach and the copperhead. . . . And for the Teuton. . . . Well, Walther von der
Vogelweide wrote "Tandaradei," but for the most part the
Teuton has a world-ache to get away from his forests and
heaths and to be off thither, thither with his *Geliebte*. . . . In
any case, for Northerners, Nature is something large, boundless, beforested, be-pampased, be-prairied, heathy, hedged, taken
up by commons, gorse, alder-swamps—generosities! The enemy
in any case of Thought and the Arts. . . . Thus the Londoner's ideal is to drive into his city vast tracts of green-ness that
shall never know plough nor spade nor secators, nor formalities,
nor shrines, cloisters, statuary, nor memorials to thinkers, nor
frescoes, nor gravelled walks nor inscriptions bidding you keep
off the lawns. . . . Spaces in which you may imagine yourself
in Sussex or Bucks or the Dukeries. . . . And with what a painful awakening. . . .

For the Provençal—as for the Italian in a less and, I am told, for the Chinese in a greater measure—Nature is a matter of little squares in the orange, sun-baked earth. . . . You go out at dawn from your *mas* that has frescoed walls; between a forgotten shrine that contains a IXth century Christ and the field from which they are just disinterring the Venus of Arles who looks upon you with sightless eyes; with a tiny knife before the

Detail of Cloister at Arles

dawn is up you remove an infinitely tiny but superfluous leaf from a tiny plant; between clods the countenance of every one of which is as familiar to you as the face of your child and that tomorrow you shall reduce to fine earth, you lead with your hoe threads of water to the base of every plant that is as familiar to you as the clods, your children and the names of your saints, bull-fighters and poets. The sun rises and scorches your limbs whilst you prune your vines; your throat knows the stimulation of the juice of your own grapes that you have pressed, of the oil of the olives you have gathered and crushed, of the herbs you have grown in the mess of pottage of your own beans, of the cheese whose whey was pressed from the milk of your own goats. You lie for your siesta through the torrid heat of the day in the shadows of the cloister of St Trophime watching how in the orange stone of the capitals Adam delves, Eve spins and the Maries come up from the sea to Arles. You go

Procession. The Maries come up from the sea

back to your work past the Greek shadows of the columns of the theatre made by the Phoceans; at the day's end in the golden aureoles of the dust you cast your *boules* between the stone chest that is the tomb of a captain of the Tenth legion that had "*Valens, Victrix*" for its motto, and another stone chest with a curious ribbon pattern that once held the ashes of a paladin who died beside Roland at Roncevaux. At night, by your hearth, your youngest daughter spells out for you

PROVENCE

O Magali, me fas de ben! . . .
  Maitre te vèire
Ve lis estello, o Magali,
  Coume an pali

and for the three hundredth time you tell your family how the poet said *"Coquin de sort!"* to you when you had knocked over his coffee cup whilst he was playing backgammon in the Café du Forum. . . . And on Sunday there will be the *mise à mort.*

I do not say that you will have all those things; but that is your ideal of what Nature can do for a man. You do not need to win the *Gros Lot* to achieve it. You only need not to have the *maladie* among your vines for one season when the vines of most of your neighbours have shrivelled under the *mildiou,* the *oidium* or the *pourridié.*

And that is Nature and how men wish to live with Nature for Provence and all the world to the East of Provence—for the Riviera, for Italy, for Greece, for Stamboul—for all the great belt of land that was once the Great Trade Route. . . . Into Cathay.

I do not again say that the Chinese go to bull-fights on a Sunday or drink French wine or turn the sods in the shadow of Provençal shrines that were set up by your ancestors a thousand years ago. Being Chinese you will prefer to see crickets or quails or sticklebacks fight in little paper-cages or glass bowls. But—so I am told—you will love your tiny square of hot earth and it will appear finally beautiful in your eyes when by industry, self-sacrifice and an infinite frugality you will have succeeded in placing at one corner of your plot a little paper shrine in which shall burn for ever a little light to the greater glory of your ancestors from ten thousand years back—a little paper shrine painted according to the laws of the arts, the requirements of beauty and the divine dictates of Nature and the beloved earth.

CHAPTER III

DARKEST PROVENCE

THE DARK AGES must have been darker in Provence than in any other quarter of the world. Belgium has been called the cockpit of Europe but the triangle to the East of the Rhone was the stamping-ground for all the nations of the then-known world—the cockpit of humanity. There fought their battles in that unfortunate territory before the Western World tidied itself out into some sort of pattern, not merely Romans, Celts, Franks, Teutons, Ostrogoths, Visigoths, and Celtiberians, but Africans, Asiatics, Arabs, Moors and Levantines who became generically known as Saracens and for centuries caused the more poignant troubles of a martyred country.

By 476 A.D., as we have already seen, Odoacer,—or Odovaker,—the chieftain of the German mercenaries in the employment of Rome, had deposed the Emperor Romulus Augustulus and had become Governor of the Empire with the title of Patricius. But already sixty years before, and five years after the sack of Rome by Alaric, which took place in 410, a king of the Visi (Western) Goths called Walja had founded a kingdom of Toulouse which, at first nominally under the supremacy of Rome, very soon became independent. Behind him the remainder of the Visigoths under two successively murdered kings, Athaulf and Sigric, had already established the Visigoth kingdom of Barcelona, and a little later Genseric, king of the Vandals, took Carthage and established the Vandal kingdom in Africa—a kingdom which lasted from 429 to 534. Becoming a great naval power they initiated the African practice of plundering the opposite shores of the Mediterranean—which continued for almost exactly thirteen centuries and which exercised so fatal an influence on both the history and the aspects of Provence. . . . That kingdom was founded in 429.

One may hazard the interpolation that it was exactly twenty years later that the celebrated, if legendary, Hengist and Horsa appeared on the London scene, the unfortunate Britons, left undefended by the Romans, having called in those noted pirates, the Angles and the Saxons, to defend them against the equally noted land-robbers, the Irish Scots and the Scottish Picts. The Anglo-Saxon anarchy in Britain lasted almost exactly six hundred years from, say, 440 to 1016 when Canute appeared on the scene. By that date Provence was already suffering severely from the crusades against the Albigenses.

For ten years after 476 Provence proper was still tenuously attached to Rome, but by 486, the Franks who had driven the Romans out of nearly all Northern Gaul finally defeated the Roman governor Syragus at the Battle of Soissons and Provence became threatened from the North. The Frankish leader was Clovis, or Chlodwig. He became a Christian ten years after the battle of Soissons and four years after that defeated the Burgundians near Dijon.

In the meanwhile war had broken out in Italy between Odovaker or Odoacer the Patricius of Rome and Theodoric King of the East, or Ostro, Goths. This began in 489 and ended in 493 with the victory of Theodoric who became East Gothic king over most of Northern and Middle Italy. So hordes were preparing descents on Provence from three directions—from the Ostro Goths in Italy, the Western Goths in Spain, where they had established a kingdom at Toledo, and from Clovis in the North.

That founder of the Merovingian dynasty defeated the Goths of Spain who were invading him, near Poitiers in 507 A.D. and his hordes straightway poured down into Provence.

Theodoric, called the Great, then, with his Italian Goths, came to the rescue of his Western connections, and Spaniards and Italians together defeated Clovis at Arles and drove him through Narbonnic Gaul—which by then was called Septimania—on the right bank of the Rhone—back into his Frankish territory.

It was the dream of Theodoric to re-establish the Roman Empire of the West under Gothic auspices and immediately after the battle of Arles he assumed the guardianship of Septimania and Spanish West Gothland on behalf of his grandson Amalaric. He died however in 526 and murders and family feuds split up the Gothic dominions, the Eastern Goths coming to loggerheads with the Byzantine Empire which, under the great Belisarius and then under his successor Narses, destroyed the East Gothic kingdom in 555 A.D. and re-established for a time a Byzantine-Roman domination of Italy and Provence.

But within a very few years tribes from the Danube under the leadership of a king called Alboin and generally known as Langobards or Lombards overran and subdued the whole of Northern Italy as far as the Tiber, Ravenna, Venice, Naples and Calabria alone retaining allegiance to Roman Byzantium and Rome itself gradually establishing an independence under the Popes. The Papacy was now about to become powerful in the affairs of the world.

From 590-604 Gregory I—the Great—was bishop of Rome. The title of "Papa" or "Father" had until the seventh century been given to all bishops but in Gregory's day it began to apply solely to the successors of St Peter. The Roman church was already wealthy. After the conversion of Constantine that Emperor and the noble or wealthy families of Rome and the Empire had, as the saying used to be, vied with each other in showering gifts on the Roman bishops and, though this property had been threatened by Huns, Goths, Vandals, Visigoths and other conquerors, by the time of Gregory the Great, at the beginning of the seventh century the landed estates of the Pope were sufficient to constitute the Papacy one of the largest private landowners in the world of that day. The property consisted in farms, arable lands, forests, mines, charitable foundations and even whole towns. Over these domains the Emperor in Constantinople asserted certain claims, the Byzantine sovereign being represented in Rome by a functionary of vague powers called at one time 'exarch' and at another 'Patricius'. Byzantium used its powers to impose taxation which was at times very oppressive on what was called the Patrimony of St Peter. Occasionally, too, the Eastern Emperor asserted claims to modify the doctrines of the Church. The Emperor Leon III—the Iconoclast—brought about, if indirectly, the temporal power of the Papacy by sending troops to besiege Rome and take possession of the person of the Pope, Gregory II, who occupied the Holy See from 715-731. This pope who was one of the foremost opponents of the Iconoclastic heresy—it was approved by the Council of Constantinople and denounced by that of Nice—applied to Luitprand king of the Lombards for help. Luitprand drove away the Byzantine troops but refused to restore to the Pope the lands he had rescued from the Byzantines and his successor, Gregory III, found himself between the devil of the Constantinople Emperors and the deep sea of the Lombards.

The Papacy turned for help to the Franks—and in sufficiently happy hour. For Pope Stephen II, fleeing into Gaul, menaced by the Lombard king who had taken possession of Ravenna, found the Franks assembled at Soissons and in process of getting rid of the last of the Merovingian shadow-kings and electing to the throne the Mayor of the Palace, Pepin the Short. Nothing could have been more propitious for such a usurpation than divine sanction and, Pepin having promised help to the Pope, Stephen himself consecrated at St Denis not only the king but his two sons Charlemagne and Carloman. This was in 754.

Pepin then three times sent ambassadors to the Lombard king, Astolf—one of the earliest instances of Nordic attempts to settle delicate matters by diplomacy rather than by pouring aimless hordes into a disputing territory. Pepin demanded that

Astolf should return to the Pope Ravenna and such parts of the patrimony of Peter as the Lombards had seized. Astolf refused. Pepin crossed the Alps and besieged Astolf in Pavia, which capitulated. The Isaurian Emperor of Constantinople then remembered that he had rights over the cities of the Patrimony and demanded that Pepin should surrender the papal lands to him. Pepin replied that he had laboured not for the Emperor of Constantinople but for St Peter and for the remission of his sins. He bestowed upon the Pope the exarchate of Ravenna and the sovereignty over twenty-two towns, including Rimini, Ferrara and Ancona, laying the keys of the cities on the tomb of St Peter. So were founded the Papal States. According to some German authorities Pepin retained for himself the sovereignty of Rome, according to others he did not. In any case it was as Patricius of Rome that Charlemagne afterwards interfered between Pope Leo III and his relatives, being in return crowned Emperor of the West at Rome in the year 800 A.D.

In the meantime a new and formidable religion was being founded in the East. The fleets of the Vandal kingdom of Carthage had, as we have seen, already frequently plundered the shores of Provence to which the Northern shores of Africa for centuries provided formidable neighbours. The prophet Mahomet was born in Mecca of a wealthy merchant family, in 571 A.D. By 629 he had conquered Arabia and converted its inhabitants to 'submission to the will of God'—or Islamism. He died in 632 and Islamism was immediately divided into two parties. That part of it that acknowledged the Caliphate of Osman proceeded to the conquest and conversion of Northern Africa between 644 and 656; and in 711 the battle of Xeres de la Frontera put an end to the kingdom of the Visigoths and, as we have seen the Moors who had invaded Spain established in 756 a separate Caliphate at Cordova under Abd-er-Rahman. In the meanwhile, in the East the Mahometans under Omar had conquered Syria, Palestine and Phoenicia and destroyed the Persian Empire of the Sassanidae. They had thus more than half-encircled the Mediterranean with Mahometan powers and they were to proceed to the subjection of nearly all the shores of Provence, establishing themselves for a time inexpugnably in the mountains still called Les Maures between Toulon and Cannes. In 814 they entrenched themselves in the heights above Monaco —in Eze, la Turbie and Ste Agnèse.

Tower at Le Revest les Eaux

It was Guillaume I, comte de Provence, who finally expelled the Saracens from les Maures, and Ghibellino Grimaldi, a Genoese, afterwards Prince of Monaco, who performed the same service for Eastern Provence, both Princes leaving today in the legends of the Provençal peasantry an aroma like that of fading lavender. . . .

For myself the memories and the traces of the Saracens in Provence have something particularly moving. To come suddenly on a Saracen tower on a lonely hillside, amongst the rose-

mary and thyme of the Alpilles or amongst the great congeries
of towers Roman and mediæval of the great outer walls of Carcassonne is to feel a singular emotion of the enlargement of the
horizons of my world. It is much as when from the coast of
Kent I suddenly see France, or when, on the dock at Calais I
notice a Pullman car labelled Warsaw, Buda-Pest and Constantinople . . . A sense of enlargement. . . .

And in Provence the feeling is peculiarly vivid. It is not
merely that the mind is taken towards the Orient; indeed I feel
a certain dislike for my mind being taken towards the Orient.
But it is as if it was welcome, in the middle of the memories of
the ignorant butcheries and wanton horrors that in all those
centuries raged over poor Provence, to remember fearless men
with a set and coherent theory of civilisation, with knowledges,
philosophies and courages, sitting in those lonely towers and
feeling for the savage hordes that beneath their feet ravaged
the gentle contours of the land much such a contempt and
hatred as the Roman captains must have felt when looking
northward from the wall that spanned Britain. . . . Or indeed
much such a hatred and contempt as we ourselves, as thinkers
in the lovely towers of Provence, may well feel for the rag-heap
of confused philosophies and ignoble preparations for butchery
that is our civilisation of today.

I feel a certain contrition: it is perhaps not fair to introduce
thus suddenly to the unsuspecting reader what is really the basic
note of this book. But indeed, for some hours, I have been feeling what every decent butcher must feel when he is leading a
lamb to the slaughter. It is obviously not fair to introduce you
suddenly to History when what you desire is modern instances.
And indeed were the affair of poor Provence a coherent matter
say of precedent broadening down to parliamentary government
my conscience would not have let me do it. . . .

I was talking yesterday afternoon to a nice young—but not
too young—English political thinker with whom I had by accident renewed acquaintance in a Bond Street picture gallery. We

stood before some pictures of flowers and Sussex farms that were as it were indescribably amiable but completely without meaning or purpose. Without, as it were, religion. It was difficult to see why the painter had painted the things; they were neither sufficiently representational to serve as records nor sufficiently arbitrary to enliven a room or a restaurant car and, I being a man of violences, they filled me with a sense of depression.

My mind had hitherto resisted the London afternoon. In a London mood damp shoes and a be-drizzled darkness setting in at three are things that I can very well, he-mannishly, resist. But, under the impression left on me by those applications of paint to canvas, I baulked at the sight of the wet street and, in the ante-room of that gallery, clung to the society of my old acquaintance who had rescued from a damp commissionaire a wet mackintosh. So I brought out then and there a question that I had intended to save up for a time when we should have more leisure to go into the matter.

I said:

"Tell me, because you know. You're buried in young things; you're the guide and counsellor of young things. You're a leader and an animating spirit. Then, what in the world's the matter with the young things of this city and day?"

My companion paused in opening her umbrella and gave me a long, queer look.

"You should know," she said. "They're suffering from what we—H.G. and the rest of us, used to say was the matter with you, years ago. . . . They don't know what to think. . . . About anything. . . ." Then, suddenly and determinedly as if she were challenging me and taking her place beside her young things, she asked:

"And who does?" and strode purposefully into the outer drizzle.

It was a curious chassé-croisé to have been brought about by Time. Because I knew exactly what to think. And standing there in that hesitant place in a city whose main note was not so much the fear that haunts all the rest of the world as a vast hesitation, I knew, as if in a streak of sunlight amongst rocks, more vividly than ever, what, as you might say, we must do to be saved.

Amazing things about London today are the kindness of its inhabitants, its domination by the figure of Christ—and then, above all, to an old, hardened-in-the-grain Londoner—its hesitances. In my day in London one—if you will pardon the expression—bloody well knew that London was the bloody world and if anything went wrong anywhere one said that something must be done about it. And one wrote to the *Times* and something was done about it. That at least was the frame of mind.

But today it is impossible to find so much as a leader. I don't myself want a leader, but the spectacle of an immense city drifting not merely rudderless but as if she had never had a rudder is of a depression almost infinite. One asks: Is it for this that all the martyrs died? All the sufferings of Provence alone should have sufficed to give the world of today some light. But there is no light anywhere and least of all beneath the lowering skies of Thames valley.

I am not, you understand, a pessimist: I don't want our civilisation to pull through. I want a civilisation of small men each labouring two small plots—his own ground and his own soul. Nothing else will serve my turn.

All the same, if you have once loved something it is at least sad and puzzling to return and find what was once confident, resolute and on the whole well-meaning, become, not so much emaciated or enfeebled but just simply hopelessly puzzled— even as to the possibility of so much as being well-meaning. In my day we had King, Lords, Commons, the Book of Common Prayer, the London County Council, the Metropolitan Police, the Home Secretary—and Christ Jesus Who had died to make us and our vast Empire what we were. Now all those first attributes of Londonism are as dim as figures seen through the steam from a kettle-spout. And the Saviour Himself if His crucified arms seem to spread across the whole London sky as never before they did is nevertheless dimmed too, like a Byzantine Pièta from which the gold-leaf should have been removed by the attrition of the ages. The Londoner, today, models himself on Christ as never he did before. Yet he has given up the idea that the Redeemer of the World will ever by miracle take sixpence off the income tax, re-assert the old good law of supply and demand or set the Lancashire cotton spindles working as they used to work. I doubt if even the London charwomen today will say that under Christ and by virtue of her worshipped specific one day the pain in her back will be diminished. It is more likely that she will talk of vitamins—and disbelieve in them.

You say: That is the work of the War . . . But, good Lord, there have been other wars that were followed by no such collapses. . . . For three centuries the poor Provençal, Albigence-Cathare-Iconoclast, fought all France, all Christendom and the Papacy and, after he had been 'wiped out' at the treaty of Paris under Blanche of Castille, managed to put up still so good a fight that it took St Louis himself to clean him off the face of Provence and leave the world purged of di-theism and free for Christianity. . . . Why, by twenty years after the end of the Napoleonic Wars London had gone far towards saving foundering Europe by her example, calling the New World in to redress the balance of the old and, firm-based on the new twin faiths of Electoral Reform and Free Trade which was then almost a *fait accompli* was ready, with the law, as already adumbrated, of supply and demand, to set forth on her glorious march towards imperial destinies and the industrial hegemony of a tottering world.

So do not say that it is the War . . . Say, if you will, that it is due to loss of Faith, or to the loss of a generation, or to the development of the natural resources of the poor United States, or to cheap labour in Japan or to confusion in the minds of the Fabian Leaders or—and that is the more likely—merely to the growing indigestibility of her food . . . And indeed it is no doubt caused by a fusion of all those factors. To them I must return. For the moment it is sufficient to say that London is at her darkest and to repeat the question: Why did all those tough heretics die in darkest Provence if London was to come to this? For, be one as Papist as one may, a little of the heresy of per- fectibilism will yet creep into one's view of things. And London was until only the other day one of the outposts of Latinity and Provence, that broad stretch of the Great Trade Route through which Latinism must pass to get to the outer, Northern world.

The heresy of the Albigenses is one of the most curious and suggestive forms of near-rationalism and even as is the vast hesitation of London today it was a product of a civilisation that was in the throes of disappearance. It was as if London, or the world today, should develop a faith of negation and quietism that, to the horror and reprobation of those seeking to re-estab- lish the Old Method by means of a New Plan, should run through parts of the world as if with the afflatus of a divine impulse. . . . As if we thinkers should be listened to!

For you may well ask: Provence as the vast pleasure farm of the Roman Empire must have contained a great population of highly civilised and reflective beings. What, when the world went mad and became an enormous battle ground across which in the darkness charged the aimless hordes of Vandals, Huns, Ostrogoths, Visigoths, Franks, Burgundians and Germans—what did that population of artists and thinkers do? What was their attempted contribution to the saving of the world?

They evolved the civilisation and poetry of the Troubadours, the heresy of the Albigenses and, for as long as they could, let the legions thunder past. And by the time Provence was ceded to the Franks as a price of neutrality by the Ostrogoths who were fighting the Byzantine Emperor of Constantinople and who had no right to Provence—by that time already a subter- raneous civilisation native to that land was already well under way.

PROVENCE

2

The civilisation of Provence—the civilisation of the Troubadours and of the Albigenses—was a duplex affair dependent as
much as anything on the geographical features of the valley of
the Rhone. The history of Provence during the Ostro-Visigoth
and Frankish times is a very unknown affair because Goths,
Huns, Vandals and Franks and still more the Franco-Imperial-
Papal combination that finally martyrised Provence, were plun-
derers of a type to leave no traces behind them. The Church is
an admirable body but it is no part of its business to be fair to
its opponents and, since the history of these times was written
exclusively by Churchmen, the Provençal civilisation obviously
did not receive much tenderness at the hands of the historiographers. As well expect Cotton Mather to write with fairness
the history of Quakerdom or Bismarck to weep tears over the
Latin civilisation that his Brandenburgers wiped out.

It is however possible for the scientist to derive the whole of
the diplodocus from the inspection of one of its spinal joints;
so it is possible for the humanist to evolve from the few poor
traces left by SS Dominic and Louis, what was the nature of the
civilisation they wiped out as thoroughly as Bismarck wiped out
the Second Empire.

The valley of the Rhone, then, is distinguished by substantial
peaks and pinnacles of rock. The original Roman conquerors
had already taught the Provençaux the value of heavily fortified
points of vantage and for centuries after the fall of the Empire
colonies of Roman-minded and Roman-educated citizens continued to hold Roman-fortified valley and hill-towns like Vaison, Riez, Nîmes, Arles or Fréjus. To mere barbarians un-
equipped with siege trains such fortified spots were impregnable.
Their tides flowed past.

What became of the countryman is not more difficult to
conjecture. In Provence vegetations grow with extraordinary
rapidity; it is possible to snatch three or even four crops off the

same plot of land in the course of the year; the plebeian Romans of the villa civilisation were inveterate and skilful gardeners and a great deal of their skill must have remained to such of them as stayed in Provence after the fall of the Empire—as indeed it there remains to this day. And it was no part of the job of a Vandal or Hun trooper to occupy himself with the destruction of growing crops and, since he had no occasion for hatred of the populations between which he passed he had little temptation to give himself the trouble to commit acts of gratuitous *Schreklichkeit*. So, when Northerners were about, the agricultural populations retired into the shelter of the fortresses and walled towns—which in return they provisioned against the days when they must close their gates.

The towns and fortresses having, in the meanwhile, an easy life and much opportunity for leisure, employed themselves on the arts—those mostly of music, song and architectural decoration—whilst, life being almost equally leisurely in the sunlit fields, and apparatus for music and architecture being there relatively to seek, the mind of the countryman turned rather to pure thought or metaphysical speculation. So on the one hand you had the Troubadours and, on the other, the Albigenses. The Troubadours developed gradually into a local aristocracy; the Albigenses became more and more an agricultural commonalty. There developed thus an uncommercial and uncoded feudalism that was without regulations as without fixed prices, the aristocratic Troubadours according their protection to the Albigenses, the peasants provisioning their protectors.

And the whole social cosmogony was salutarily latitudinarian, the knights being without discipline, the rural thinkers without prejudices as without puritanism. It was that that so infuriated the Northern and the Eastern religious when at last they had time to devote their whole attentions to this peaceful and prospering community. For the peace and prosperity of another are already cause for hatred but when that prosperity and that peace are secured without the expenditure of the effort, self-denial and discipline which Destiny has made our lot, the necessity for wiping that other out of existence becomes a monomania. We shall never rest until we have applied our torches to his infamous thatch.

It is to be remembered that a great many heresies divided the early church even before it finally divided into the Eastern and Western rites. The heresy of Arianism was condemned under Constantine the Great at the Council of Nicea in 325 but it continued to flourish for many centuries in North Africa, Spain and even in Southern Russia. The heresy of Iconoclasm was condemned at a council held in the same place in the eighth century but it continued to corrupt souls not only in Provence but in Bohemia and England for a number of centuries. The heresy of Catharism, of Slav and possibly of Judaic origin, began first to become formidable in Bulgaria, the home of its birth, in the ninth and tenth centuries. It passed to Provence and through Provence to the outer world at about the date when Canute on Dover beach first commanded the sea to be still.

Albigensism, called from the city of Albi where in the ninth and tenth centuries it was gradually evolved, united in itself a little of all these heterodoxies. But its main characteristic was that it was eminently suited to the temperament of a leisured and contemplative peasantry of sufficient education to regard with scepticism a faith that was adopted as a passport to success by the most dangerous and most bloodthirsty of its would-be persecutors. For, to a thinker as opposed to a man of action or financier, the spectacle of a Clovis, baptised by St Rémy, incited not merely to adore what he had burned but to burn what he had adored and then, in the name of the Prince of Peace, burning with extreme success and efficiency everything within sight from Soissons to Arles—such a spectacle was not one to inspire with enthusiasm a thinker, whose roof Clovis had burned over his head. Nor could the subsequent view from the high towers of Albi—that of Theodoric the Great in conjunction with his relatives of Spain falling, in the same Name, upon Clovis at Arles and driving him back past Albi itself—be anything other than confusing. And the confusion might well be added to by the fact that the orthodoxy of both Clovis and the united Goths was constantly and with clamour impugned by the Byzantine branch of Christendom which eventually under the heroic Belisarius and Narses completely wiped out the Eastern Gothic faithful near Vesuvius.

So, from the soil round Albi sprang the faith in defence of which such enduring and useless heroism was displayed. . . .

Both by Catholics and by their most prosperous opponents of today Albigensism has been called consistently "Protestantism." I open a history of the Church and see the heresy defined as a branch of the organizations of Huss, Wyclif, Henry VIII and Luther; I open a Protestant writer on the subject and read:

"When the powerful family of Trencavel"—that of the viscounts of Albi—"and the counts of Toulouse embraced Protestantism in the XIIth century. . . ."

Catholics, in short, are anxious to credit to Protestants whom they hold obnoxious anything in recorded History that they have found obnoxious. Protestants, on the other hand, anxious to claim for their heredity anything that in ancient times inconvenienced the march of Christianity, accept the gift, if not with enthusiasm, then at least without distaste. It would be as well if sundered and confused Christendom were to establish once for all the fact that Protestants are the supporters of the signatories of the Protest that was signed in the castle of Marburg and that neither Albigenses, Anabaptists, Wycliffites, Hussites nor yet the communicants of the Greek Orthodox Church can be logically or scientifically accorded that appellation.

It is one that is particularly hard on the poor Albigenses who were not even Christians. They expressly disavowed the doctrine of the divinity of Christ, advocated a strong application of laws of both physical and mental purity and professed disbelief in any personal deity. They substituted for that article of the Creed, a theory of two first Principles, the one of good, the other of evil. That last belief, as indeed the first one, the original Bulgarian founders of the catharist sect are, by Greek Orthodox writers, said to have drawn from the perusal of the first chapter of Genesis and other, obvious, Jewish sources. Catholic writers on the other hand assert that the Albigenses believed in two Gods as well as in race suicide and worse practices, asserting that the Provençaux—or at least all such Provençaux as did not survive the attentions of SS Dominic and Louis—were never really converted to Christianity. They retained, said the clerical writers, the doctrines of polytheism, the practices of easy divorce and the unmentionable vices that disgraced the classical era. And the Catholic writers have the situation so well in hand that even today and even in perfectly unsectarian works of reference you have to put up with reading that the Albigenses were pagans who believed in two Gods and condemned the pro-creation of children.

In any case, once proclaimed in and round Albi, the doctrine spread like fire through all Provence and as soon as the con-verted heathen of the North and East had leisure to take their eyes from each other's throats they perceived that there existed a great menace to their newly found prosperity-mascot . . . Nîmes went Albist, Arles, Narbonne, finally Avignon and all the territories in between. There was danger that the new rational-latitudinarianism might cross the mountains that lay between Provence and Rome and extend even to Burgundy. There is evidence indeed that it penetrated the Alps as far as the canton de Vaud and influenced the peasants who later became the highly puritan Christian Waldenses. . . . I remember read-ing in the archives of the city of Carcassonne the cross-examina-tion of an Albist deacon who had twice suffered conversion and as often repented. On his second trial he was accused by the Inquisitor of having gone into the Alps and got together small bodies of peasants to whom he had preached his heresy. That however is not to confuse Albigensism with Waldenism—a mistake that is frequently made. The Albigeois were non-Christian, the Waldenses being Christians of the strictest complexion and Waldenism did not penetrate into Provence until a century after Albigensism had been completely extirpated along with all its adherents by St Louis and the inquisitors. . . . I may add the chronological note that Inquisitors into irregularities of faith were first appointed by Innocent III in 1203; St Dominic had been born in Castille thirty-three years before; the Order of St Dominic was founded in 1215. The Holy Inquisition itself was instituted as a regularised tribunal by Gregory IX in 1229 . . . the religious arm being thus called in to complete the extirpation of those that the sword had failed to destroy. For it had been supposed and is still usually believed that that poor faith had been put an end to by the Treaty of Paris in that year. In any case the Pope instituted the Holy Office to do what we used on the Somme to call the mopping up. Thus the occasion of the institution of that body was not the heresies of Spain and the converted Jews in the sixteenth century, as is generally supposed, but the ending three hundred and fifty years earlier of the last civilised state and creed that Europe was to know. That sad honour may as well be claimed for those who so amply earned it.

I can no longer re-capture what it was that in almost my earliest days aroused my affectionate admiration for the Albigenses—but it is more years ago than I care to remember since I studied the archives of the city of Carcassonne for traces of their passage through the world. And, if at that date I was ready to undertake a work that must be tedious to one of my temperament, I must already have had some enthusiasm for that poor lost cause.

And, when I come to think of it, attentively, remote fragments of memory come floating up like small straws and fragments of detritus that at last form a dam across a trickle of water such as, in Provence, we use for irrigation of the red earth. . . . It begins of course with the line:

"Avenge, Oh Lord, Thy slaughtered saints!"

—the slaughtered saints being the Waldenses.

I do not know that I ever read another word of the poem but whenever I have occasion to think of that sect the line comes automatically into my mind. . . . And almost immediately a picture of my grandfather's comes to reinforce it—or rather I see the characters of one of the descriptive cards that Ford Madox Brown used to have printed to accompany his pictures. At the top of the card, grown brown with age and handling, I see the line about the Waldenses because my grandfather who admired the Ironsides and Dutch William and people of that sort had had printed at the head of his card the whole of the sonnet of Milton about the Waldenses . . . at least I suppose the poem to be by Milton and to be a sonnet for I never took any interest in Milton except as writer of Latin prose and what you could do with a line like that except follow it up with the remaining thirteen lines of a sonnet I do not see.

The picture, then, represented Cromwell, jack-booted, spurred and with all the appearance of having come in from a hard gallop, sitting astride the end of a table. At it, with a great white Peter Pan collar sits the poet Marvell, taking from the dictation of the blind Milton the latinised version of Cromwell's proclamation to Louis XIV . . . in favour of the Waldenses. Cromwell listens in a silence that must have been much like the bellow of any other person; Milton raises his hand with the gesture of one who deprecates interruption; Marvell looks at him over his shoulder. There is a great patch of orange sunlight on the back wall of the room. Why it should be there I never understood; it in no way helps the composition. Perhaps it is intended to symbolise the wrath of God at the persecution of those Swiss heretics though, since, as far as I know, my grandfather did not believe in God, I do not see why he should have troubled to depict the shadow of His wrath. I used, I remember as a boy, to resent the depiction of Marvell in that company. I know of course that Marvell was a secretary of the Roundheads but it used to seem to me to be a sort of hitting below the belt to represent him earning so questionably his living—as if you should represent Buonaparte trying to enlist in the British Army or any other episode in the discreditable parts of the careers of the Great . . . Didn't Marvell after all write:

"The grave's a fine and private place
But none, I think, do there embrace"?

So one day my grandfather let himself in at his front door whilst I was standing in the hall where there hung a large reproduction of that picture of his . . . It must have been painted fifteen or twenty years before. . . . Whilst he was letting his old Inverness down from his shoulders his eyes fell on the reproduction; then he looked at it with attention. Finally he made the remark that we all one day or another have to our sorrow to make: He said:

"To think that I could paint like that so long ago!"

He must then have been about seventy—and still experimenting as all artists must do to the end of their days if they do not wish to die from the root upwards. So he thought himself a better painter at past three score than at two score and ten. But that was one of his bad days; he was tired by his walk on Primrose Hill and a Manchester friend had lately told him that the Manchester Town Council actually intended to carry into effect their resolution to whitewash out his frescoes in the Manchester Town Hall and replace them with advertisements of the merchandise of the Town Councillors. That was a threat that he had borne with equanimity but of course it must be saddening to have threatened with destruction the productions of twelve years or so of your life.

The young however are merciless and I began to tease him about Marvell's being a better poet than Milton and Cromwell's having no right to interfere in the internal affairs of another nation—and the like manifestations of juvenile Tory-Papistry. . . .

I don't know how deep my Tory-Papistry of those days went, but I know that my manifestations of that spirit of lost causes gained a good deal in what we used to call cockiness, from the fact that my cousins, the young Rossettis, lived next door but one and made my life rather a burden with their militant atheism and anarchism.

I must have said something particularly disagreeable about the Waldenses. My grandfather was as far as the poles from either Toryism or Papistry but he used as a rule to listen to me with liking or at least with amusement and toleration. He stood on this occasion, still with his blunt-topped bowler hat pressing down his white hair that was cut à la King of Hearts and leaning on his stick, a vine stock the crook of which smelt with a faint sweetness of the turpentine he used for painting. And suddenly he snorted. I don't know what I had been saying to goad him to contemptuous answering and I don't know exactly what he said though I could no doubt re-construct it, since the rhythms of his speech and his characteristic phrases are still singularly familiar to me.

It was something to the effect that if I was such a dam fool as to think that decent people would stand for the six hundred years of butchering and plundering the Roman Church had inflicted on the innocent Albigenses who were all the same as the Waldenses and on the entirely delightful Troubadours as to whom my father could have told me something . . . Look, he continued at that most attractive of all the Troubadours, the good King René, whose life he had painted in Fitzroy Square and who had been not only poet but painter, architect, musician and king. . . .

I had him of course then and at once came out with my German-inspired facts: the Albigenses had no spiritual or actual kinship with the Waldenses, being non-Christian; the good king

René was largely a legend; he did not paint the picture in Villeneuve-lès-Avignon which my grandfather in returning from his studentship in Rome had gone specially up the Rhone to see. It had not been the Good King who had built the castle at Tarascon but his ancestor Louis I of Provence. King René had done little more than renovate and redecorate it when by his defective generalship and want of popularity with his subjects he had lost the greater part of his realms. And finally King René could never have presided at any Court of Love since the Troubadours were exterminated in 1229—or at any rate in 1247 when St Louis burned Carcassonne, whereas King René was not born until 1409. . . . My grandfather had been sketching a design shewing the Good King presiding at one of the Courts of Love when the firm of William Morris and Co had come abruptly to an end and no more furniture was constructed with panels for Ford Madox Brown to decorate with designs shewing events in the lives of his favourite historical characters.

He stood there silent. Once or twice he dug the end of his vine stock into the tiles of the hall . . . You see, he considered that he had a sort of divine right to be an authority on Albigenses, Waldenses, the Courts of Love, the Good King. Had he not, as a young man, followed in the footsteps of that King; hadn't he in his strong prime listened for hours into the night to my father, the Great Authority, talking about Guillem de Cabestanh and the *Sanh del Trobador?* . . . I can still hear his voice as he says "Cabes . . . taing'g." Couldn't he invent a date or a coincidence? . . . Was I the one to tell him that Cromwell and Milton and Marvell and Dutch William had been wrong to interfere with the butchering of the Waldenses by Louis XIV and the Papacy? Why Cromwell and his company did it in the name of the Good King René of Naples, Sicily, Anjou, Bar and Lorraine! In the name of the Troubadours as to whom my father had been the greatest living Authority of his day! In the name of all the Arts!

My grandfather however said never a word of all this. I let

off the final insult . . . The Good King preside at the Courts of Love! I exclaimed, or words to that effect. Who was he to talk about love? Why, he could not even beget a child on either of the two women whom he married and professed on paper to have loved with such passion! That was why his kingdom of Provence had fallen into the ravening maw of the dukes of Anjou and France. That was the cause of all the trouble!

My grandfather opened his mouth to speak. But no sound came and he shrugged his shoulders and stumped heavily up the stairs to his studio. For at least a fortnight he spoke to me only with the very frostiest politeness. Then I suppose he forgot it. . . . As for me I went and looked up in every authority I could get hold of the subjects of Arianism, Arminianism, Albigensism. I was anxious to build up an always stronger case against his picturesque inaccuracies.

I do not think that there is much of my life that I would care to change if I could. But that at least is a memory I should be glad to be rid of. It was, I suppose, a sufficiently familiar sort of skirmish in the never dying religious warfare that goes on between youth and age. Today I am particularly prone to the assaults of young American journalists who have spent six weeks or two months or three in London, Paris or Berlin. They come to see me here in my garret with the fog drizzling outside. They lecture me about European nationalities, gradually getting back to the causes, events leading up to, strategy, tactics and demeanour of troops in the late war.

I stand it with equanimity for an hour; for three quarters; for two hours or two hours and a half according to the number of fools I have already had to suffer on that day. Then I begin mildly to suggest that I too have been in Arcady. They say: You, you doddering old fool . . . Haven't we been in Europe for three weeks, or two months or five, as the case may be? Haven't we had all the Authorities giving us all the documents all the time? . . . Of course the French invaded Alsace three days before the Germans had to defend themselves at Gemmen-

ich in August . . . Of course the British were forced back a
mile and a half on the Somme on the 13th July, 1916. . . .

I say with some heat—like my poor grandfather who had
visited the Rhone and seen the picture at Villeneuve-lès-Avignon
—that every dawn here when I am awakened by the crash of the
milk-cans in the street below or at dawn at home when a squad-
ron of aeroplanes brushes the top leaves of the oak under which
I sleep I start up and think it is the French seventy-fives with
their Marseillais gunners locked wheel to wheel behind our
trench on the Somme and firing without pause. And certainly
our trench was in the same place at dawn of the 14th as it had
been at dusk of the 13th.

They say: "You poor old fellow . . . We know you are
wrong because we have *read* about it . . . Any one can *see*—
who isn't purblind with ocular presbytism and reading too much
Latin—that the only way to save Europe is by washing out the
last trace of the classics from her mentality. . . ."

"You mean," I exclaim then sardonically, "by giving France
to Mr Hitler to play with."

They answer that it is I that say it, not they. And after all,
why should not ancient crimes be expiated? . . . When, in July
1914 M. Poincaré went to Leningrad and plotted, as they had
read, with Iswolsky . . . But of course I did not know that
Poincaré had been to Leningrad in July 1914. . . .

Then, remembering my grandfather slowly and depressedly
stumping up stairs in silence, I let them have it. No retreat for
me!

I do not mean to trouble the reader with the account of my
deeds in those particular skirmishes in the sempiternal war between youth and age, between classicism and the Old Teutonic
Gods . . . Only, when the New York Press falls on the head
of this writer like a house of cards overwhelming a tin soldier
let him remember that there have been old battles long ago, the
causes of, and the events leading up to, that War having been
the sack of Rome by Alaric and his Goths, the defeat of Clovis

at Arles, the extirpation of the Albigenses at the battle of Muret, the letter of Cromwell, the execution of Maximilian in Mexico, the forged telegram of Ems, the cooking of the chef of the *White Heather. . . .*

I have been wanting for some time to make this note:

I have somewhere related how when I was about eighteen, I went to my confessor and recounted that I was unable any more, not so much to believe in, as to compass the idea of, the Third Person of the Trinity. He being old and wise and having the interests of the church cannily at heart, replied: "Calm yourself, my son; that is matter for theologians. Believe as much as you can,"—since when I have never given a personal thought to matters theological.

Of course that visit of mine to old Father Peter of the Passionists of the Avenue Hoche was by way of expiation to the shade of my grandfather who was by then dead. He was not of course any sooner dead than I was more anxious than I can say to be at one with his benignant spirit; for I knew then that forty years after that day I should still have to look in vain for a more chivalrous, benevolent and Christian man—in all the world. Speculating, then, on the nature and doctrines of the Albigenses, Waldenses, Arminians and the rest, it had come into my head that, if you could without falling from Grace expunge from your consciousness the Third Person, you would be left with the belief in two first causes, the one vengeful, the other infinitely forgiving; the one Jahweh, the other Elohim; the one creating Provence, the other, the rest of the Great Trade Route. Thus there appeared to be no reason against the reconciliation of St Louis and Raymond of Toulouse; no reason why one should not, if one were Romantic, confuse the painters of the *atelier* of Avignon with the builder of the bastide at Tarascon and the president of the Courts of Love; or the Albigenses with the Waldenses. It is probably the better way to take one's history. For if one can fuse the Albigenses into the Waldenses there is no reason why one should not like the Waldenses—which is a good thing to do because they were slaughtered saints or at least brave men. And, if you can like the Waldenses—as I have done since that day—you might with practise come to like Milton, if not his verse, and eventually Cromwell who, if to the Kings of France, Spain and the rest of Christendom he must have presented the aspect of a seventeenth century M. Hitler, could yet utter as his last words the conviction of his personal salvation. And it is probably the conviction that one is in tune with the Universe that will most surely make of men good citizens—and save the world.

CHAPTER IV

COURTS OF LOVE

I AM giving you my Provence. It is not the country as made up by modern or German scholarship; it is the Roman Province on the Great Trade Route where I have lived for nearly all my spiritual as for a great part of my physical, life.

I drink deep into my lungs wind that I know comes from Provence;
From that country everything that comes gives me pleasure
And listening to the praises of her I smile.
For every word of praise that is said I ask you for a hundred
So much am I pleased by the praises of that land.
From the mouth of the Rhone to Valence, between the sea and the
     Durance!
In that noble land did I leave the joy of my heart.
To her I owe the glory that the beauty of my verses and the valour
     of my deeds have gained for me,
And, as from her I draw talent and wisdom. so it is she that made
     me a lover and, if I am a poet
  To her I owe it.

I am reminded of Henry James saying that he had loved France as he had never loved woman. Like the Author of "Daisy Miller," Peire Vidal who is for me *the* Troubadour as for me Henry James is *the* Expatriate, was when he wrote those lines away from the country he loved, though no further away than in the castle of la Louve, in the Black Mountain, behind Carcassonne, in the Narbonnais. To be sure St James's Park where the Master of the London novel spoke those words is no further away from France than is Carcassonne from Tarascon. But, just as poor dear old London is a Paris without effervescence so the Narbonnais, like a cake that has been baked in a too slow oven, is a heavier Provence. Running water cuts off the power of witches—which is why you must always make a hole in your egg-shells—so the Rhone and the Channel form barriers for lightnesses.

It is queer what powers of insulation those waters have. I sit here in my garret and hammer at phrases; I walk these streets with the dove-coloured paving stones, bemused; if I want to see anything I must make an effort of the will; if I write a sentence it comes out as backboneless as a water-hose; to give it life I must cut it into nine. It is no doubt no more than indigestion; when I get back to Provence the world will be astonishingly visible. I shall write little crisp sentences like silver fish jumping out of streams.

There is contagion in that land. But, if, as I shall in an hour or two, I get up from my table in these dimnesses and take a walk. . . . What? I shall cross Fitzroy Square. There is my grandfather's house, the house with the urn. From the windows behind it I had my first view of life. It consisted of doves in the enormous plane trees. And the planes *are* enormous—as big to me now as they come back to me in memory. That seems odd; usually, when you come back to what to you as a child seemed enormous it will appear ludicrously small. But these trees have had to grow and to keep pace with my enlarging views of life. . . . Say half a century, and planes grow fast. Not as fast as walnuts. In forty years a walnut will be as large as a two century oak. Ladies should never plant walnut trees when they are young. . . .

I suppose that behind that urn I must first have heard the first poem that imprinted itself on my memory:

> A mushroom springs up in a night;
> Take warning, little folk.
> An oak it takes a hundred years to grow
> . . . But then it is an oak!

Certainly it was behind that urn that I first saw Christina Rossetti—that poor half-Greek, half-Italian, expatriated like Peire Vidal or like Henry James . . . or like Mr Pound, but inversely . . . She frightened me a good deal, I suppose because of her Latin-Hellenic origin and particularly because of her fluting, exact voice and dark, always inward-smiling eyes. She moved one hand towards me presumably to draw me towards her. That frightened me out of my life so that I ran behind the easel that had upon it the picture of the good King René, whilst his wife kisses his cheek, drawing his plans for the castle at Tarascon. For my grandfather, just about then was painting that panel. . . . When I emerged she called me her 'dear young connection' with the air of enjoying a holy joke.

She had that in common in her aspect, with Henry James. Both used exact phrases with the air of savouring them, like a bull-finch cracking hemp-seed. . . .

"One evening," says Mistral, "when sowing was on, watching the ploughmen who sang whilst they followed the plough I broke, glory be to the Highest, into the first song of 'Mireille.' This poem, the child of love, opened peacefully like a plant, little by little, leisurely, to the breath of the land breeze, under the heat of the sun, beneath the tempestuous mistral. And all the time under the direction of my father who at the age of eighty had grown blind I superintended the work of the farm. . . ."

I wonder what Christina or the author of the "Golden Bowl" would have made of things if they had written—and lived all their lives—on a farm, under the heat of the sun, beneath the tempestuous mistral—in the valley of the Alpilles, which says Mistral, he had always beneath his eyes, at Maillanne.

Instead there is something cruel about both of them—something cruel that finds utterance in the fact that her masterpiece is "Goblin Market" and his "The Turn of the Screw." That is the most cruel thing that was ever written—if it isn't the "Four Visits," which is more pitiless than it should be permitted to a human being to be . . . Talk about bull-fighting! . . . In that story the Master kills a spring lamb with all the torture and the gusto of El Greco's Torquemada . . . Well, I suppose that if you live in a cellar you must expect to have poisonous mushroom growths on you.

At any rate those two who are for me the most—the only—significant figures of London Literature in the XIXth century, lived in Chelsea, Bloomsbury, and the parish of St Marylebone, where I sit; and they only rarely saw the sun and never felt the mistral.

> . . . One day, remembering her kernel stone
> She set it by a wall that faced the South.
> . . . It never saw the sun,
> It never felt the trickling moisture run
> While with sunk eyes and faded mouth
> She dreamed of melons. . . .

But if she had lived at Cavaillon she would have seen whole streets heaped with melons as you see whole quays piled with cheeses in Holland. And we may say that her whole life of writing poems on the corner of her Bloomsbury wash-stand was one long obsession of longing for that South that begins after you have passed Valence—*entre la Mer et la Durance.* . . .

> "Raise me a dais of silk and down,
> Hang it with vair and purple dyes,
> Carve it with doves and pomegranates
> And peacocks with a hundred eyes . . .
> Work it in gold and silver grapes
> In leaves and silver fleurs de lys
> Because the birthday of my life
> Is come, my love is come to me."

I don't know what Dr Freud makes of all that; for any normal person it is the obsession of an exile for the land of Peire Vidal, of the contests of the troubadours. If you like, of the courts of love which no doubt hardly existed save in the fertile brain of the brother of Nostradamus of St Rémy de Provence. Of not merely an exile but of a blood descendant. For Christina is the hundred-times great, grandchild of Dante who was the son of all the writers of Provence from Bernard de Ventadour who loved Agnès de Montluçon, wife of Viscount Elbles, to poor Guiraud Riquier who sang a perpetual swan song to his empty purse. Indeed, no sooner was poor Riquier dead in 1294 than Dante came on the scene with the "Vita Nuova" and knew the bitterness of eating another's bread and climbing the stairs of exile.

As for Henry James, I do not so much know. The passionate pilgrim from barbaric Washington Square, he went in search of deportment, prunes, prisms and peeresses from Manhattan, by way of Boston Common, Geneva, Montparnasse and Montmartre—which shocked, shocked, shocked him—to De Vere Gardens and lay on his death-bed in Chelsea S.W. with the Order of Merit pinned to his breast by Professors Gosse and Kerr . . . I don't know what he had done to deserve *that* but I equally don't know what, exactly, is his connection with Provence. He might have liked to call on Petrarch at Vaucluse and have Laura come in to tea. Though, exactly what he would have made of the relationship of that couple I hardly dare think. . . . I know that Andrew Lang's translation of "Aucassin and Nicolette" really appalled him and, in the fact that that work became during his life-time an Anglo-Saxon classic, he discerned evidence of the eventual decay of our far-flung, sister-cousin seed. . . .

"What have I to do with Paradise," quod Aucassin—*Aucassin, li biax, li blons, li gentix, li amorous!*—"I have no desire to go to Paradise; but vouchsafe to me Nicolette, my sweet friend. I will tell you what make of folk it is that do go into Paradise, and they only. There go old priests and the halt and the crippled such as day-long and all night cower before altars and under vaults; there go the threadbare and those in rags; on that pilgrimage the company is made up by those who have no clothes, walk bare-foot and crusted with sores; those who have starved and frozen and died of thirst and of despair.

It is they who make up the hosts of Paradise; what have I to do with them? Hell is my chosen destiny. Thither go plump clerics and gentle knights such as died on the tented fields and in great wars; good soldiers and goodly men. Let those be my journey-mates, and, with them, such fair and gentle ladies as have two lovers or three besides their husbands. And there you shall find gold and silver and black fur and grey"—and vair and purple dyes—"and jongleurs and minstrels and the Kings of the World. . . ."

What wonder that that famous passage was the despair of the author of "The Great Good Place"; it shocked even Walter Pater who speaks of "the influence of that faint air of overwrought delicacy, almost of wantonness which was so strong a characteristic of the poetry of the Troubadours. . . ." But, if in revenge you could have heard Mr James' remarks on Mr Pater's paean to the Northern companion poem of "Amis and Amile!" Mr James took it to be a paean to homo-sexuality, into such queer blind alleys will moralising lead you. . . .

Mr James once called on the painter who painted behind the urn in Fitzroy Square. He was distressed by what he considered to be the squalor of my grandfather's bare working studio, being used to the gilt dome of Sir Lawrence; the stuffed peacocks of Sir Frederick; the oriental draperies of Sir Edward. And he was more than distressed by the *King Renés* and the *Death of Tristan* and the Saracen-Jewish features of *Elijah Carrying the Widow's Son* down a ladder from a loft whilst a hen—to symbolise the Church—screams to her chickens to hide from the Prophet beneath her wings. Mr James was used to the *Visit to Aesculapius* of the one KT., P.R.A. (Knight, President of the Royal Academy) or the *Perseus and Andromeda* of the other KT., P.R.A. The one shews a number of naked ladies standing up before an aged doctor; the other, one naked lady reclining, almost unconscious, on rocks, before a young Academy model and a ptero-

dactyl. But why should Mr James be genuinely pained by the
spectacle of a Hebrew prophet and a hen and not shocked at
all—but neither was Queen Victoria! who knighted the painters!—by the spectacle of all those naked ladies? That is a
problem in aesthetics that we may well leave to Dr Jung and
Professor Babbitt. . . . But perhaps it is really a problem in
anaesthetics.

And the horrid thought strikes me that just as Christina
Rossetti was descended through Dante from Arnaut Daniel,
Peire Vidal and Marcabrun who was murdered by his lord
because his tongue was too sharp, so Mr James through the
Mayor Guiton of La Rochelle may descend from Paul of
Samosate, the Catharists of Bulgaria, and all the other founders
of the polychromatic sect of the Albigeois of Provence . . .
'Catharist' at least means 'Purist' and Mr James' Huguenot
ancestors came from La Rochelle to Washington Square where
Henry James, Sr. presided over a sect of Purists all his own.
. . . And the Huguenots of La Rochelle are said to have descended straight from the Paulicians, the Catharists, the Albi-
geois. . . .

At any rate I imagine that if Mr James had sat habitually
in the sun before the Café—*de Paris* of course, not *du Commerce*—and had discussed French as spoken in the law-courts
instead of morals and manners at the tea-table of Mrs
Humphrey Ward . . . well, in that case, I imagine that his
sentences might have been more like little silver fish. And
the history of London would have been different.

Let us however continue our walk through this storied
district—in search of literary contagions. There is, I was told
the other day, not far from the house that used to be my
grandfather's, a brothel exclusively patronised by the richer
intelligentsia of the city. I have not visited it so I do not really
know. In Fitzroy Street, going South I once called on Mr
Wyndham Lewis (Percy) who was of opinion that the other
inhabitants of the house were very wicked people and was

taken to call on Miss Nina Hamnett who was seated on a bed entirely surrounded by empty sardine tins. . . . So one finds a little of the atmosphere.

I came yesterday, also in Fitzroy Street, at a party, upon a young Lady who was the type of young lady I did not think one ever could meet. She was one of those ravishing and, like the syrens of the Mediterranean and Ulysses, fabulous beings who display new creations to the sound of harps, shawms and tea-cups. What made it all the more astounding was that she was introduced to me as being one of the best cooks in London —a real *cordon bleu*, and then some. She was, as you might expect, divinely tall and appeared to appear through such mists as surrounded Venus saving a warrior. But I found that she really could talk, if awfully, and at last she told me something that I did not know—about garlic. . . .

As do—as *must*—all good cooks, she used quantities of that bulb. It occurred to me at once that this was London and her work was social. Garlic is all very well on the bridge between Beaucaire and Tarascon or in the arena at Nîmes amongst sixteen thousand civilised beings . . . But in an *atelier de couture* in the neighbourhood of Hanover Square! . . . The lady answered mysteriously: No: there is no objection if only you take enough and train your organs to the assimilation. The perfume of *allium officinale* attends only on those timorous creatures who have not the courage as it were to wallow in that vegetable. I used to know a London literary lady who had that amount of civilisation so that when she ate abroad she carried with her, in a hermetically sealed silver container, a single clove of the principal ingredient of *aioli*. With this she would rub her plate, her knife, her fork and the bread beside her place at the table. This, she claimed, satisfied her yearnings. But it did not enchant her friends or her neighbours at table.

My instructress said that that served her right. She herself, at the outset of her professional career, had had the cowardice to adopt exactly that stratagem that, amongst those in London who have seen the light, is not uncommon. But, when she went to her studio the outcry amongst her comrades, attendants, employers, clients and the very conductor of the bus that took her to Oxford Circus, had been something dreadful to hear. Not St Plothinus nor any martyr of Lyons had been so miscalled by those vulgarians.

So she had determined to resign her post and had gone home and cooked for herself a *poulet Béarnais*, the main garniture of which is a kilo—two lbs.—of garlic per chicken, you eating the stewed cloves as if they were *haricots blancs*. It had been a Friday before a Bank holiday so that the mannequins at that fashionable place would not be required for a whole week.

Gloomily, but with what rapture internally, she had for that space of time lived on hardly anything else but the usually eschewed bulb. Then she set out gloomily towards the place that she so beautified but that she must leave for ever. Whilst she had been buttoning her gloves she had kissed an old aunt whose protests had usually been as clamant as those of her studio-mates. The old lady had merely complimented her on her looks. At the studio there had been no outcry and there too she had been congratulated on the improvement, if possible, of her skin, her hair, her carriage. . . .

She had solved the great problem; she had schooled her organs to assimilate, not to protest against, the sacred herb. . . .

Freshened by that stimulating thought let us proceed down Fitzroy Street. Here once lived and worked Etty, R.A.; Dyce, R.A.; D. G. Rossetti, P.R.B.; Maclise, R.A., who had trouble with his bath. . . . There are no memorial tablets on these houses.

I gather no literary contagion from Charlotte Street but my New York friend who is accompanying me points out that this thoroughfare exactly resembles the more squalid streets round lower Sixth Avenue. That is true but not astonishing, because the builders who built all this parish like those who erected the greater part of Lower New York, Boston and Philadelphia, got their measurements, proportions, brick, tile and woodwork specifications from the same Builder's Manual which was published on both sides of the Atlantic at the beginning of the XIXth century.

Where Charlotte runs into Percy you get a little of the effect of a French *place* and there are one or two *bistros* and *gargottes* of a certain, and one or two public houses of extreme, nastiness that do duty for cafés—with all the disadvantages of insane and ridiculous licensing hours invented for poor, patient London by Welsh-Scotch-North-Irish-Nonconformity. Here you will occasionally meet a being of some intelligence walking along the pavements, as is the case on the Boulevard Montparnasse or on Fifth and Sixth Avenues below Twenty Third Street.

It is, in short, this *place*, the heart of the Arts for London—but what a tiny heart; in a breast of what squalor, feebly pulsing to send how thin a trickle of the faint silver blood of civilisation through the flaccid veins of this enormous city. Like a vast narcoticised body thrown across the valley of the Thames and from there into what soiled remotenesses! . . . A flaccid jelly of a body with organs of assimilation, of some sort of digestion, of some sort of circulation, of some sort of consciousness, ninety miles across by sixty, and, with a heart the size of a hen's egg, for all salvation.

Standing as it were—for of course I am really bending over paper and looking across the way at the small windows of the brick boxes opposite. Two foreign looking dark women occasionally lean bounteously out of one of them, one at each small window and each accompanied by an amusing cat— But standing as it were in that *place* I feel my mind run over London. The southward-going streets here make a sort of bayonet turn into . . . I can't remember the name of the street. There was a time when, except for Conduit Street which I always confused with Coventry Street, I hardly knew the name of any street in London though I could have found my way blindfold from Shepherds Bush to Bow Church by way of Tite Street and Primrose Hill supposing you to have challenged me thus to zigzag . . . Why should I have known the names of streets? If I wanted to go anywhere I took a cab and so kept my mind free for matters more necessary than the names of streets. Alas, for '29 on Wall Street! Now I have to go afoot and even to ask my way . . . Positively, yesterday, in a street that I understood to be called Cheapside I had to ask a City Policeman the way to the Guildhall! My New York friend had wanted to see if the Guildhall was *really* as fine as the Town Hall in Brussels!

So I cannot call to mind the name of the street that connects Charlotte with Oxford Street. It is distinguished by a colour-shop where my grandfather used to buy such paints as he did not mix or grind himself . . . And of all the acres of the faded gumminesses that, under the guise of British Art, the A.R.A.s; P.R.A.s; R.A.s; K.T.s and O.M.s, are now displaying at Burlington House, my grandfather's *Work*, the *Last of England* and the *Pretty Ba'a Lambs* are the only pictures that have not so hopelessly faded as to give you no idea what poor old London-British Art was originally meant to look like. The moral is that if a painter wants his pictures to look anything like, in fifty years, what he wants them to look like today, he should at least mix, even if he does not grind every brush-full of paint that he puts on his canvases—except when it comes to the simplest earth colours. As to them, if he takes a gun and, holding it at his colourman's head extracts from him a written statement that his pigments contain nothing but the earths that they purport to be . . . he may buy them.

Going then down Rathbone Place . . . for if I do not load my head with the names of streets I provide myself copiously with address books and works of reference . . . And I will

here repeat what I have often said that if, for your private
occasions, you need a memory you should never, never, never,
load it with any details that you can find in an address book
or work of reference or calendar or dictionary of dates. As far
as I am concerned I have never troubled to retain a single date.
Occasionally some will spring unbidden to my consciousness.
Thus I happen to be aware that from the birth of Guillaume IX
of Poictiers to the death of Guiraud Riquier was exactly 207
years, Guillaume the first of the known *contefablistes* of
Provence being born in 1087 and Guiraud, the last of the Troubadours, dying in 1294. And I know that the order of birth
of the most notable Troubadours was: Bernard de Ventadour,
Marcabrun, Jaufré Rudel, all born in the same year, though
what that year is I do not know—only that it was before 1150—
and then Peire d'Auvergne who called himself the Master of
the Troubadours; and Guillem de Cabestanh and Richard Coeur
de Lion—to whom Blondel was presumably a contemporary—
and Peire Vidal and Bertran de Born, Folquet de Marseille, the
Bishop of Toulouse who was one of the fiercest persecutors of
the Albigenses and Rambaut de Vaqueiras and finally poor
Riquier. That seems to me to be not only the sort of thing to
remember but enough . . . Oh, the first three were born in
1140, Ventadour dying aged fifty, Marcabrun being murdered
at forty-five and Jaufré Rudel—who loved the Countess of
Tripoli all his life though he never saw her till he lay on his
deathbed—at the age of thirty . . . I have of course looked up
those dates since writing the preceding sentence. With regard
to Memory I shall here insert in a note a story called "The
Darky Who Had a Good Memory." It is dear to me since it
was told me by an English North Country old maid whom I
had never met before and never saw again, on the battlements
of Carcassonne in a snowstorm . . .[1] That I imagine must be

[1] A Virginia country gentleman once sold his Darky's soul to the devil as
against certain temporal advantages. On the appointed day Satan appeared
and claimed his wage of the Virginian. No, says the Virginian, you kehnt
hev that Darky's soul. That Darky has such a good memory that I couldn't

a concatenation of circumstances that the law of probabilities would scarcely permit to recur in less than a million years. For how many Yorkshire old Maids know anything about Virginia or would tell stories in a snowstorm in Carcassonne, snowstorms happening there once every forty years or so? That was in 1913 when I was refreshing my memory as to the Albigeois martyrs of that city and when I saw inscribed on the end wall of the soldiers' refectory in the Citadelle the words: *"Soldats: deux étendards de votre régiment sont dans le musée de Potsdam. N'oubliez jamais!"*

So, in pursuit of literary contagion let us go on down Rathbone Place . . . We arrive at De Quincey's stony hearted stepmother . . . But if it had been under the trees on the Rochers du Dôme that he had slept, awakening to see the great stretch of the Rhone, and the snows on Mont Ventoux, and the Tower of Philippe le Bel and the acres and acres of walled ground of the castle of Villeneuve-lès-Avignon and the bridge of St Bénézet, he would have gone down into the town humming, and the market-women would have called out: *"Ohé, Poète"* and would have filled his hat with tomatoes and olives and little fishes fried ready, and peppers and a square yard of the garlic-and-anchovy cake that they call *Paradis de Nice*, and a bottle of Tavel, and a paper cup to drink it out of. And he would have gone back to the steps of the Castle of the Popes and, sitting there, would have thought out a poem in continuation of *"Sur le Pont d'Avignon."* So there would have been one poet

run my farm without him and that would mean the loss of all the advantages you conferred on me . . . I must hev'm says the Devil. . . . I always thought you were a Gentleman, said the Virginian. A Gentleman does not take back what he once gave. . . . Well, says the Devil, I come of a gentlemanly family. Let's see if yo' Darky *hes* such a good memory.

So the Devil went down to the fence where the Darky was ploughing in the potato-patch and calls out. "Yo laike aiggs?". . . . "Sho'" hollers the Darky. . . . Satan he went away for a whole yeer. Then he went down to that fence again. The Darky was ploughing the same patch—I hope for something else than potatoes or what becomes of the rotation of crops? The Devil he calls out: "Ha.ow?" and the Darky Hollered back: "Fr.r.a.i.ed." So the Devil judged that that Darky's memory was good enough.

the more and, thank God for the imagination!, one English Essayist the less. . . .

You do not believe that? I will tell you. It was in the days when we still wore across our stomachs golden watch-chains, and having caught and broken my chain scrambling up hill to the Castle of Roumanille—where, as you remind me, the Courts of love were holden—I went to a jewellers to have that chain repaired. When I fetched it and asked the price that descendant

The Castle of Villeneuve-lès-Avignon

of Maître Anseau le Tourangeau exclaimed: "*Mais, monsieur, Monsieur est poète* . . . One does not charge Poets for the work one does for them!" . . . And he had put in two links of solid gold! . . . I was shortly afterwards arrested by a romantic gendarme . . . as being the Duc d'Orléans! That is what the suns of the South do for you. . . .

Well, in De Quincey's Oxford Street dwells Mr Compton Mackenzie to whom I owe two of the greatest pleasures of my life . . . For it was when I was writing about his "Sinister Street" and complaining that his talents had been for too long unacknowledged that I wrote the sentence: "But even Miss

Genée had been dancing for ten years before she was discovered." The printer turned the last word into "divorced" and so I had the privilege, during a visit of apology, of learning that I was too old and too fat to become a clog-dancer . . . And it was at a cocktail party at Mr Mackenzie's the other day that I was introduced to the gentleman who introduced me subsequently to the young lady who gave me that splendid tip about *allium officinale* . . . And when I come to think of it I have this confirmation. In the towns of the South on Fridays there is *aioli* on the menu of every restaurateur, and every soul in private lunches on that succulent and perfumed mayonnaise which is compounded at the rate of twelve cloves per person. Yet the air of the crowdedest tram car, of the most packed cinema, of the most popular barber and of every place where men most densely throng is as sweet as the breath of a day old child! . . . On looking up the word *ail* in a medical work of reference I read: *"On s'en sert comme vermifuge"*—which in itself is valuable. Of it you can also make one of the very strongest forms of glue . . . It is however best not used for gumming up sachets of lavender to be placed in linen cupboards.

Casanova once lodged in the street that connects Oxford Street with Soho Square and advertised in the *London Mercury* for the return of a parrot that had deserted a celebrated courtesan who lodged in the same house . . . No, not *that London Mercury* of course. There is no memorial tablet on that house any more than there is over the door in Oxford Street on whose step slept De Quincey.

In the south-east corner of Soho Square once dwelt T. E. Hume. There is a memorial tablet next door to an engineer but none to Hume. In the north-east corner of the Square once lived a publisher who paid me real money for a volume of poems. (No Tablet.) That apartment is now occupied by an extension of the French Huguenot Church which, in its varnished, pink brick looks as if it aped the Alhambra—of Leicester Square . . . Oh, shades of the Albigenses! . . . But see how

Provence keeps creeping in! . . . In Dean Street is the house where Hogarth threw his brush at the gouty toe of Sir William Thornhill, thus becoming his son-in-law . . . No tablet!

There are restaurants in Soho but no . . . vermifuge . . . That perhaps accounts for the present pensivity of London literature, most of our *intelligentsia* there resorting to breathe in the Latin atmosphere that is so corrective of our allusiveness . . . But unless the house be blessed, the builders build in vain.

Piccadilly Circus, London

You emerge in Shaftesbury Avenue and are shocked at the callow juvenility of the traffic cops. That nerve-racking job should be given to grown men. They are abolishing a famous variety house at the Piccadilly Corner of the Avenue. The *Eros* is back but, as Biala shews us you cannot see the Circus for recommendations to stop that cough, clean your teeth, drink malt liquors and avoid sleeplessness.

It is at this point that my New York friend remarks that the famous streets of London if not undistinguished are at least indistinguishable . . . *Haow* can you tell Piccadilly from the Strand? What is the difference in local colour between Regent

Street and High Street Kensington or between King Street St James's and Earl's Court Road? . . . They all tell you that it is now time to drink malt; that you are suffering from night starvation; that you 'can't'; that you ought to drink more milk. . . .

And that New Yorker will remind me of a story of Mr— afterwards Sir—Edmund Gosse and Professor W. P. Kerr that I once told. The two—but so differing—literati were hiking it in North Wales where it is mostly precipices. Scrambling round a mountain-face on a path a handsbreadth wide they came suddenly up against a precipice-face inscribed in immense letters— letters twenty feet high: PREPARE TO MEET THY GOD . . . "And at such close quarters, too!" chirped Professor Kerr as he supported a pallid Librarian of the House of Lords.

All of London, said that New Yorker, was like that precipice—and indistinguishable . . . I muster some of the superiority of the hardened European addressing the Transatlantic transient . . . I say:

"Of course for you . . . who don't see the atmosphere, the glamour, the old traditions, the literature, the Art that are behind it all—circumambient. . . ."

The New Yorker answers:

"Well, if you were dropped in a parachute into Piccadilly what literary circumambience would let you tell it from Madison Avenue? . . ."

I say:

"Hang it all . . . There's . . . There's . . ." And desperately: "There's Fortnum and Mason's . . . And . . . And . . . Fortnum and Mason's. . . ."

That visitor from Gotham says:—would you believe it?—

"The butcher's shop where you buy candy! . . . Well, I'll admit you can't buy candy at a butcher's shop in Madison Avenue but otherwise I can't see any different circumambience . . ." . . . But you can!

And he adds:

"I'll tell you what . . . Next door to Fortnum and Mason's is . . . what do you think? . . . The principal agency of the P.L.M. from where you can make reservations right to Tarascon without changing. I guess if they dump you in front of the Café du Commerce you'll know where you are . . . Let's go and look over their travel pamphlets. . . ."

And we go. Under the flaming posters of the Promenade des Anglais and the View from the Corniche and the young lady pointing from under the umbrella pines of St Jean Cap Ferrat at M. Reinach's Greek villa on Beaulieu point we look questioningly into each other's eyes and plan our progress to Bignor and Chichester and Newhaven and the rue Madame and the Place des Ducs de Bourgogne at Dijon, and Valence, and Vaison, and Orange, and Avignon . . . And it is pouring on the jammed, huge, scarlet cubes, in their mastodon confusion in front of dripping Burlington House . . . And a miserable fellow with one arm is breaking one's heart trying to sell us plush toys from a tray suspended to his skeleton neck . . . Oh, Clio, Muse of History, daughter of Jupiter and of Mnemosyne, Goddess of Memory, give strength to my poor pen . . . So, on the last Sunday in May, we shall see Lalanda and Chicuelo at Nîmes. Yes, as the poet sings—any old poet: "Fill up my empty purse and let me go!"

Poor dear old London is like that . . . A good place in which to dream of the glories of Peire Vidal and Bertran de Born, but no city in which to walk the streets in search of her own glories . . . There is a statue of Shakespeare in Leicester Square and another in the wall of a public house on top of Primrose Hill . . . But if you let your thoughts wander over London they have to go by air if you wish to find traces . . . There is the house that Thackeray built himself near Kensington Palace—the house that he built and then for the rest of his life lived in in torture for fear his popularity should desert him so that he should not be able to run that house on the scale suited to a member of the Athenaeum Club . . . And somewhere behind the Law Courts is the putative house of Dickens' Little Dorrit.–Or perhaps the Old Curiosity Shoppe . . . And Johnson took a walk down Fleet Street . . . And Shakespeare must have worshipped in Southwark Cathedral. Perhaps not by inclination but because all the players at the Globe in his day must by law attend divine service in that fane on Sundays and be shut up in a pen in front of the tomb of Gower . . . *"Quite the Hitler touch!"* says my New Yorker . . . And then what? . . . I believe there is a memorial to W. H. Hudson in Kensington Gardens . . . But there is also one to Peter Pan. And poor Huddie suffered agonies of depression and poverty for years in the shadow of St Luke's Church, Bayswater; whose spire you can see rising above the northern end of the Serpentine. There's circumambience!

There is however a touch of art that makes Piccadilly one with Provence: The rocks at Vaucluse, above the fountain of Petrarch, are so covered with publicity-inscriptions that you might well believe yourself gazing at it beyond the Eros on the other fountain. So at least it was when I first saw it . . . Hear then the expatriate lover of Laura:

"This is my life," says he, "I rise at midnight and at dawn I go a-walking. But in the countryside as in my house I study, I meditate, I read, I write. All day long I walk on the bare mountains, the green valleys and the grottos; I go along either bank of the Sorgues, alone, having with me no companion but my cares, which however grow less and less galling every day . . . Here I have made my Rome, my Athens, my native land. All the friends I have had, not only those I have myself seen or who have protected my life, but also those who lived centuries ago and are known to me only by their books, the men whose actions, characters, life, manners, language and genius I admire, differing friends come from all over the world and from all the ages–all these I gather round me in this narrow valley."

So it was in that Provençal valley that the language of Modern Italy was formed. That is only another instance of the backward and forward trend of civilisation–backwards and forwards through Provence—but always with that country as its halting place, its shelter and its nourishment.

Petrarch has always seemed to me a very alien character in the valley of the Rhone, I daresay because of the Coney Island display of publicity of one kind and the other that decorates the rocks of Vaucluse. This is not as silly or as arbitrary as

Mistral. A Statue to the Poet

it seems. A great man cannot get off the responsibility for the quality and behaviour of his admirers, because his poetry or doctrines will have had a large share in moulding their characters and demonstrations. You will see troops of the faithful surrounding a Great Figure, treading on tip-toe with their fingers to their lips so that no syllable of his utterances shall be lost. But a Great Figure who, if he wants to, cannot make his mark for himself in general company or before the world, had better keep out of, say, the studios of Paris and avoid publicity in New York. Even so great and unconcerned a character as Mistral has suffered in public estimation from the character of his worshippers. It is impossible to go into any city or hamlet in the valley of the Rhone without seeing a statue to the poet of a grotesqueness that cannot but give you what London housemaids call "a turn." He is usually represented as standing on a rock and fiercely affronting, with flying cloak, the gusts of the wind from which his family took its name. But the author of "Mireille," like every other sensible human being, when the mistral blew, kept himself as much as possible in his sunny *caniche* and employed himself with his enormous correspondence until it stopped . . . Mistral nevertheless passes amongst those who have not read him for a romantic of the vein of Hugo or Dumas at their worst. He was actually one of the greatest and simplest of renderers of the intimacies of human life and natural vicissitudes. I am ready however to confess that, though I once heard Mistral himself read a considerable portion of "Calendal," I was misled by his romantic personality—he was like a Mr Pound with a more rotund vocal organ—into sharing the common, uninstructed opinion. Indeed, though, as I have said, I can and could then, understand fairly well—or at least get the general tenour of—the Provençal dialect as spoken in the plains round Tarascon that was a very different thing from understanding a swift reading of the very flexible and complicated language—for it was a language, not a dialect that Mistral had evoked for himself and his brothers of the Félibrige . . . *Félibrige*, by the way is a word of no particular significance, that occurs in the burden of a popular ancient ballad. The seven Provençal poets who with Mistral at their head met at Châteauneuf de Gadagne on the 21st May, 1854 to found a society of poets of the Avignonnais were in want of a name. They happened to sing the old—religious—ballad and, the burden being *"Félibri, félibra"* they adopted those syllables as their slogan.

Mistral is generally reproached with having invented a sort

of Wardour Street jargon; but that is not at all what he really did . . . Provençal was by no means a dead language; it was like one of those plants of its own hills, of an enormous toughness of rootage. The French would decree its extermination—under Louis XI, under Francis I, under Louis XIV. But still like those plants after periods of drought when all trace of them has been lost, it would crop up again in the suddenly green valleys, in the mists of the lonely mountain tops. And all the while it was being used, desperately, as an organ for verse—by shoemakers, by fishermen, down the centuries. SS Louis and Dominic might root out the Albigenses and, in the process, get rid of the courts of the little princes and viscounts in which sang the Troubadours and the village *places* where the *contefablistes* singing and reciting and acting their romances in alternate prose and verse passed such innocent and happy days as the French, the Kaiserliks and Papists would leave them. All that—the whole civilisation—seemed to be wiped out. Nevertheless, subterraneously and passionately it continued—in Arles, in Avignon, in Marseilles, even in Toulon, where you had poets like Bellaud de la Bellaudière, Gaspard Serbin and Etienne Pelabon in the XVI, XVII, and XVIII centuries; and many more, mostly working men, to support them . . . A baker at Nîmes, a stonemason of Toulon, a street porter of Marseilles, a tailor of Aix, until you come to the great Roumanille of St Rémy de Provence, the son of a gardener . . . In Marseilles, even, towards 1848, there flourished an *Athénée Ouvrier*, a workman's Athenaeum all of whose members were poets though these for the most part wrote in French . . . It is in fact a people that loves verse.

But naturally, in the course of centuries, and as happened in every country in the world, great local changes took place in the language. Just as the Kentish peasant today cannot understand the Yorkshire workman, or the Kentucky small-farmer understand the New York journalist, so the fisherman of Marseilles and the arsenal worker of Toulon could neither understand the one the other nor yet the vine-grower of Vaison in the north. On the other hand the Provençal of the plains round Tarascon which contained Maillanne, the birth-place of Mistral, could be perfectly understood by and could understand all the three . . . I had a curious illustration of a similar state of things a couple of years ago when motoring from New York to the depths of Kentucky. My companions were all New Yorkers, but I had to act as interpreter and guide. My language steered a middle course between the two extremes . . . But indeed the long-suffering New Yorker of this book completely —and I daresay obstinately, since there is such a thing as being too long suffering—refuses to understand Virginians whose language and accent are at least as clear to me as those of the policeman at the corner. The policeman at the corner speaks Devonshire with that dreadful accent of south–east Essex which is called Cockney but which is nothing of the sort.

So what Mistral had to do—and did—was to form an academy which should codify the language as far as it is good for a language to be codified. He rejected Gallicisms and Italian and Spanish phrases and restored to literary uses classical Provençal words and expressions the use of which may have died out in the country round Maillanne. To some extent also he tried phoneticising the spellings of words so that today Provençal is a language as liquid and as calculated for the expression of fine shades as any language that exists. The whole of his labours in this direction are enshrined in the great dictionary known as the "Trésor du Félibrige."

For the enormously impressive thing about Mistral, the man, was his colossal industry in the reorganisation of his country. There was a time when Mistral, after the publication of "Mireille" enjoyed a white flame of popularity such as would have destroyed the equanimity of most poets. Paris indeed was prepared for his advent by the momentary popularity of Jacques Boé, known as Jasmin, the Barber, a coiffeur born at Agen, who wrote admirable light verse in the patois of Gascony. But

Mistral never lost his head and instead of remaining in Paris and—again as most poets would have done—becoming a hanger-on of Lamartine, George Sand and the Princesse Mathilde, he returned to his Provence and spent the rest of his days over his wonderful labours of writing poetry and organising the literature of his country.

It might be too much to say of Mistral as was said by that beautiful poet, the Comtesse de Noailles

> Ton coeur enveloppe ta race
> Et ton pays descend de toi

and it might be too much—though perhaps it is not, to say, like the author of "Dans l'Ombre de la Bastide":

> Et tu viens d'acceuillir le verbe qui résume
> Le mètre de Virgile et le coeur de Jésus.

But the authentic note of the great poet is to modify for you the aspect of the world and of your relationship to your world. This Mistral very astonishingly does. I have said that for a great many years I misestimated this great poet. But of late I have been reading him a great deal—notably since I have been in this city . . . And the curious effect has been to render London infinitely more supportable. It is, I suppose, because Mistral is the poet of little, unassuming people who are near the earth and have no claim to dictate destinies to their fellows . . . Whilst the High Gods thunder above, they find cracks in the earth in which to play their concertinas and carry on the arts, the amenities and the realities of life. London is more stupidly mis-governed than any place on the earth simply because its people are so docile and contented with so little that it should be easy to make of the Thames valley a paradise of harmony. It is in-stead one vast blunder—an immense muddling through about which its kindly people go with for ever on their lips the shib-boleth:

"You can't bloody well have everything."

I think if the politicians of Westminster and the ediles across the Thames could be removed to a desert and shut up in cells with nothing but"Mireille" to read and the "Trésor du Félibrige" to help them out in the interpretation London might get its desserts. For though it may be an exaggeration for M. Turle to say that Mistral puts the soul of Jesus into the measures of Virgil it is nothing but the truth when he says:

"Tu ne pourras pas vivre ainsi que de coutume
     Si les chants de Mistral t'ont chanté dans l'oreille . . ."

. . . You cannot continue in your old, bad courses once the songs of Mistral have sounded in your ears.

CHAPTER V

CHURCH AND STAGE

THE bloodiest wars in the world have been fought for spices.
For spices and religion, it being difficult to know which
comes first. For the question of spices and religion is inextricably mingled so that it is difficult to say which has caused
the most bloodshed. All that it is today safe to say is that
the civilised races are those that use spices and cook their food,
barbarism being denoted by the eating of barely singed meat or
matter out of tins.

The sequence is inevitable. A diet without spices causes indigestion—and, my New York friend remarks, night starvation.
Indigestion and its ally cause religious and homicidal mania; religious and homicidal manias are at the root of religious warfare. When you have waged a successful religious war you take
possession of all your opponents' spices. They, being short of
condiments, become once more constipated, melancholiac, homicidal and again fit to wage war for their beshadowed creeds.

Of that Provence is the great exemplar. Provence is the
one country in the world to contain a sufficiency of all spices.
So the Provençaux are the one people that only once in recorded history issued from their own boundaries in an aggres-
sive war. It is true that she does not grow the nutmeg nor
the clove, nor yet cinnamon. But with mint, thyme, taragon,
verjuice, verbena, fennel, lime-flowers, bitter oranges, lemons,
absinthe—the plant not the beverage—olives, basil, garlic and
an innumerable company of minor pot-herbs down to pimento

and the peppers—and mustard, all growing in profusion and without cultivation over her rocks and, with saltpans all along her shores the Provençal digestions are tranquilised and her populations content to stay at home.

It is true again that the bloodiest wars in the world, the most atrocious religious massacres, have occurred in Provence and the Narbonnais. Provence, as we have said, is the one country in the world of which no history has been written; but that is not to say that she is one of those happy lands that have no history. It is merely that the history is so bewildering that no one human brain has yet been able to take it all in. That is because life, religion, the arts, thought, love, assassination and all the attributes of human existence—even to cookery—have been so inextricably mingled in the story of her wars. It is like trying to decipher fifty fishing nets superimposed and inextricably tangled the one with the other. When we Northerners wage war we put from us all thoughts save those of butchery—and of course plunder, with a sub-flavour of rapes. But during the 2,500 years when Provence was being harried she evolved two magnificent literary traditions, an architecture unsurpassed in even Italy, a number of beautiful and humane schools of religious thought and a local civilisation that, if we except that of Periclean Athens, has been the only real civilisation that the world has yet seen.

Yet, when I look at the notes as to Provençal history that I have made for my own purposes I find them to begin—without any moral faking of my own—with the massacre and expulsion by the Massillians of the Greeks who had colonised the Héraut—the part of Langue-doc that surrounds Montpellier—and to end with the massacre by Northern French Royalists of Bonapartists at Avignon, Tarascon, Nîmes and throughout Provence and the Narbonnais.

In the intervening twenty-five centuries what incursions, massacres, expulsions and occupations! They came from every imaginable quarter of the globe and were perpetrated by men of all colours and of every imaginable religious complexion. You have Greeks, Etruscans, Ligurians, Gauls, Afro-Semitic Carthaginians, Volces, Romans, Afro-Vandal Carthaginians, Ostrogoths, Visigoths, Celt-Iberians, Saracens, Franks, Lorrainers, Burgundians, all struggling into the country, struggling against each other. Only the Romans left any permanent traces, the rest being expelled one after the other until little by little the North French of the Ile de France establish a footing that finally becomes a stranglehold from the Pyrenees to the Maritime Alps. The Visigoths who had established themselves at Toulouse took Carcassonne from what was left of the Romans in 413 A.D. . . . I do not apologise for repeating all this catalogue here in slightly differing language. To get any pattern at all out of these confusions it is necessary to go through them several times from different angles . . . In 418 the emperor Honorius ceded to the Visigoths Aquitania with Toulouse for their capital. The North French King Clovis took Toulouse from them at the beginning of the sixth century, nevertheless they held Carcassonne and the country round until 713. Then they were driven out by the Saracens who in turn were driven out by Pepin the Short. Avignon was twice taken by the Saracens and twice re-taken by Charles Martel. Roussillon was taken and nearly burnt out by the Saracens from Africa. On the next day what was left was burned to the ground by the Normans, originally from Denmark!

The dissolution of the Empire of Charlemagne gave Provence to the Germans. The treaty of Verdun divided that Empire into a territory made up of the Western Frankish lands under Charles the Bald; another made up of the Eastern parts of Germany under Ludwig the German; and a third under Lothar, called Holy Roman Emperor who took central Germany, the left bank of the Rhine, Burgundy and Provence, thus giving his Empire access to the sea through that unfortunate land. At the same time, by this family arrangement, his brother, Charles the Bald took Septimania, or the Narbonnais. Thus on the one side of the Rhone you had the Kingdom, on the other, the Empire—a distinction today merely mental but one which, the reader may perhaps remember, still divides the ideas and interests of the two ancient countries. For still, as I have said, the fisher beside the bridge at Beaucaire, spits towards Tarascon in Provence; and the Tarasconnais, looking towards Beaucaire, exclaims distastefully:

"*Sacr. r. ré Royaume!*"

Both countries however on emergence from the Dark Ages developed a common characteristic. Having somehow to rule their relatively distant dominions both King and Emperor had to appoint governors of districts who were called Counts, had vice-regal powers, and had as lieutenants, governors of lesser districts who were called vice- or Vis-Counts. These dignities were much sought after by the strong men of both countries. Thus, as we have seen when the Berengers of Barcelona and the Baux family were contending for the County of Provence, Raymond Berenger went to the Emperor Frederick who was holding court at Milan, and being accompanied by a company of Troubadours so charmed the Holy Roman sovereign that he was at once appointed, to the rage of the Baux, Count of Provence, being afterwards confirmed in that office.

But no sooner was Berenger or Baux or Tancarvel, secure in his office than he developed a passion to declare himself independent and thus from the Maritime Alps to the Pyrenees and beyond there sprang up the bewildering intricacies of small courts, mostly on rocky pinnacles crowned by citadels into which, when attacked, the peasants, merchants, shepherds and craftsmen of the surrounding districts could crowd for protection whether against their master's North French Royal, or German Holy Roman Imperial, over-lords. Or against the neighbouring Counts or Vicomtes or as was more frequently and terribly the case, against the Saracens. These last again and again sacked the deserted countrysides lying between the towns, taking sometimes even a castle and penetrating as far up the

Rhone as Orange itself. Such inhabitants as they did not slaughter they took away into slavery.

Thus arose the popular Romances and half-sung, half-recited pieces of which the most famous is of course the story of Aucassin. But the peasantry and labourers and small tradesmen of the villages of Provence continue to make up these pieces or to modify old ones. You may still, if you have a good deal of luck, hear the peasants and fishermen of the foothills not only rehearsing but adding to the *pastorales* that they still act and sing in Latin, Provençal and French. It is not two years since I was privileged to attend one of these occasions . . . I owed the privilege not to the fact that I am *poète* but to my local reputation as a *chef* who can dispute as to the correct preparation of *bouillabaisse* through a whole afternoon and far into the evening. These rehearsals are kept rather secret and are held in the *calanques*, the inland arms of the sea between the wine-red cliffs of the promontory near Marseilles. So they can only be approached by water.

The poetry of the songs sung on this occasion was often very exquisite, the interspersed prose being, as was fitting, such as should be recited by liberal shepherds getting the words from two thousand years back.

Amongst the *dramatis personae* were Caius Marius; St Mary Magdalen, St Mary the Virgin; a Jew; a Saracen; an Emperor; a Negro Sultan; a Chinaman . . . and Bismarck. He appears in a piece that was interpolated in 1870.

Thus we had a specimen of a living art, not a mere survival. For you might just as well have been listening to the story of Aucassin and Nicolette; the two pieces might have been written by the same hand; the songs in the old piece were introduced just as they are today by the words: *On se cante:* 'Here one sings'; the prose by: *On dient et content et fablent:* "Here they say and tell and make fables." The subject only differs.

It might be as well here to adumbrate the theme of Aucassin, for it occurs to me that, after all, a few of my readers may not have read it . . . Indeed if I consider how few French people seem to have heard of it at all and how many, if they have heard of it, consider it to be a child's story of the rank of "Red Riding Hood," it may well be that its fame is less extended than I had taken it to be.

The conte-fable begins by purporting to tell the story of the war between the aged Count Garins of Beaucaire who owns no overlord and the wicked Count Raymond of Orange, an equally independent sovereign over an ant-hill; you have the Viscount whose functions are merely administrative. The Count's son loves Nicolette and, because she is refused him on account of her unknown origin, she having been bought of the Saracens, he voices opinions that represent the Albigence peasants' contempt for the priests and their heavens. And you have a battle that might be Uccello's own and Aucassin leading prisoner by the nose of his helmet the wicked Count of Orange; and prison in the White Tower that you see from Tarascon, and moonlight and the nightingale, and escape and the guards coming with their weapons beneath their cloaks. And adventure by forest and sea, and grotesque magic of the paynims, expressive of the peasants' deep pacificism . . . And of course the happy ending with the suspected Saracen maid turning out to be the daughter and heiress of the Emperor of Carthage and cousin to the Sultan. That of course is another expression of religious indifference.

"Here they speak and say and make fable:

The ship sailed until it came under the walls of the City of Carthage. And when Nicolette was aware of the walls of the fortress and of the country around, she remembered that there she had been a child and had been carried away from there. Nevertheless she had not been so small that now she did not know that she had been daughter to the King of Carthage and that in that city she had been a child. . . .

And Nicolette smeared her hair and her clear face till she was

[168]

dark. And she got for herself a cape and coat and shirt and breeches and so took to herself the disguise of a minstrel-youth. She took a viol and went to a ship's captain and so pleased him that he gave her passage . . . over the main of the sea to Provence. And she went down from the ship with her viol that she played upon through the land until she was come to the castle of Beaucaire where Aucassin held his court. . . .

There was in fact about the country of the Troubadours little of the oriental languour and wantonness that Mr Pater chose to attribute to them. And, if they seldom felt the desire to invade other lands they fought enough among themselves. Enough, certainly, to keep them healthy. Thus it is difficult to apportion their time between love and its courts, the writing and recitation of sirventes, the holding of tournaments of verse, the combatting of sea-pirates and the commission of acts of land-piracy in their own country. Mr Pound, who is the greatest living authority—or at any rate the best living writer—on Troubadours, speaks somewhere of the boredom of their lives. But I think that there he lets his pen slip. That the Minnesingers and Trouvères of Germany and North France passed ages of boredom shut up in their castles during the winter, with all roads impassable to a knight in armour, with fantastic and indigestible foods and with no occupation in castle-rooms through which the winds incessantly howled—that is true enough. It is indicated in their architectural details as in their personal ferocities and accounted for by their incredible menus, since, having nothing to vent their nerves upon they had to find excitements from the excruciation of their tongues and gastric juices.

But in Provence the knights, like the bees, could work all the year round, as my friend and bailiff Standing of Bedham put it. For in Provence as in the Narbonnais there is no winter and with the Roman tradition of horticulture they had always green vegetables. Moreover, inured from birth to the use of the innumerable herbs and spices of Provence, they had no need for the sadic flagellations of their tongues and intestines to which the cuisines of Anglo-Saxondom and to a less extent still of Germany bear witness. Being therefore spared the Northern tortures of ennui and indigestion they did not have to suffer from the thwarted ferocities that gave rise to the Gothic in North Europe and to the sadically mad cruelties of the Northern Middle ages.

Thus in Provence you will find the jovial and the libidinous. But in the cathedrals of Provence you will see almost no leering gargoyles and almost no vomiting peasants, copulating apes and be-pitchforked fiends such as make horrible the miserere stalls and architectural intimacies of the Northern Gothic fanes . . . It is indeed one of the chief joys of that sweet land that the Gothic there has practically no existence. And the grotesque as a characteristic is as absent from the lives of the Provençaux as from their arts. They had instead traditions of beauty, discipline, frugality and artistic patience.[1]

[1] I do not mean that the knights of Provence or their retainers were too delicate to fight or could not indulge in appropriate cruelties in their male pursuits of circumstance and gold. It was merely that, eating frugally of properly seasoned and usually fresh foods, they had none of the incitements to sadic indulgence in cruelty as an art that distinguished their Northern contemporaries—and some of their descendants. I have tried for a long time to think of a better summing up of this male and go-getting side of Provençal life than is that of John Addington Symonds, speaking of the turbulent family of les Baux—the heroes or business men who lost the Count-ship of Provence because they would not send troubadours with their embassies to the Emperor Lothair. But, as I can find no better words of my own, it seems fairer to the reader, much as I dislike quotation, to quote him here.

"The real temper of this fierce tribe was not shown among troubadours or in courts of love and beauty. The stern and barren rock from which they sprang and the comet of their scutcheon are the true symbols of their natures. History records no end to their ravages and slaughters. It is a tedious catalogue of blood—how one prince put to fire and sword the whole town of Courthézon; how another was stabbed in prison by his wife; how a third besieged the castle of his niece and sought to undermine her chamber, knowing her the while to be with child; how a fourth was flayed alive outside the walls of Avignon. There is nothing terrible and savage belonging to feudal history of which an example may not be found in the annals of les Baux as narrated by their chronicler, Jules Canouge." "The Renaissance in Italy," Vol. I.

It is a great pleasure to me to name the book and transcribe the prose of a writer whose prose and books were one of the greatest pleasures and

So, distinct from the conte-fables and romances of the populace the poetry of the Troubadours came into being—a poetry
that at once raises all the problems of that art which has never
yet been defined. For in poetry as in all the affairs of life and
indeed more than in nearly all the other affairs of life the
eternal conflict between the professional practitioner and the
gifted amateur who writes with the vine-leaves in his hair and
solves .the problems of the universe by his inner lights—that
eternal conflict is most strikingly in evidence.

The poetry of the Troubadours was, almost more than any
other manifestation of the Arts, governed by a very definable
technique; its hearers—for it had in its own day almost no
readers—paid almost as much attention to, and got as much
pleasure from, the skilful accomplishment or circumvention of
a technical point of rhyme, rhythm or metre, as they got from
the actual content of the work to which they listened. The content, that is to say, of the poem of Guillem de Cabestanh that
I have already quoted must have been completely threadbare
to all his knightly hearers. It expresses Guillem's passion for
Berangère and the deeds he is prepared to undertake in her
service or the sufferings his passion causes him, over and over
again—and the expression of similar passions, achievements and
sufferings must have been made a thousand times before by
his contemporaries and predecessors. It thus becomes, like the
representations of millions of virgins and children of another
mediaeval and renaissance art a variation on a given theme, the
delight of the hearers being won by what we may as well
call the craftsmanship, the ingenuity, the patience which could
let a knight find images, thoughts and metaphors for seven
hundred lines each repeating the rhymes of 'ire' and 'en'.

influences of my childhood. . . . It remains however to be said that the Baux
family really were amongst the chief go-getters of their day and country and
in that they differed from, say, Counts of Toulouse who staked and lost
their all on the cause of the Albigenses who were actually indifferent to
them. . . . In the XII century they possessed twenty-nine towns and castles
. . . and bore the titles of Princes of Orange, Counts of Provence, Kings of
Arles and Emperors of Constantinople.

To call, as Mr Pater does, such work either oriental or wanton is merely to beg the question. In fact it is better to regard the noble authors as craftsmen gaining by that ingenuity and patience their itinerant livelihoods; their fame that has never died; their temporary glories and affluences and their license which outpassed the farthest bounds of the poetic. And it is to be remembered that though the actual performances of the sirventes, canzos, tenzones and the rest were knightly and chevaleresque occasions, the art itself was, as all arts must be, essentially both aristocratic and democratic. An English ship's engineer, like Mr Burns, may rise to be President of the Board of Trade; any American may travel from a log-cabin in Kentucky to Washington itself. But the guerdon and fame of the Troubadour were the product equally of the rhyme, the metre and the metaphor that were open to gentle and to simple alike. That art procured for its practitioners of the lowest origins not merely fame and wealth but privileges of a distinguished singularity. It is true that the husband of Berangère des Baux murdered Guillem de Cabestanh—but the Baux family as we have seen were grim of complexion. The gentler Lords and those whose temperaments were normal to their day supported the addresses paid by these bards to their womenkind not merely with equanimity but with enthusiasm. The noble husband of the lady of Peire Vidal who, though of no particularly blue blood was the terror of the noble husbands of his day, remonstrated as we have seen with La Louve for shewing insufficient favour to the troubadour whose mere visit secured deathless fame for the twin castles of Las Tours in the Black Mountain behind Carcassonne; the Marquis of Montferrat supported with equanimity the spectacle of Rambaut de Vaqueiras, though but a peasant protégé of that noble house, yet sleeping with the Marquis' sister; Jaufré Rudel loved hopelessly the Countess of Tripoli and when he came to lie on what was thought to be his deathbed the Count sent his lady to gladden the Troubadour's dying eyes; Folquet of Marseilles, to whom

Dante allots, alike for his sweet songs and his ruthless persecution of the Albigenses, a distinguished place in Paradise, loved
Adélaisie wife of Bérald des Baux and, in spite of the fiery
nature of that family was granted singular privileges. In return
he wrote for the husband after the death of Adélaisie the celebrated "Lament of Bérald des Baux" which has earned for
Bérald, though the meanest of traitors, an immortality at least
coeval with that of Folquet himself. . . .

Provence being thus rendered fit for poets gained speedily
the condemnation and hatred of the outer world. As I have
already pointed out, if it is true that *"mal d'autrui n'est que
songe"* it is infinitely more certain that—and today more than
in the Dark Ages—the happiness or prosperity of another nation
cause in every other people a nightmare so atrocious that they
will have no peace till that evil is remedied. Though it cost
them all their fortunes and all their lives they will do it. Still
more is this the case should that prosperous and happy people
ignore the economic-moral laws of the nations that surround
them. It is well-known that disrespect for the laws of marriage
is ruinous here on earth and the cause of eternal damnation in
the hereafter. It is well-known that Christian morality is the
sole road to material well-being in this vale of tears. Poetry also
is an invention of Satan . . . But here was a people of an infinite complication of gentle and non-ascetic heresies who earned,
by adulteries poetically supported, not only fame and immortality for all parties but even places in Paradise . . . Cursed
then be they in walking, in standing, in sitting, in sleeping.
Cursed be they in planting their vines, in ploughing their fields;
in their recitations and whilst singing. All Christendom echoed
with the cry. No fires from heaven however consumed the
fortress of Les Baux, the walls of Avignon, the castle of Roumanille where were holden the Courts of Love.

Then Provence—or rather the Narbonnais—being itself for a
little time, made its solitary incursion into other territories. For
you can hardly call the sack and burning of the Temple of

Delphi by the Volces Tectones a Provençal manifestation since the Volces themselves were interlopers in Provence and, for the vindication of the outraged Gods, the sunken spoils of Delphi were taken from them by Scipio when he in turn sacked their capital, Toulouse. Nor indeed was the obscure crusade against the Bulgars, those loathsome purist heretics, in which fell beside his lord the Troubadour Jaufré Rudel, a real expression of Provence. For Provence itself was at least as over-run by the Catharist heresy as were the poor Bulgars to whom the out-raged Christians assigned the promotion of a vice that has ever since borne their name . . . Rudel, by the bye, must have been sufficiently cured by the sight of the Countess of Tripoli to get up from his bed and die in harness.

Christendom was however too preoccupied by the peace and prosperity of the Saracen civilisation to trouble for the moment about the Albigenses. The infamous followers of Mahound must be stripped of their cities and their fortunes before any decent man could think of lesser booties. So, the first Crusade being preached by Peter the Hermit and a great meeting held at Clermont to the North of the Narbonnais at which assembled all the princes spiritually subject to the papacy, in 1095, that great emprise set forth next year.

Raymond IV of Toulouse, a really important prince, was one of the chief supporters of Urban IV, preaching the Cru-sade at Clermont. And he was one of the five most important champions of Christendom who set forth for the redemption of the Holy Sepulchre. He took a hundred thousand south-erners with him. The greater number perished in transit. Per-haps their hearts were not in the enterprise, their lord being the chief protector of the Albigenses and they themselves for the most part tainted with that heresy. And, as you have seen, cousinship to a Sultan being in the case of Nicolette no bar to nobility or to her marriage with the Count of Beaucaire, there was no innate hostility between the Provençaux or the Narbonnais and the followers of Mahound. They disliked being plundered by corsairs but seldom accused the corsairs of being non-Aryan or even pagan. And, when occasion served, they were perfectly ready to trade with them for Christian slaves and other commerce, vessels sailing freely between Carthage and the Bouches du Rhône.

So, as might not be unexpected, Raymond IV of Toulouse seems to have double-crossed both parties in Palestine and, had he not died at the siege of Tripoli in 1105, might very well, by betraying Godfrey de Bouillon, have lived to become indifferently either King of Jerusalem or Emir of Trebizond. As it was, his conduct added, in the eyes of the respectable, unpopularity to the County of Toulouse and the cause of the Albigenses.

And, as we have seen, the poor Provençaux were soon taught to keep their eyes in their own boat by having the most brutal of all the Crusades waged against them . . . Whilst they had been being harried by pagan Ostro-, Visi-Goths, Vandals, Franks and Germans their orthodoxy had been beyond suspicion. Their martyrs as we have seen had been many and had supplied admirable sport for the populace. From the third century onwards they had been indefatigable in spreading the teachings of the gospel. The saints of Provence are innumerable; the islands of the Lérins off Cannes were the Lindisfarne of the Southern Sea; in 314 the council of Arles condemned the pestilent heresy of the Donatists, who had the audacity to demand that whoever administered the sacraments must himself be holy of living and who, in Carthage, considered that their priests alone had the apostolic succession. But, after two centuries of their acquiring fame by the writing of ingeniously rhymed and imaged verse and of enquiring as to the nature of Love, Satan, as we have seen, must find some work for their idle brains. So they had thought out the group-heresy of Albigensism—which, as we have said, was a gentle union of various scepticisms with, one would have thought, little locomotive or contagious power. It spread nevertheless like a flame until nearly all the cities and countrysides from the Spanish borders to Avignon itself embraced one or other of its branches of tenets. And the swiftness of its spread is witness to the unpopularity that the Popes and their supporters had earned for themselves in the country of the martyrs of Lyons—the most striking expression of which is of course Aucassin's.

Provence nevertheless continued to fill, on the great Trade Route, its rôle of handing on to Septentrional lands the flame of Latin civilisation: Béra, Count of Barcelona founded an Abbey for the learned Order of the Benedictines at Aletz; Arles

The Bridge of Avignon

became the capital of a kingdom celebrated for its devotion to poetry; Toulouse suffered a great deal from North French and Spanish attempts to suppress religious speculation; Pope Urban II visited the city and preached against the Albigenses on his way to preach the first Crusade in 1095; Montpellier founded its School of Medicine in the 12th century and grew from a village to a capital town from the number of students that came to it. Avignon became a separate Republic or Commune. In 1172 the last Count of Roussillon, dying childless, bequeathed his sovereignty to the King of Aragon. That King with his subjects became tinged with the heresy. From 1177-8 St Bénézet, a shepherd boy, according to some as a result of a heaven-sent dream or, according to others with the co-operation of the Devil, succeeded in building, across the intolerably swift Rhone, the Bridge of Avignon. The French set up on the other bank protective fortifications to prevent the inhabitants of Provence from dancing into the Royaume; in 1215 the University of Toulouse was founded; twenty years before, Raymond VI of Toulouse had built at Vaison, near Orange, a fortress supplementing the fortress already founded by the Romans—to strengthen his resistance to the French King.

It was time. A Crusade—even more formidable and even more bloodthirsty than even those that had been sent to the Holy Land—was preparing outside Provence, ostensibly against the Albigenses. The Chief Crusader was Simon de Montfort the fitting father of the celebrated Earl of Leicester, the English Reformer who earned our odium when schoolboys by drawing up the Provisions of Oxford which one confused with the Constitutions of Clarendon on examination days—and who founded in 1265 the first of all Parliaments. The inspirer of this sinister undertaking was St Dominic himself, the employers were the Holy See under Innocent III and North France under Philippe II (Auguste)—the King who disagreed with John Lackland.

In 1207 that father of the English Reformer took Béziers, in the Narbonnese triangle, out towards Spain. The entire population of the city—60,000—was massacred, seven thousand at once being killed with swords in the Church of Ste Madeleine; the minor clergy of the church of St Nazaire continued to ring the passing bell in that steeple till all the congregation were killed and were then killed themselves. This is not as astonishing as it seems; many of even the Catholic clergy of that date were tainted with the heresy and in the enthusiasm of conversion nice distinctions were hard to draw. Even the figures of the killed are difficult to establish. The chief official chronicler of the affair, Aubry des Trois Fontaines, gives them as the above sixty thousand but he was anxious for the credit both at Rome and in Heaven of the Crusaders, each of whom earned several centuries' remission of the pains of Purgatory per ten thousand killed. Other contemporary chroniclers put the figure at 38,000. The papal legate, the modest Arnaud Amauri, Bishop of Cîteaux, in his report to Innocent III claims credit for only 20,000 preventive executions. . . . It was he who, when the victorious crusaders asked him how they should distinguish heretics from faithful, replied: "Kill them all; God will know how to choose His own." In any case no man, woman or child was left alive in Béziers after that day.

In 1211 de Montfort took Castelnaudary, an unfortunate city which was re-taken from de Montfort's son by Raymond VI, all the inhabitants being exterminated. In 1355 it was burned to the ground by the Black Prince. In spite of that cassoulets are still made at Castelnaudary in whose neighbouring castle of Burlats Constance, wife of Raymond V and sister of Louis VII of France, and Adelaïde, Viscountess Taillefer of Albi, held a nearly authenticated Court of Love even whilst crusaders were sacking the lands and cities of their husbands.

In the same year—1211—de Montfort essayed the taking of the Maiden Castle of Carcassonne, the fortress that was never taken. That strong place was held for the heretics by Raymond Roger, fourth viscount Tancarvel and his Troubadours. Finding the place a tough morsel even for Crusaders, Simon invited the knights and the viscount to a peace-conference. But you do not keep troth with heretics and, as befitted the father of a Reformer, the Crusader seized Raymond Roger and hung all the Troubadours, expelling the whole population of the city and fortress in their shirts and shifts, so easy was it for the Faithful to obtain new clothes. De Montfort then poisoned Raymond Roger in the Painted Tower on the walls of the Citadelle and proclaimed himself Viscount of Béziers, Carcassonne and Razès, a title in which he was confirmed by Philippe the August. This fief was inherited by the son of Simon Sr who wielding rather the pen of the reformer than the

Crusader's sword was unable to retain it against the assaults of Raymond VI. He therefore ceded his land to the King of France and, by way of Gascony, returned to England in 1253 to open, five years later, to the dismay of the English schoolboy, the Parliament of Oxford.

. . . One may interpolate that, at about that date, the University of Oxford knew its greatest fame, being the asylum of Friars Bacon and Bungay and of Matthew Paris and the reputed temporary refuge of Dante himself. At about the same date too the romances of Arthur were being collected from Brittany, Wales and Cornwall and modelled on the romances of Guillaume IX, to be eventually, as it were, codified by Malory. The "Mabinogion" also heralded the revival of Welsh literature and the Chronicle of Geoffrey of Monmouth was in the writing. . . .

. . . And one might as well also interpolate that by about this date the art of pre-explosive fortification had reached a very high pitch that was only to decline after the invention of cannon in the early fourteenth century. In the day of Simon de Montfort the Citadelle of Carcassonne may well have been reputed impregnable or 'Maiden,' every stratagem of the attacker along the great extent of walls having been anticipated by its designers. The protruding towers, serving also for the storage of supplies in enormous bulk, permitted arrows to be shot along the faces of attacked walls; the machicolations were on the wall-tops, as it were balconies without floors, through whose orifices boiling liquids and missiles could be dropped on to the heads of besiegers; the walls were also tapped by crenellations for giving cover to archers and those using the mâchicoulis. There were the ascending, corkscrew roads, walled high on each side, down which immense stone balls could be rolled on an ascending force of attackers; the drawbridges before the gates; the portcullis behind the drawbridges. A second portcullis behind the first formed the *souricière*—a chamber into which the attackers having penetrated, the outer portcullis was let down so that they were in a trap exposed to the boiling oil, flaming tar, arrows and bolts of the guards crouching in the apertures above. . . . And after all these were forced, inside was just such another, smaller *enceinte*, fortified in exactly the same way and within that the barbican, the last stand, within which were the apartments of the lord of the place. This too was exactly similarly fortified and even higher and thus more difficult to take. Defence had in that day so outstripped attack that it is no wonder that the casualties amongst really determined attackers in the thirteenth century were pro rata anything from twenty to eighty times as great as was the case in the ranks of the attackers of Verdun during the ten months of the siege of 1916. . . .

The victories of the Crusaders continued then for years, being varied of course by defeats. In 1213 there took place the great battle of Muret in which forty thousand Spaniards, Narbonnais and Provençaux took the field under Pedro of Aragon and Raymond VI of Toulouse. They were confronted by 1,000 Crusaders. . . . It is perhaps unnecessary to say that the numbers of the troops engaged and the account of the battle are those of the monkish chronicler, Guillaume de Puy-Laurens. . . .

According to the rules of tactics and in honour of the Holy Trinity the thousand Crusaders marched in three columns of three hundred and thirty-three men each, the odd man being presumably de Montfort as commander-in-chief. In addition St Dominic was in support. He and his retinue of several hundred clergy retired into the church of Muret and "cried to the Lord and sent up such outcry that it seemed they rather bellowed than prayed."

According to the shocked chronicler the enemies of de Montfort and the Almighty behaved exactly like Shakespeare's French before Agincourt, there being a singular unanimity or a singular lack of invention in the chroniclers of great victories from those of Alexander to that of Sedan. They ate and drank, wooed without sentinels their mistresses and, when they saw the enemy in motion ran to their arms and rushed without order to the attack without listening to either King or Count.

"The champions of Him who was crucified 'on the other hand,' had chosen for their battle the feast of the exaltation of the Holy Cross . . . They confessed themselves; fortified themselves with the saving bread from the altar and girded themselves seriously for the battle. Simon led the attack on the city of Muret with a thousand men at arms, seven bishops and a great multitude of priests and monks. All that company had not the steadfast confidence of Simon. Whilst they were riding to the attack a cleric tried to dissuade that Count from risking a battle with so few men against such a copious multitude of enemies. But the Count drew a letter from his wallet.

" 'Read,' says he, 'this writing which has fallen into my hands.' The priest saw that it was a letter addressed by the King of Aragon to a noble lady, wife to a gentleman of the diocese of Toulouse. The King in it said to this lady that he was coming for the love of her to rid her country of the French and a thousand things of a similar nature.

" 'Well,' said the priest, 'What do you make of that?'

" 'I make of that,' cried Simon, 'that I scarcely need to go in fear of a King that marches against God for the sake of a scarlet woman.' "

Cromwell said the same thing before Naseby—but by that day the Scarlet woman was on another side. . . . The heretics had learned of St Dominic and it was they, more Nordic still, who by then longed for the spices which the less Northern religions had won on the field of Muret.

De Montfort thus became master of all the territories of the Counts of Toulouse. Nevertheless the towns permitted their Lord to keep up a goodly struggle for a number of years. Simon de Montfort, I am glad to say, was killed by a stone, five years afterwards at the siege of Toulouse itself. And, since his son Amaury was unable to keep up the fight against Raymond VII, that egregious family were shorn of all their Southern possessions—their ill-gotten gains, as the saying used to be.

Never was catchword more apt. For all religious wars are

atrocious, but I permit myself to hazard the aphorism that, although the Almighty may desire a plague on both houses in a religious conflict, He reserves for the winners a special murrain —a murrain that negatives all their efforts here on earth and sends them eventually to that Other Place where special attentions are reserved for their discomforts. One should not desire another people's spices. Perhaps even one should not desire to keep one's spices from the other fellow. SS Pothinus and Blandina along with Maturis and Sanctus who provided for the pagan spectators a good afternoon's sport at Lyons in the second century are doubtless more to be commended than the Albigenses who protected with all the weapons at their disposal and with an infinite endurance and courage their anti-papal indifferentism. . . . Let us by all means be passivist, non-resistant, anarchist-quietist or follow whatever counsel of perfection may be vouchsafed to us; but when human nature can no further endure and we take down from the wall our rusted fowling piece, polish up and remove from the muzzles of our verdigrised cannon the wooden stoppers and put an edge to our scythes, let us at least kneel down and offer to the Ancient of Days our humble petition that we may not come out the winners. For it is better to be "enclosed in a net and thrown to a bull" and "after having been long tossed by the animal" to expire at last, amidst the plaudits of the Saturday-afternoon football crowd, rejoicing yourself as if you were going to your marriage feast than by a single nutmeg or one clove of garlic to profit from the defeat even of an oppressor. For that would be to make yourself one with St Dominic striding across the field of Muret and setting his feet on the faces of the dying Albigenses who there lay—or one with John Knox victoriously thundering from his Edinburgh pulpit against one more martyred civilisation. Or at any rate let your generous impulses in any war for religion or for gain, or in the sacred name of sport . . . Let your generous sympathies go with the loser— with Pompey as against Caesar; with Anthony as against

Octavian; with Romulus Augustulus as against Odoacer; with the Albigenses as against the Catholics; with the Catholics as against Knox; with Charles as against Cromwell; with Napoleon as against the Holy Alliance; with Lee as against Grant; with the Second Empire as against the big battalions; with the South always as against the North—and even with Carpentier as against Dempsey. Always and for ever.

For you may be sure that in almost every victory in this category of contests the defeated cause fails because it stands for a higher civilisation. . . . I was reading only yesterday in a French paper the account of a boxing match. The expert critic wrote with extreme disapproval of the loser because, said he, that fellow thinks too much. A boxer's brain should be completely empty of every thought—of every desire even, except that for slaughter. Thought is heavy; it adds to the fatigue of combat; thought is relaxing, it slows down the speed of blows; thought softens, it leads you to think that you have punished your adversary sufficiently. . . . That is true. As a former judge at I do not know how many Army boxing contests I confirm every word of it. I don't mean to say that a poet-philosopher with longer reach, better legs, more intensive training, deeper lungs, keener eyesight and a more intelligent coach—that such a civilised being could not knock out a short-sighted, brutal and rachitic bantam with no more training than ideas. He could. But how many such poet-philosophers would think such a game worth a farthing dip or is not aware that God is, in the end, not on the side of the big battalions?

2.

The best thing that was ever written about the Troubadours is Mr Pound's chapter on them in his "Pavanes and Divisions." I do not of course profess to have read everything that was ever written. I once saw, in Jena, a collection of doctoral theses every one of them conjecturally amending the text of one Troubadour or another, and numbering over two thousand. I did not read them. But except for Mistral, and his writings on those poet-actors are fugitive and occasional as a rule—except for Mistral, Mr Pound is the only supremely great poet who ever took the trouble eruditely to study their works and then to write about them and their lives at once lucidly and with humanity and humour. I don't of course forget the Dante of "De Vulgari Eloquentia" or even the Browning of "Sordello." But both those poets approached their predecessors from a different angle—and neither of them, nor yet Mistral, had the advantage of having been professors of the Romance languages in a trans-Atlantic university prior to professing poetry. And I have been informed—again in Jena, which should be good enough—that, as an authority of the Romance Mr Pound is perfectly "sound." The two testimonies from such extreme poles of the world of letters—for surely no one could more than this writer differ from a pre-war Professor Wirklicher Geheimrath —two such testimonies might be sufficient to send the reader who wants more as to the literary characteristics of Peire Vidal or Arnaut Daniel to the writings on the subject of the author of the "Cantos." And whilst he is about it he might as well read Mr Pound's book on poor Gaudier who, as a Marseillais, was one of the most brilliant geniuses that Provence has produced.

As to his design in writing the section on the Troubadours that I have mentioned Mr Pound says:

"My purpose in all this is to suggest to the casual reader that the Middle Ages did not exist in tapestries alone, nor in the XIV century romances, but that there was a life like our own, no mere sequence of citherns and citoles, nor a continuous stalking about in sendal and diaspre. Men were pressed for money; the chivalric singing was devised to lighten the boredom; and this very singing became itself in due time, in the manner of all things, an ennui."

I differ from Mr Pound in the incidence as, except for the matter of the Troubadour literature, I differ from him as to everything else. With the matter of the 'boredom' of the little courts of Provence I have already dealt. As compared with the courts of the North they cannot have been bored at all; they led very busy lives; there was always—and all the year round—a fight ready for them with a neighbouring Count or Viscount. No doubt as is the case with every man of a fairly civilised and enlightened people they had periods when they felt the monotony of life. Even Mr Pound has felt that; it would be interesting to know what exact percentage of his poetry—and still more of his battleaxe that he calls prose—is not an irritant reaction to the boredom of his circumstances—ever since he first wrote:

"Damn it, how all this our South stinks peace" or words to that effect.

The Provençal courts in fact were as little bored as it is possible to be with life during the day and as is the case with every tolerable civilisation they had to find occupation for their nights between rising from the last meal and going to the practises of Love. So to the conte-fablistes who preceded them they added the invention of the Troubadours. The only sure and solid pleasures of life—the only ones of which you cannot be deprived by any metaphysician—are those of the chase, of war, of love, of the table, of religious intolerance and of the stage. And, if we lump together the conte-fablistes and the Troubadours we get stage conditions that went as far as the aspirations and mechanical possibilities could reasonably go. And to them you could add jugglers, proprietors of dancing bears, conjurers and a host of what today we call musical or vaudeville turns.

You should, in fact, regard the recitals or contests of the Troubadours as stage performances in which the aristocracy of literary skill took part whilst the performances of dramas like "Aucassin and Nicolette" gave in market-places shows that, though the performers were small people, the Quality condescendingly patronised. Then at once the position becomes plainer. The Troubadour appears as taking the place of the Hollywood star—but of the Hollywood star who should be not only performer but the extraordinarily skilful author and composer of the piece. And it is to be scored to the Courts of Love and of Provence that they valued the creative artist above the non-creative lute-player or citharist. As writer and performer Peire Vidal was the equal of the highest in the land and the terror of noble husbands though but the son of small trades-people. Had he been merely a good actor, executant, or capable only of adding a line or two to the folk-productions in their continual modification, he would have taken about the rank of a good footballer of today who, when the days of his active life were over should return to the status of his father the furrier.

Provence of that era is today called the "Provence of Bertran de Born and of Arnaut Daniel" who died in 1189 and was an admirable performer of sestinas incomparably improvised in the lists to *bouts rimés*, much as fifth century B.C. Athens was the Athens of Sophocles, Euripides and Aristophanes or as Antibes of the first century was the Antipolis of the Northern boy who "*bis duobius*" danced and gave pleasure. So also sixteenth cen-tury London was the London of Shakespeare and of Ben Jonson with his learned sock, both of them having firstly been public performers. And early Victorian London is the city of Jenny Lind and Taglioni, the performer gradually taking precedence of the creator. The city of late Victorian days assumed gradu-ally the aspect of a desert of houses before the shining dais of Ellen Terry, Mrs Bancroft and Mrs Kendall, all in the tradi-tion of Mrs Siddons. And so London of my more active days was the London of Adeline Genée, of Miss Marie Tempest, of Victoria Monks, of 'Mrs Pat' and her author, Pinero. He too in his day had been an actor. . . . Or Paris was the city of Sarah Bernhardt, Réjane and Yvette Guilbert, or New York the appanage of Blanche Bates and Edna May. . . .

It is after dinner, you are young, you have effected your digestion in your stall or in your gallery seat, the theatres are emptying, the lights whirl over the Great White Way, you stroll in the tepid night towards what adventures! But above all things immediately visible, there will be at the back of your mind the other lights in which sits Paula Tanqueray with her dreadful whisper: "What's to be done? What's to be . . . *done?*" or Blanche Bates, leaning against the door-post of her log cabin apostrophising in her thrilling tirade the red sunset seen between the practicable trunks of the far Western cedars. . . . Or it may be *la Genée*—the white moth behind the dimmed footlights. . . . Those visions shall accompany you through your whole lives until the visions of all your other glories have faded. . . . It is the tribute humanity pays, eternally, to the sisters Euterpe, Thalia, Melpomene and Terpsichore—and to its lost youth. . . .

For I suppose that if you mentioned to a hundred men of my generation Queen Victoria, Darwin, Thackeray, General Gordon or Samuel Smiles you might awaken here and there a flicker of interest or memory. . . . But just whisper "The Second Mrs Tanqueray!". . . . And so thousands of men in each generation—but millions!—languidly touched by the names and deeds of world heroes, remain to the ends of their lives mindful of the slightest gesture of the successors of the Northern Boy and for them even the Great Trade Route and its Successor are mere backgrounds for such memories. There will be changes but those will always be constant—and the changes will be almost unobserved.

It is, I imagine—or indeed I am certain that it will be in August—just twenty years since I made any protracted stay in our poor dear London, once the city of the Empire Promenade. That was, I assure you, nothing like the boardwalk of Atlantic City. Of course in pursuing unceasing gyrations on that modified Route I have made frequent enough swallow flights across the oval spread of bricks in our familiar, be-misted, valley. But, re-visiting one's birthplace with leisure to take stock, one may expect to be overwhelmed by emotions, to have to make mental re-adjustment, to be flooded with memories. . . . Above all to observe changes!

But I don't observe, here, any changes worth, as you might say, writing home about. London will always be, as she always was, "just London" . . . a vast thing, ending one does not know where, beginning haphazardly and haltingly at no known point in the soiled green of unknown fields . . . a Gargantuan rag-bag of a place; the eternal char-lady in a mackintosh of the great cities past and to be. But because of its climate, its cookery, its indigestions, its vastness, its easy going progressions, its toler-ances . . . for a hundred reasons one feels here no emotions. And memories are, in consequence so thick and unmarked that they seem to plaster all the dun house-fronts and to die away into the always present mists of the familiar vistas. In the bright light of Provence the change of a stone in the façade of the Maison Carrée will affect you as a world disaster and even in the

The Maison Carrée at Nîmes

nearly as bright light of New York you are appalled, as if by an earthquake at the idea of making changes in the front of Washington Square. . . . But I hear that there is a law before Parliament for pulling down the British Museum and, for the convenience of the public and the nippies, replacing it by one immense Corner House. . . . I read a head line in the *Daily Telegraph* yesterday which said: "LYONS PROVED IMPREGNABLE TO AIR RAIDS: Three Hundred Bombers Foiled," and marvelled at the thoughtfulness of our Government. . . . Well, they will pull down the Museum after three retired colonels will have protested in the correspondence columns of the *Morning Post* and thirty thousand ratepayers have supported the project in other journals. If we are any sort of a civilisation we are progressive. . . . And in a fortnight after the builders' hordings have been taken down no one will remember what once stood where rises the marble lined cathedral of pink terra cotta.

Changes in a great city establish themselves with a marvellous rapidity. It is for a couple of days disagreeable to see one's historic landmarks overtopped, as they all inevitably become by whitish masses waiting for grime. Regent Street does not seem to merge its streams in the swirling pool of Piccadilly Circus at just the angle one expected. The sky line at Swan and Edgar's corner isn't the glamorous serration that it was when I was a boy: but all the houses of the Circus are so obscured by the names of specifics for sleeplessness and sluggish internal organs that one cannot be certain either of what architecture is behind them or of how it formerly was. . . . And even Baker Street Station has become a Junction with fast trains that do not stop at St John's Wood—which seems to me to be rather fussy and plebeian and must be confusing to country cousins going to the Eton & Harrow. . . . Still, even the leg-theory has known modifications.

The first time I saw the Tower on this visit, going to Mark Lane on business, I was annoyed. Behind that heaping together of mediæval grimnesses and *enceintes* and barbicans that could well stand up beside the fortress of Carcassonne itself, against the livid skies towered one of those immense, formless lumps of white building that give to certain districts of London the aspect of being a throwing together of unfinished wedding cakes. I had seen the Tower once; I had gone, as a good Londoner, forty years before, to shew it to an American relative. I had ever since thought of it as solitary and majestic. So I was annoyed.

But on my second visit—this time with my unfortunate New

Yorker—it did not seem to matter. It stood there in front of that white sort of Mappin's terrace and was just there in a London that was just the old London that no one bothers about. And I will confess that before that poor Transatlantic—who, like Stephen Crane takes very little stock of corner lots and battlefields—before that worn out individual could get out of that fortress we had changed rôles. It was I that wanted to see more and always more morgensterns and blocks and thumbscrews. A strange emotion for a born Londoner!

. . . But I think that the strongest emotion I have lately had in London came when suddenly Mrs Patrick Campbell appeared on the films. . . . On the films and in the "Empire" of Genée! All one's youth and all the romance and glory that once were London's awoke with the first deep and glorious thrilling from behind that sheet of the voice of . . . Paula Tanqueray!

I have said that London cannot feel emotions, but she can know extraordinary stirrings of a sort of ground swell. Or could. You have alas to be well into the fifties of life to remember the sort of queer whisperings and almost uneasinesses that went through the vast place before the first appearance of Mrs Patrick Campbell. . . . Or of Mrs Langtry at Devonshire House!

The Professional Beauty preceded the Stage Star as the Stage Star preceded the cinema *vedette* and the reasons for the glamorous whisperings that went through the city before that last social appearance of a small black, puritanically simple figure—on a husband's arm—on the broad marble steps of a vanished house beneath the eyes of "All London"—those reasons are part of a social life so vanished that it would take the pen of a writer of historic genius to disinter them. . . . London whispered and the Jersey Lily mounted the staircase and someone else must say why.

But the reasons for the emotion that heralded the appearance of the being who afterwards became our "Mrs Pat" are less

difficult to discover. We whispered for weeks before we saw
"Paula." The Stage of those days under the aegis of ladies like
Mrs Kendall and Mrs Bancroft demanded an infinite Victorian
respectability of its female representatives. . . . Nay, it did until
not so long ago. . . . I remember, years later, suggesting to
Mr Granville Barker when he was running his glorious seasons
of Shaw and Galsworthy and himself and the rest at the
"Court" theatre that he should put on John Mabbe's translation
of the wonderful Spanish play, "Celestina," which is like a trans-
fusion of all Shaw and Galsworthy and Maeterlinck and "Mrs
Tanqueray" with real genius to weld them together. Mr Granville Barker said it could not be done. In the first place English
actors cannot speak blank verse; and, in the second I seemed to
have forgotten that English actors and actresses were ladies and
gentlemen—the full title of the Spanish classic being: "Celestina
or the Spanish Whore."

At any rate Mr Pinero and George Alexander had found
insurmountable difficulty in casting the character of Mrs
Tanqueray because the acknowledged Queens of the Stage
would have nothing to do with the representation of a character who was not quite nice. Publicity in those days may not
have been what it is now but the late Mr Pinero and the later
Sir George managed pretty well to let everybody in London
know of that difficulty and, later, that they had found a
heroine of transpontine and provincial melodrama to accept
the part.

Mrs Campbell was then playing in a real blood-and-thunder
melodrama in one of the popular theatres on the other side of
the river and for a week or so it became the fashion for the
young bloods of the West End to cross the bridges. Mr Frank
Harris who in those days conducted the *Saturday Review* with
the voice and gestures of a cross between a Napoleon and an
Elizabethan roaring boy with a nice nose for mundane sensations—Mr Harris then, guessing what was coming, ordered Mr
Shaw who was then his dramatic critic to undertake the danger-

ous crossing of the river and to give an account of the as it were unborn Mrs Pat. Mr Shaw didn't go, I think. I did. . . .

The other day I had a date with someone at a palatial cocktail bar whose walls are laved by the smiling Mediterranean. The someones were rather late and, exclaiming hurriedly: "She's waiting for you!", they hustled me into a car and drove with as much speed as, taking into account the safeties of millionaires temporarily overcome in winding streets, the law allows. They drove me into the circular and circuitous by-lanes of that Provençal peninsula where, as was the case with Alice in the garden, every time you set out to go somewhere you find yourself walking into your own back door. . . .

I had no idea of whom I was being taken to see and didn't much care. But in a few minutes it was like being mad. I was walking out of Mrs Pat's back door into a garden where at an immense table sat . . . Mrs Pat as Alice. . . . It was the more exactly that since in that corner of the Riviera everybody is either mad or asleep or Anglo-Saxon. . . . And that table was covered with an infinitude not only of cups and saucers but of improbable viands—ham and caviare and peaches and rose-leaf conserves and cheshire cheese and plum cake and iced lampreys and stewed finnicopters. . . . And that glorious voice from beneath the largest black hat that I have ever seen was asking me WHAT I HAD SAID ABOUT HER IN NEW YORK. . . .

You perceive how, sit as I may in the W. 1. district of London, my memories take me round that beaten track from the "Empire" of Adeline Genée by way of Southwark to the Mediterranean littoral and then the Manhattan Island of Aimée Macpherson. . . . And even to Winchelsea whose pews in the church are made of tulip wood brought back from New England by the ships of the Pilgrim Fathers. . . . Because whilst I was telling Mrs Pat what I could recount of her adventures in New York I was remembering Miss Ellen Terry in Winchelsea.

I was walking on one side of her, Mr Henry James being on the other, in front of the Winchelsea post office. . . . Mr

James had paused in the middle of one of his unending cadences of speech and we were all standing still waiting for the continuation. . . . And suddenly and simultaneously round the feet of that lovely and adored lady lay a black silken something. . . . Mr James' eyes bulged out of his head as he regarded me; mine I daresay bulged out of mine. Tiers of faces looked at us from the post office windows; Mr James and I synchronised our bending one from each side of her so exactly that our foreheads came smartly into contact the one with the other and we recoiled exasperated and empty handed. But Miss Terry exclaimed: "It's only a *petticoat!*" with a royal contempt for her escort. And bending down, recovering the garment and slinging it over her arm all in one gesture she moved on uttering the words . . . "As you were saying, Master! . . ."

You will see the connection between that and the Alice-Pat tea party in Golfe Juan a little later. . . . For it is in that way memory works. . . .

Whilst I was in the stalls at the "Empire" yesterday and suddenly heard the organ tones of Mrs Pat I was seeing an "Empire" of thirty years ago and a stage rather darkened and a white moth flying round and round on the boards. . . . And a man beside me—a rather hearty, hard-boiled millionaire, but with the tears streaming down his face because he was so in love with a Genée he had only the courage to see across the footlights.

It is only with such symbols that one can hope to re-capture the queens of the stage who mark the epochs of the lives of men and of cities. . . . For London itself is truly only the London of the days of Mrs Siddons and of Jenny Lind and of Taglioni and of Mrs Kendall and of Ellen Terry and of Marie Tempest and of Genée and of Mrs Pat. . . . And then perhaps there will be no more London. . . . Just Hollywood.

I see that they are reviving Mr Granville Barker's "Voysey Inheritance." . . . May it run ten thousand nights! For there was also in those days a London of "Barker at the Court"—a day when if you hadn't seen "Arms and the Man" with Lilla Macarthey as Raïna you counted as little as if you had not made the Grand Tour—the days when London began to have the aspect of a 'world-centre' and hope stirred in bosoms and the triumph of all the Arts was just round the corner. . . . Alas! Where are the roaring boys of yesteryear. . . . Miss Marie Tempest is playing one of the most thankless parts of one of the most inane comedies I have ever seen. . . . But if in those days you had seen Marie Tempest unmasking the mendacities of Charles Hawtrey! I suppose Miss Tempest is the last exponent of the old, formal stage school.

I do not think that I ever saw English actors of the Grand Manner rehearse but I was once privileged to see M. Sylvain at a rehearsal of "Louis XI" at the Comédie Française and Mr Richard Mansfield presiding at an extra rehearsal, at four in the morning in July, of the 700th performance of "Drink" in New York. Of Mr Mansfield's methods I do not remember much except for his arbitrary manner, his flashing eyes and the fact that, it being as I have said, a July night in New York he insisted that his troupe must remember that they were ladies and gentlemen—and not perspire. But M. Sylvain, sunk deep in an armchair on the stage comes back to me with great clarity because of his extreme slowness and gentleness and the fact that on the stage there were chalk marks to shew the places for the feet not merely for himself but for those of every character that was to be on the stage at that moment. And M. Sylvain rehearsed over and over again one single gesture—that of a man, in a moment of reflection, catching the end of his own nose between his thumb and fingers and slowly letting his hand fall back to his thigh . . . that and the motions of the subsidiary characters. . . . All that in the Paris of M. Coquelin and Réjane and Sarah Bernhardt . . . for Paris, too, dates by the dynasties of its stage kings and queens.

As a counterpart I may mention a rehearsal by the Abbey Theatre players at the "Court"—a rehearsal during the short period whilst for my sins I was responsible for that Company. Miss Maire O'Neill and her sister Miss Allgood and Mr Donovan and Mr Kerrigan just strolled on to the stage, nodded the one to the other, said: "Oh, You're the Widow Quinn . . . You're Pegheen Mike" and then as if "by th' will o' God," strolled through their parts without paying the slightest attention to Lady Gregory or Mr Yeats or me or anyone else who might be supposed to be directing them. And at the end of every performance every member of that company had to have an unconditional apology from every other member.

But I do not think that their performances were in the least less real and convincing than those of the Comédie Française and M. Sylvain. . . . I was in those days a whole-hearted supporter of the natural, almost unrehearsed type of acting, the habit of which, with Duse as a protagonist, swept over the entire world. But I suppose the real truth of the matter is that unless you have a company every member of which, like the Abbey Theatre players, is a natural genius, the meticulous and back-breaking rehearsal with the places for the feet chalked out on the stage is a necessity if you are to get any sort of realism. The purpose of good, backbreaking drill in the Army—a proceeding which to the civilian seems merely pedantic disciplinarianism—is so to accustom a man to use his arms and legs and weapons that, in contact with the enemy, he will function automatically, thus leaving his mind free for any unexpected developments of combat. Similarly the use of backbreaking drill on the boards is to get the actor to go through his part automatically so that his mind may be free to take in extraneous circumstances, small accidents or the mood of the house on a given night. That is what gives you the air of being as at home on the stage as in your own bedroom.

I remember, years and years ago, Miss Ellen Terry's giving lunch to myself and a young American relative of mine who had come to London from Richmond, Virginia, by way of Paris especially to see Ellen Terry act. Miss Terry however had a cold and during lunch announced her intention of telegraphing to her understudy to take her place at the "Lyceum" that night. This was a great blow for my cousin who was leaving for Paris next morning. I was in those days a slightly privileged person with Miss Terry because when Miss Terry had been younger and very down on her luck my mother had befriended her. Indeed one of the first—the second thing that I can remember is coming to in a period between fits of delirium due to diphtheria and seeing Ellen Terry bending over me with, in her arms, an immense arum lily which she had brought to console me. . . . So, at that lunch I argued with and overpersuaded her and she good-naturedly gave my cousin—she is now so long since dead, dying in Paris just after her return—the chance to say that she had seen Ellen Terry act. . . .

And Ellen Terry acted—ah, but unforgettably—Portia with a cold. The amazing humour; the amazing soft voice that yet pervaded every interstice of enormous spaces—and the amazing handkerchief! . . . She made as much and as inevitable gesturing with that piece of lace, hanging from her closed hand, as if she had rehearsed every flirting movement with it as carefully and as long as Sylvain rehearsed the pulling of his own nose. Yet, in the nature of things, it was an accident that she could not until that day at lunch have foreseen.

The same complete at-home-ness on the boards distinguished Mrs Patrick Campbell. She wasn't, when she at last appeared at George Alexander's side, Mrs Patrick Campbell on the Haymarket stage; she was Paula Tanqueray in a great drawing-room so much her own that she moved amongst its furnishings automatically as if she had lived with them all her life. Tall, dark, tragic and sinuous she moved about, arranging flowers, lowering blinds, with all her movements so completely as it were on the side that, except as the complements of the emotions that she expressed, they did not count in the least. You were just with her in her drawing-room and her story had so completely taken hold of you that you hardly observed what she was doing. That is the highest point of art.

The most amazing feat, as the most amazing stage tribute, that I ever saw or heard of occurred on the occasion of my visit to the transpontine theatre of which I have spoken. Obviously Mrs Pat would grip you from the first moment that you saw her. That was all, as it were, in the day's journey. She was playing in some sort of melodrama in which she had, as far as I can remember, to be carried over a bridge above a millstream by a villain. And at the crucial moment—now you will see why in Golfe Juan I suddenly remembered Ellen Terry in front of Winchelsea post office—her petticoat fell off and lay round her feet. . . . And no one noticed it! She just stepped over it and went on playing. No one smiled; no one in that rather rough audience made any remark. I did not myself notice it; I only remembered it after the play was over. . . . There could be no greater tribute to the magic of personality . . . none imaginable.

There was the same magic about the air at that Mad Hatter's tea-party in Golfe Juan. . . . There was Mrs Pat, sitting like a great black Alice at one and the same time rehearsing a beautiful young, blonde, New York actress in the "Bells of Ender. r. r. by"; fluttering her fingers hospitably over, and offering vast slices of ham, pickles, rose-leaf conserve, tea, wines of the country, iced mandrake juice; pushing her enormous hat forward over her left eye or sideways over her right ear; checking the trans-Atlantic actress who was rehearsing "Ender. r. r. by" from the top of a ladder; telling in her voice that touched everyone's heartstrings how some long-dead celebrity liked lobster and abstractedly listening to me whilst I recounted to her her forgotten New York adventure. . . .

I don't wonder she had forgotten it or my part of it or Aimée Macpherson's or the snow or Miss Lawton. . . . It had gone like this. . . . Mrs Muriel Draper had asked me to dinner one Sunday. I was working at that time in my old, old apartment on West 16th Street. When I work I don't lunch, so towards seven, empty, correctly attired in Gibus, immaculate shirt front and pumps I set out to go to 41st Street. There were no taxis; new snow had been falling all the drab day between aligned snow-piles already ten feet high. My pumps full of it, I pushed against the North Wind, up, up, up, Fifth Avenue, growing hungrier and hungrier . . . hungrier. . . .

And already, outside the door of Mrs Draper's fantastic studio I heard Mrs Patrick Campbell's amazing organ exclaiming:

"I don't *want* to go and hear Aimée Macpherson. . . . I want my dinner. . . . I won't go and hear Aimée Macpherson. . . . I want my dinner. . . ."

I didn't want to go and hear Aimée Macpherson. . . . I can safely say that at that moment Mrs Campbell's heart and mine beat as one. . . . I wanted my dinner.

But Mrs Draper was inexorable. . . . Her guests had to hear Aimée Macpherson before they had their dinner. Perhaps she thought we needed conversion. . . .

I don't know who the other guests were; there were certainly some nice young men for they produced taxis, I don't know from where. But when you are in a room faced with the inexorability of Mrs Draper and the spectacle of Mrs Patrick Campbell reclining regally on a Mme Récamier day-bed, recounting her woes and calling for dinner, you do not see or know of the existence of anyone else. . . .

I don't know if even Paula Tanqueray had such woes. . . . There can never have been a reception surpassing in rapture that which had greeted Mrs Campbell's re-appearance on the New York stage a week or so before. But alas, the play she had chosen to bring over must have been the worst that was ever produced on any stage and the night before Mrs Draper's party it had hopelessly been withdrawn. And, like her Paula Tanqueray of years before, Mrs Campbell sat on her sofa and exclaimed: "What are we to do? . . . What are we to *do?*"

She said she had been shamelessly robbed by the New York furnishers; she said—in the golden light of Mrs Draper's candles beneath the high beams of the ceiling—that the golden slippers she had on had cost her $370; that she had eaten nothing for weeks and weeks; that she would give thousands and thousands of pounds and dollars to me or to anyone who would write or adapt or re-adapt or re-write or find or steal a play that had a real part for her—only it must not be a part that Duse or Ellen Terry or Réjane had ever played. . . .

But the inexorable taxis were there; we were all bundled into them. Then it appeared that Mrs Draper had not any tickets for Mrs Macpherson's church.

We arrived before some sort of East Side vast temple, towering up into the black skies, with loud-speakers bellowing across a great waste of snow and thousands of people assembled before it in the lowering gloom. Mrs Campbell in her golden slippers and I in my pumps were bundled out into a snow drift before a regular posse of policemen. Above the deep voices of the congregation singing "Rock of Ages" went the high tones of Mrs Macpherson's fioriture embellishments. Mrs Campbell told the embattled police that she wanted to go in. They said she could not; there were a million people already in the hall.

The voice of Mrs Macpherson said that the subject of her discourse would be. . . .

I told the police that that was Mrs Patrick Campbell and that they must let her in. They wanted to know who the hell I was. The snow fell. Thousands more arrived in that open space.

The subject of the discourse was to be: "The y-iternal tri-angle: Jesus Christ, John Baptist . . . an' Mary Magderleen!"

The hundreds of policemen loosened their night-sticks and gazed fixedly at me. I said we must go away; Mrs Patrick Campbell said she must go in. I have felt more worried when, later, all my money was blown into the Rhone, but not much more and I had never before been so worried.

The policemen raised their night-sticks; the blows fell as one blow on the heads of a swirl of the crowd that, impelled from one side, had involuntarily but unadvisedly intervened. I implored, pulled, pushed, panted with Mrs Campbell down through miles of snow into the door of a taxi that was miraculously in a street below. . . .

When we had laboriously climbed the stairs to the door of Mrs Draper's apartment we found the door locked. Mrs Draper had got into that temple.

We sat down on her doorstep, side by side, like two orphans before a poor school. . . . I told Mrs Campbell who I was and she told me that her formerly golden slippers had cost $3,700, so outrageous was the overcharging of New York tradesmen— and that she would give tens of thousands of pounds and hundreds of thousands of dollars to me or anyone else who would discover for her a play with a part suited to her that had never been played by Duse or Ellen Terry or Réjane or Sarah Bernhardt.

But there today, at Genée's "Empire," Mrs Pat's wonderful, familiar voice resounds. And the run of the piece is prolonged and the wonders of one's youth are renewed, for through London, like the ripple of wind through wheat, run the two questions: "Have you seen Mrs Pat?" or "Are you going to see Mrs Pat?"

No, London does not change very much.

I find I have omitted to say—for the relief of those of my readers who can sympathise with hunger, for it was then after eleven and we had eaten nothing since eight in the morning— that, after we had sat there a long time, Miss Lawton, the Ellen Terry of New York, who lived in the apartment above, passed up the stairs and invited us to follow. There, in a great room, all candles, was an immense turkey that Miss Lawton had had prepared for sixty guests. When we had done with it there was left perhaps enough for fifty-four.

CHAPTER VI

FINE ARTS

WITH the end of the Crusades against the Albigenses came naturally the end of the civilisation of the Troubadours. They had flourished in the small, semi-independent courts but by the treaty of Paris in 1229 and the subsequent extinction of the remaining small powers, under Louis IX, that whole life was blotted out. The Count of Toulouse ceded to the French king all that part of his country between the Rhone, the sea and the Pyrenees and by purchase or negotiations the Saint came into possession not only of Chartres, Blois and Mâcon to the North of Lyons, of Cahors to the North of the Narbonnais, as well of Foix and Forcalquier, and Arles itself in true Provence. In addition by exchange with Henry III of England he obtained Normandy, Anjou, Maine, Touraine and Poitou as against Périgord and the Limousin which the English preferred as giving them control of the wine of Bordeaux which they called claret because they could mull and drink it, tepid.

So St Louis had as it were steamrolled out for himself a territory running uninterrupted from the English Channel and, on the left bank of the Rhone, to the Mediterranean of the Saracens itself. In that way he could make embarkation for his last—the Seventh—crusade, this time against the Mahometans of Africa, from the port of Aigues Mortes. And in that way in Northern France there was established the foundation of one of those Great Powers whose existence has been so fatal to the peace and civilisation of the Western world. So the French

Royalists do very well to date themselves from Louis IX since he was not only a Saint, and the exterminator of a civilisation, but actually the founder of the modern world.

The end of true Provence was however, not yet come. The family of the Bérengers—whose names historians spell indifferently and on the same page Berenger, Bérenger and Béranger—had remained secure in their sovereign counties of Provence and of Barcelona during all of the two centuries that the persecutions of the Albigenses had lasted. They had had in the West to fight the Counts of Toulouse and Forcalquier during several generations and had had to withstand in the East the ceaseless intrigues of the family of Les Baux. But by the beginning of the thirteenth century they had happily withstood all the assaults of their enemies; and, taking no part with the Albigenses, Raymond Béranger V found himself at the end of the crusades in the position of a sovereign ruler over Barcelona, Forcalquier and the greater part of Provence itself. In addition he was supported by his remarkable minister, Roméo de Villeneuve, a diplomat whom Dante places, like Folquet, in Heaven and who negotiated the illustrious marriages which in the end caused the disappearance of the independence of Provence itself.

For the unfortunate Margaret of Provence, the wife of St Louis whom the saintly but jealous Blanche of Castille would not allow either to sleep or converse in private with her husband, so that the poor young couple must meet only on the back-stairway that ran between their respective sleeping apartments—that poor victim of her mother-in-law was the eldest daughter of Raymond Béranger V of Barcelona, Forcalquier and Provence. And her younger sister, Beatrice, Roméo married to the King's brother, Charles of Anjou.

Thus in due time that Prince became sovereign of Provence. He had to fight for his lands not only against *his* mother-in-law, the Countess, but against all the en-castled lords and knights and all the fortified and independent towns to the east of the Rhone, between the Durance and the sea. The fight was not easy and was only won with the help of his brother, Alphonse de Poitiers, who, replacing Raymond VI at the treaty of Paris, had been appointed by his mother, Blanche of Castille and with sanction of the Papacy, Count of Toulouse.

A few knights like the lords of Orange—who were to provide the Northern world with Williams—held out, and a few towns; but Anjou bribed the traitor Barral des Baux, then mayor, to sell Arles to him. He had three times to besiege Marseilles and to destroy the walls of that city in the ten years between 1252 and 1262 and even then that proud port would not quietly surrender to his will.

The vitriol however in the cup of the steamrolling sovereigns of those days was still the fact that it was impossible to find faithful viceroys for their more distant provinces. The kings of France from Louis IX onwards had already visions of vast tributary realms tranquilly paying imposts to a central power over which they should preside beneath an obedient Pope. But that time was not to come for centuries. At that date they began to adopt the policy of confiding their less central territories to members of their families with the result that they armed against themselves formidable rivals like the Dukes of Burgundy who were to prove so nearly fatal to Louis XI—or like the kings of Provence, Naples and Sicily.

For, inspired by his brother the Saint, Charles of Anjou thought of nothing less than of remaining a faithful lieutenant of the crown and developed for himself the ideal of becoming a great sovereign over steam-rollered territories from which all individuality should be crushed out. So as soon as he had sub-dued Provence and was in possession of her taxes he extended his power along the Italian Riviera and, occupying the hinter-land behind the formidable republic of Genoa, seized the sov-ereignties of Naples and Sicily. So was founded the dynasty that gave to the world and to Provence the good Queen Joan and the good King René and which sold Avignon to the Popes, thus giving to Provence one more legendary Golden Age and one more immense castle—that which frowns over the Rhone from above the bridge of St Benézet.

Charles of Anjou, I am thankful to say, did not enjoy his ill-gotten sovereignties in much peace and on the 31st March, 1281 his subject Sicilians testified their want of appreciation of having the brother of a saint to extort taxes from them, murder their sons and outrage their womenkind. That 31st March was an Easter Monday and as the bells were ringing for vespers the Sicilians rose throughout the island and massacred the entire body of French that had been its garrison for Charles. At Palermo only two knights out of several thousand French escaped with their lives. So the phrase "Sicilian Vespers" passed into the language of Christendom to be a warning to conquerors. It has been superseded only in Anglo-Saxondom and Protestantism by the affair of St Bartholomew's day. This is rather a misfortune. St Bartholomew's was not much of a success, the Huguenots having, as we have seen, remained masters of the field, whereas the Sicilian Vespers were for all time an adequate warning to conquerors from the North.

In any case the Angevin kings, during the eighty years or so that their sovereignty lasted, never re-conquered Sicily but, continuing to extort taxes from Provence, spent them in Naples which they made the seat of their government.

Queen Joan I of Naples and Provence led an agitated existence. Having occasion to murder her first husband she was under the necessity of being pardoned by the Pope who had been exiled from Rome. She therefore ceded to the Papacy her city and territory of Avignon as against 80,000 florins of gold—which were never paid. She received nevertheless the pardon for having murdered her husband, Andrew of Hungary and a dispensation for her marriage to her cousin, Louis of Tarentum. In 1348 she had taken refuge in her good country of Provence which had received her with enthusiasm and which to this day venerates her memory. She returned then to Naples and reigned over the two kingdoms for thirty-four cheerful and dissolute years. She was then strangled by the orders of her other cousin, the Duke Charles of Durazzo, the reputation of her beauty and kindnesses surviving her to this day.

There ensued for the unfortunate kingdom of Provence a period of distraction enlivened by massacres. The good Queen had left her inheritance to her cousin Louis of Anjou which accounted for the perhaps legitimate irritation of Charles of Durazzo who was nearer of kin to her. Immediately on her death atrocious fighting broke out between the partisans of Charles and Louis, the fields being even more deeply encarnadined by the exploits of brigands, led by a German-descended adventurer called Raymond de Turenne. Louis I—who really built the castle of the good King René at Tarascon—was sufficiently successful in the prosecution of his claims, to die in Naples. . . . His widow and her young son continued the struggle, also with some success and in 1387 that son, Louis II, was able to seize Aix-en-Provence and to become undisputed ruler of Provence and Naples. Nice however and a couple of towns of the Provençal Riviera refused to swear allegiance to Louis and gave themselves to the Duchy of Savoy, under Amadeus VII, the Red Earl. Nice remained separated from Provence until, after many adventures, all of them blood-stained, she was ceded to Napoleon III by Victor-Emmanuel of Savoy in 1860. It is cheering to think that the inhabitants accepted the cession with rapture, 25,033 inhabitants voting for it and 159 against.

Louis II nevertheless remained in more or less peaceful possession of his territories from 1387 to 1417 when he was succeeded by his son, Louis III who reigned for 17 years when he died and left the two thrones and the Duchy of Anjou to his brother, the Good King René. . . . The good but unfortunate king was deprived of Naples by Alphonse V of Aragon, known as the Wise or the Magnanimous, and of Anjou by his nephew, Louis XI of France who, as is well known, worshipped leaden medals which he kept in his hat-brim and is less celebrated as having initiated the posting-service in France. . . . It was thus manifested that Wisdom and Magnanimity, aided by Superstition and the Post Office, will triumph over Goodness and a devotion to the Arts.

That the Good King, who finally took refuge amongst his faithful Provençaux, was devoted to the Arts there seems to have been no doubt, in spite of the mirage of legends that blurs the outlines of his figure. In Tarascon he surrounded himself with a real Court of poets, painters and musicians and, though it may be doubted that he painted the great picture in the Hospital of Villeneuve-lès-Avignon, he has left sufficient in the way of verse and of illumination to bear witness to the peacefulness of his aims and the beauty of his aspirations. And, if he did not actually build the foundations of the Bastide that goes by his name and is one of the most beautiful of all the monuments of Provence, the beauty of proportion and of the ornamental details that he added to it may well leave him with the deserved reputation of a skilled and enamoured architect.

I have spoken already of his renown as a justiciar. Whether all the judicio-penological problems of today could be solved by his device of punishing all crimes by fines and amercements is a matter rather for criminologists. The invention seems to me to be logical in a world the great majority of whose crimes, if you include wars, are committed for the sake of gain. If you can, by process of remorseless law deprive the criminal not only of his gains but of even more, thus leaving him poorer than when he set out upon his enterprise, it would seem to be reasonable to expect him to give up a career of depredation which can only in the end utterly impoverish him. For myself I have always been averse from every kind of punishment whether regarded as a deterrent or as a revenge on the part of a presumably outraged State. In the one case punishment has no deterrent effect and at worst serves as a hypnotic inducement to others; in the other, the State degrades itself to the condition of an executioner whom it is human to regard as the lowest of mankind.

The answer to that argument is that, if the State does not occupy itself with punishment, the Public inevitably takes the matter in hand, so that you get a condition of lynch law in which more often than not it is an innocent party that suffers.

That answer appears to be incontrovertible. But it seems to me that if the Public can be brought to see all criminals reduced to begging by a wayside which itself has been furnished, embellished or improved by the penalties inflicted on wrong-doers the Public should be induced to give up degrading itself to the status of a murderer. At any rate in the golden reign of the good King the Provençaux saw their roadways improved, their public buildings embellished, the functions of the State carried on with smoothness and all that without undue exactions in the way of taxes from themselves. There is then no wonder that they and their descendants to this day considered and have continued to consider René of Provence as a lawgiver equal to Solomon and as a ruler giving to his country a Golden Age such as history has known neither before nor since.

It would be agreeable to consider that the life and reign of the good King coincided with the other Provençal Golden Age—that of the Popes at Avignon. . . . Alas. The first of the Popes to occupy that city was Clément V who was elected in 1305 and the last of the Anti-Popes, Benedict XIII, died in 1411. And René was not born in Angers till 1409, dying in Aix-en-Provence in 1480, coming to his poor thrones—of Sicily and of Naples over which he never reigned, in 1434, and of Provence which has remained faithful to him ever since, in the same year.

Nevertheless there was an intimate relationship between the Golden Age of the Good King and that other of the Avignonnais pontiffs, let alone that it was his ancestress, the good Queen Joan, who confirmed the Popes in their occupation of the happy city. . . .

"He who never saw Avignon in the days of the Popes, never saw anything . . . From morning to night it was processions, pilgrimages, streets strewn with flowers, bordered by the tall lists: the arrival of Cardinals by way of the Rhone, banners in the wind, galleys dressed in bunting; the soldiers of the Pope sang Latin in the *places*, to the sound of the rattles of friars mendicant . . . and the tic-tac of the lace-bobbins, and the rustle of the shuttles weaving the cloth of gold chasubles, the little hammers of the goldsmiths tapping the altar-cruets; the lutes and recorders a-tuning, the canticles of the warp-throwers; and over all the sound of the bells and always the under-sound of the tambourines coming up from the Bridge. For, in our country, when the people is glad, there must be dancing, there must be . . . dancing! And, since in those days, the streets of the city were too narrow for the *farandole*, fifes and tambourines kept to the Bridge of Avignon, in the fresh breezes of the Rhone and day and night was dancing; was . . . dancing! . . . Ah, happy days, happy city! The pikes that did not cut; the state prisons where wine lay cooling! . . . Never famine; never wars . . . That was how the Popes of the Comtat knew how to govern their people; that is why their people has so much regretted them!"

Those words of Daudet must have been the first of French that could be called Literature that my eyes can have fallen on, so that here with fair confidence I can translate them out of my head. And that perhaps is why, be my days never so dark, I cannot enter the walls of Avignon without becoming glad—and why, no doubt, I am writing all this book.

I went to school at a time when the first waves of belief in German education were welling across a hypnotised world—and indeed the first school I went to was kept by the favourite pupil of Froebel at Folkestone—a very great educationalist, Mrs Elizabeth Praetorius from whom I suppose I learned everything that I ever learned in school, except the writing of Latin verse in which I have still some skill. So, by a very tender age I could speak both French and German with as much facility as English. I can still remember standing when I must have been ten or eleven by the desk of one of Mrs Praetorius' ushers—David Watson, B.A., of Sir J. M. Barrie's Thrums—and teaching him French out of the novels of Jules Verne—our favourite book being "Les Enfants de Capitaine Somebody" . . . perhaps "Grant." It had to do with North Polar Exploration and I know we preferred it to "Twenty Thousand Leagues Under the Sea" and to "Round the World in Eighty Days." . . . And one of the minute incidents of childhood comes back to me with startling vividness. . . . I was standing by Mr Watson's pulpit on a clear day. We were puzzling over a singular word "Hein!" that Captain Grant was always using—it was an ejaculation that in those days was in fashion but that I had not yet come across. Mr Watson—who had enormous blood-red ears and who must have been very young—was sharpening lead pencils for the drawing class. Very long, thin points he could make. Suddenly his hand holding a pencil was poised over my hand which lay on the desk. He jabbed the pencil into my hand; the long lead broke in, and to this day after half a century or so the lead is still visible under the skin. . . .

In any case when I eventually went to the ancient public school where very properly all education except the teaching of Latin verse and the reading of Plutarch was treated as a joke I was put into a French class with boys extremely above my years and we were set to read in a book called "Ausgewaehlte Erzaehlungen von Alphonse Daudet," annotated and "verbess-ert" by a Professor Hauser of, I think, the University of Tuebingen.

So there, in the dim, whitewashed rooms of a city school, beshadowed by steeples and what the French would call "crasseux"; with inkstains on the desk and bars before the windows I made my first acquaintance with the suns of Avignon whilst a Big Boy who did not approve of my being in his class and disliked me because I would not indicate to him the more salacious passages of "Tom Jones" was twisting my arm behind me.

Nevertheless, in spite of the pain—or indeed ignoring it—

I let my arm be twisted and read on with my torso over the desk.

"Ah, l'heureux temps; l'heureuse ville! Les hallebardes qui ne coupaient pas; les prisons d'Etat où l'on mettait le vin à rafraîchir. Jamais de disette; jamais de guerres . . . Voilà comme les Papes du Comtat savaient gouverner leur peuple. . . ."

I don't know what it was that engrossed me—the idea of the sunlight in those glooms; the idea of a land where there were no oppressors. . . . But still more, I am sure, the rhythm of Daudet's piece. Nothing, I imagine could be much more exciting than after the good household article of Jules Verne's prose, to come suddenly upon:

"c'était encore le tic tac des métiers à dentelles, le va et vient des navettes tissant l'or des chasubles, les petits marteaux des ciseleurs de burettes, les tables d'harmonie qu'on ajustait chez les luthiers. . . ."

The massing and the sparkle of the objects presented, the hurry of the prose culminating in *l'on y dansait, l'on y dansait.* . . .

I don't know to what extent Professor Hauser, supposedly of the University of Tuebingen, had "verbessert" that passage. I remember that, from time to time, on his platform M. de Bovis who presided over our studies, would spit and mutter under his breath and re-amend one of the "improved" passages.

For with the sturdy English common-sense that let us be taught with seriousness nothing but the writing of Latin verse, the authorities of that school disregarded the pressure from above of a practically German Court and tradition and let us, for the time, have a Frenchman to teach us French. And M. de Bovis was an ardent Méridional and a very distinguished philologist whose name is still remembered with a certain consideration in places where dictionaries are compiled—a little, dark man, with a black, square-cut beard, dark-black eyebrows and vivid scarlet patches of subcutaneous blood on his vertically wrinkled cheek bones.

He used to curse and spit—into his handkerchief—at the changes that Professor Hauser, with all the contempt of a Tuebingen Don for a mere modern French conte-writer, had made in Daudet's and Molière's texts. When he calmed himself he would tell us about Nîmes where Daudet had been born and Font-Vieille near Tarascon in whose mill Daudet had not written his "Lettres de Mon Moulin," since actually they were all written in Paris or in the house of friends who lived near the mill. And he would pull papers out of his tail-pockets and read us passages from the Félibristes, commenting on the language of Provence and criticising, as philologist, the phonetic spelling that Mistral had invented for his language. . . .

I think that a little after my leaving that school he succumbed to Teutonic pressure and resigned as a protest against being forced to teach French classics out of cheap German textbooks. . . . Or it may have been before I left. I remember at least, after I had been taken off French, hearing boys still in the French-class complaining that they had a master called Bluecher who made them read "Le Philosophe Sous Les Toits" —a work that they called piffling—from an edition annotated and improved by himself. . . . Dr Bluecher comes back to me as a very tall, corpulent and stooping figure, with an immense faded-blond beard, red eyelids behind spectacles and disagreeable personal habits as to which the boys complained a great deal.

However that may be unfair, for we all preferred de Bovis who to the spitting animation of a cat added a great knowledge of the things of the world. I remember that he earned all our gratitude by getting out of trouble with extraordinary sangfroid and velocity a very Big Boy called Hutchinson who was the school hero. He had got into a mess with one of the Bad Girls who used to beset the elder boys on their way back home from school. . . . You should have heard the whispers that went from desk to desk!

I have to confess that, even at that tender age, I did not like Daudet. . . . And if you have read the earlier chapters of this book you will see that my prejudice against him still prevails whilst in earlier years I was heavily belaboured by the New York press for confessing that I used to differ from Conrad in my estimate of the author of "Jack." . . . I cannot account for the dislike.

Yet he has written passages that will never die as long as writers like Prosper Mérimée are read. . . . Last October, on a very hot day, I was sitting in front of a café on the main-road through Arles. Suddenly the uphill horizon was obscured by a great cloud of dust filled with swaying, half-seen dark forms, as you might have thought, those of camels on the horizon. . . . Then there ran anxious dogs, their red tongues descending almost to the dust. They were seeking ways through the arrested traffic of automobiles and threshing machines; seeking to open them. And then a great tide of great, horned rams; then sheep, their lambs beside them and immense men in great bérets falling over their ears, in great cloaks, directing with their great staves and their enormous hoarse voices all those vehicles into channels for the passage of the sheep. And then, in a bulk of camel-like forms the great dark mules, each swaying with a pannier on each side of it, and in each pannier two new-dropped lambs, the dams trotting with noses against the mules' fetlocks. And, in the golden haze of the final dust more shepherds, carrying in their great cloaks the sock lambs whose mothers had died giving birth to them on the blazing roads.

And immediately there rose in my mind:

"Il faut vous dire qu'en Provence c'est l'usage, quand viennent les chaleurs, d'envoyer les moutons dans les Alpes. Bêtes et gens passent cinq mois là-haut, logés à la belle étoile, dans l'herbe jusqu'au ventre; puis au premier frisson d'hiver on retourne au *mas*, et l'on revient broûter bourgeoisement les petites collines grises que parfume le romarin. . . ." [1]

It was the *retour des troupeaux*—the return of the flocks from the High Alps where they had passed the hot summer. . . . I do not profess to have remembered more than that passage there in Arles. But I did and do remember. . . .

"Il faut voir quel émoi dans la maison. Du haut de leur perchoir, les gros paons vert et or, à crête de tulle, ont reconnu les arrivants et les accueillent par des formidables coups de trompette. . . ."

And the sheep-dogs returning to the farm. . . .

"Useless for the watch-dog to call to them from his kennel; the clear cold water in the pail from the well winks at them in vain; they will see nothing and hear nothing before the herd is in the byres; the great latch dropped on the little, grilled door and the shepherds seated at table in the low hall. Then only they will consent to go to their kennels and there, lapping their bowlsful of soup they will tell their comrades of the farm all that they have done up there in the high Alps, a black country where there are wolves and great foxgloves, all purple, filled to overflowing with dew."

In this London garret that grows sadder and sadder as we approach the Spring—for how is it bearable to support the thought of Spring in the parish of St Marylebone!—I have no copy of any work of Daudet but I would not mind betting that within a word or two those quotations are letter perfect. . . .

It becomes however time to think of testing quotations and dates and, having written the above words, I look up and say to my poor New Yorker who has chanced in on my labours:

[1] "You must know that in Provence it is the custom, when the great heats come, to send the sheep into the Alps. Beasts and men pass five months up there, sleeping in the open air, in the grass that reaches to their middles; then, at the first breath of autumn, they come down again to the farm, to return and unromantically to browse on the little, bare grey hills all scented with rosemary. . . . What excitement there is in the farm-house. From their high roosts the great green and gold peacocks with crests of tulle recognise the returning flocks and greet them with formidable trumpetings."

"It is time that I went to the Museum Library. . . . You had better come along too and look up those drawings you want to see."

That patient transatlantic looks down at shoes, stockings, lower garments and, emitting a "Huh!" of want of conviction ejaculates:

"I guess they won't let me in. . . . I look like a tramp. And you are not to call it much better."

I exclaimed with my usual impetuosity:

"My amiable Huron from the Bronx, don't you even yet realise that you have come to a civilised country? . . . Isn't it you that have said that this place is the last stronghold of the spirit of Christianity? Isn't it you—not I—that have said that its inhabitants are of an unimaginable kindness and that the public servants are such servants of the Public that contact with them is like receiving the kisses of the blessed angels? . . . Remember the soft, gentle customs house officer who came all the way from Mark Lane to Victoria to throw himself at your erring feet! Remember the cop at the corner of Trafalgar Square—*not* Trafflgàr—who with the languid Harrow manner and the exquisite Oxford intonation explained over and over to you the writings on the road that you found so confusing, what time he held up all the traffic in an inextricable and shouting confusion. Remember the bus-conductor who, because you had no small change, stopped his vehicle at the top of Regent Street for nearly a quarter of an hour whilst he went to a distant tobacconist's and came back soaked, with the change for your five dollar bill. . . . And then refused your tanner. . . . And is it to be imagined that, if these illiterate underlings waft you so blissfully upon your lawful occasions, the great scholars and almost too delicately civilised officials of the Mecca of the world of learning will not fall on your neck? . . . Why at the mere production of your card and at the first whisper of your distinguished name, the great doors will fly open; you will be wafted to the softest of seats and before you, in the twinkling of an eye, there will arise stacks and hundredweights of the learned and decorated books that are your desire and delight. . . ."

2

I have spoken with some contempt of scholars and scholarship. Nevertheless during all my life I have been aware—or it might be more true to say that I have had the feeling, since never till this moment have I put it into words—that there are in this world only two earthly paradises. The one is in Provence with what has survived of the civilisations of the Good King, of the conte-fablistes, of the Troubadours and of the painters of Avignon of the Popes. The other is the Reading Room of the British Museum.

It is—it has always been—to me delightful, soothing like the thought of a blessed oasis in the insupportable madhouse for apes that is our civilisation, to remember that, rage the journalists how they may, there at the other end of the scale sit in an atmosphere of immutable calm, in that vast, silent place, all those half-brothers of the pen intent on the minutiae of the arts, the sciences and of pure thought. I think they must be the next to most happy people in the world, bending above their desks whilst the great clock marks the negligible hours of the next to Best Great Place. It is like the other consoling thought that I have always not very far from the back of my mind—that of innumerable nuns in forgotten convents praying for the redemption of all our miserable souls. . . . Yes, yours as well as mine and that of my patient non-Anglo-Saxon New York friend . . . who would really rather be damned than saved by the intervention of the pale daughters of the Scarlet Woman.

I don't know that the application of scholars is of more service to the arts than the supplications of the Praying Orders are effectual in changing, here in earth, our hearts. Nevertheless, just as praise is due to the poor dear old Church for the invention of those Orders, so the evolution by the poor dear old rag-bag that London is, of the British Museum Library may be accounted the one just act that, according to the Russian liturgy, may just save her soul. And in the long roll of her citizens that on the last day shall be offered to the Recording Angels, I do not believe that any two names could more fittingly head the list than those of Sir Anthony Panizzi [1] who began and of Dr Richard Garnett who completed the task of making the Reading Room fit for scholars. It would be a good precaution for they at least are certain to be acceptable as the two just men that will be necessary to save our poor, ragtime Sodom.

It is of course absurd to decry scholarship. Accuracy of mind and a certain erudition are as necessary to the imaginative writer as is native genius. But I was born in the days of the full desert breath of the terrible commercial scholarship of Victorian times. In those days it was sufficient to have prepared— say in Goettingen—a pamphlet about "Shorthand in the Days of Ben Jonson," "Shakespeare's Insomnia, Its Cause and Cure" or "A Tabulation of the Use of Until as Against That of Till in 'Piers Plowman' "—and you were at once accorded the right to improve the prose of Daudet, correct the use of similes by Shakespeare and bury to the extent of a page to a line the poems of Chaucer and Arnaut Daniel beneath your intolerable annotations. . . . Those fellows must have done more to contribute to the barbarism of our day than all the brutalities of ten thousand big battalions thundering across a shuddering earth. For how can the English be civilised beings if they do not know the wisdom, the good-humour, the human instances of the "Knight's Tale" which is the supreme monument of the letters of our country? And yet how could any man who was a boy

[1] Anthony Panizzi, the first Librarian of the British Museum to have left any mark and the friend of Prosper Mérimée who published a volume called "Lettres à Panizzi," was born in Brescia three years before the end of the eighteenth century and so carried to his task the classical tradition and the spirit of the last of the great centuries. He began the cataloguing of the Library, a task finished so brilliantly by the never sufficiently to be lamented Dr. Garnett and, more important still, they bequeathed to the Reading Room that spirit of urbane serviceability that most gives to London the right to assert that she is a centre of civilisation.

when I was a boy have any idea of what lay buried beneath those absolutely unreadable annotations as to Chaucer's employment of the Mittel-Hoch-Deutsch 'v' for the Greek digamma in dialect passages. . . . No, as Marwood used to say, we could not bear—for sheer boredom—to think of either Shakespeare or Christ because they had the faces, for us, of Fourth Form Masters. . . . You speak of the Lost Generation as having followed the War. Alas, it was us who were lost before ever Gemmenich heard the dawn-sound of guns. . . .

Obviously in the preparation, in the thinking out, of works of the imagination that can alone save humanity we must be fortified by erudition, if not by that of annotated books, then by that of Life. Neither Homer nor Catullus, nor yet Arnaut Daniel, Dante, Chaucer, Shakespeare, Mr Pound's friend, Confucius, or Doctor Johnson or Stendhal or Flaubert could have written their books unless they were masters of all the knowledge of their day or of how to use an encyclopaedia and to discount the newspaper accounts of current events. And the production of a great work, inspired by next-to-all knowledge and rendered beautiful by cadence, just wording, toleration, pity and impatience is the greatest benefit that humanity can confer on the Almighty. The one thing that can save a Sodom from its fate! . . .

I had got as far as that in my haranguing of that unfortunate expatriate from Greenwich Village. I seized my hat and stick and, in spite of the assurance that it was quite sufficiently cold to call for an overcoat, I exclaimed:

"Damn it all, isn't this the Spring! . . . Let's go to the Museum," and plunged down into the twilight of my rickety stairs. . . .

The great distinction of Avignon of the Popes is its school of painters. . . . The Popes of Avignon were Frenchmen. Philip le Bel—who built the beautiful tower that goes by his name, in Villeneuve over against Avignon—after having murdered Pope Boniface VIII—for to strike an old man of 84 with your iron gauntlet and to imprison him so that he died within the month was no less than murder—Philip le Bel, then, secured the election of what he hoped would prove a man of straw in the person of Benedict XI. The quarrel was of course about money, the king having exacted a tenth of the ecclesiastical revenues in France in order to pay for his wars with England and Germany. He ordered Benedict XI posthumously to excommunicate Boniface VIII and to cease from collecting Peter's Pence. Benedict refused to excommunicate his predecessor and excommunicated instead, Guillaume de Nogaret, the man who had actually struck and kidnapped Boniface. He therefore lived for a very short time, being Pope for less than a year. . . . In order that the reader should not think too harshly of Philip le Bel it should be pointed out that the Pope is the only man for whose death it is not unlawful to pray. He is certain to enter into Heaven. So that to hasten by prayer—or even by other means—the removal from the earth, which is a vale of tears, of a sovereign pontiff who is certain to taste at once of the joys of paradise is almost meritorious. . . . And Benedict XI became a saint.

To find a successor for him was not so easy and the Papal throne remained vacant for over a year, the French, Italian and German cardinals in the meantime wrangling with each other as to its occupancy. In the end, as was not astonishing since Rome was surrounded by French soldiery, the choice fell on a French patriot, Bertrand de Got, Cardinal-Archbishop of Bordeaux, in 1305. This prelate took the name of Clement V.

On the plea that Rome was 'distasteful' to him, Clement V wandered for four years in Provence, the Narbonnais and adjacent Southern countries, dispensing, with both hands, favours to Philip le Bel. He put an end to the interdiction against Guillaume de Nogaret and declared that, in having hounded Boniface VIII to death the French King had acted 'in good faith.' Finally Philip induced him to settle ingloriously in Avignon, in the Dominican monastery of that town. . . . Avignon was sufficiently near to the Comtat Venaissain of France to let the French King have the popes under his thumb. Accordingly in 1311 the Pope held, at Vienne, an ecumenical council, at which he condemned the order of the Knights Templar and delivered their estates and persons into the hands of Philip who burned Jacques de Molay, the Grand Master of that famous order—on the score of his heresy!—and took incontinently possession of the enormous wealth of the Order. His main accusation against the Templars was that they celebrated Black Masses—an accusation as to which there is no evidence whatever—but which much encourages those today desiring to practise that and similar rituals. For, say they, if the Templars who were admirable Christians and the most devout defenders of the Holy Sepulchre indulged in such practices, what better can one do than follow their examples?

It was not until 1326 that Benedict XII, the third Pope of the Exile, began the construction of the Castle, an immense, scientifically fortified pile whose main recommendation to the contemplatively sceptical is the number of secret passages that the successive pontiffs constructed in the desire to escape assassination.[1]

In 1376 the Florentines who had excited the Papal States to revolt against their absentee Father and Sovereign deputed a poor Dominican Tertiary Sister from Siena to intercede with their Holy Father at Avignon in their favour, their attempts on his dominions having failed. Saint Catherine—for it was no less a person—as became one who was later to become one of the mightiest and most gentle saints of Heaven, succeeded miraculously in her attempts. She then turned her modest suasions, her employers, the Florentines having been pardoned, to attempts

[1] I am not interested in pursuing the history of the Avignonnais popes. They numbered seven and were: Clement V (1305-14); John XXII (1316-34); Benedict XII (1334-42); Clement VI (1342-52); Innocent VI (1352-70); and Gregory XI (1371-78)—and the two Anti-Popes, Clement VII (1378-94) and Benedict XIII (1394-1411).

to induce the Holy Father to return to his faithful and mourning city of Rome. Eventually successful she led him back to Italy and in the picture of Matteo di Giovanni di Bartolo in the Hospital of Santa Maria della Scala in Siena you may see how Gregory XI, with his hand permanently raised in a gesture of benediction, rode out from Avignon, robed in full pontificals, upon a white horse, beneath a dais supported by Dominicans, followed by the Cardinals of the College on mules and accompanied by the Saint and her sisters in religion who had to go afoot.

Even the companionship of the Saint was not however sufficient to save the Holy Father, who entered his faithful city in 1377 on the 13th of January—an unlucky day. The rejoicings over the fact that the city had again her bishop and the tomb of St Peter its traditional guardian lasted more than a year and before they were finished the soul of the Holy Father had entered Paradise.

By a miracle the French and Italian Cardinals agreed upon the election of an Italian archbishop to the Papacy, and Urban VI, a saintly but dictatorial pope and one who was no friend to France, sat in the chair of Peter. No sooner did the news of the election reach Charles the Wise upon his throne in Paris than the French Cardinals, becoming wise too in their generation, developed qualms of conscience, discovered and decreed the nullity of the election of Urban. They met on the 21 September, on the feast of St Matthew, at Fondi, on the Neapolitan frontier and elected pope a French cardinal, Robert of Geneva, who took the name of Clement VII and reigned over the Faithful of France, Scotland, Spain and Lower Italy. As might be expected England supported Urban VI, together with Germany, Hungary, Poland, Norway, Sweden and Denmark and Central and Upper Italy, the alliances of the Faith modelling themselves singularly along the lines of subsequent temporal diplomacy . . . At any rate Avignon had her Popes again, for thirty-three years.

After that the city and its surrounding territory became one of the States of the Church and in the absence of the Sovereign Pontiffs enjoyed peace and a measure of prosperity until the French Revolution put an end to the papal rule, Pius VI dying a captive of the French Directorate, at Valence, where the South begins, in 1799.

To judge by the almost vanished fresco of Simone Martini in the porch of the Cathedral of the Popes at Avignon and the exquisite fourteenth century frescoes on the walls of a small room through which an intolerably loquacious and jocular guide forces you in the castle itself, the Avignon popes must have been good patrons of the arts. The castle and the cathedral, as we have seen, were begun by Benedict XII about 1326 and, Simone Martini dying about 1334, he must have been employed almost as soon as the building was begun. It was not however until 1348 that Clement VII purchased the city and territory from Good Queen Joan and building really became brisk. According to ecclesiastical chroniclers the agreed price was eighty, according to lay historians it was twenty, thousand gold florins. But since the price was never paid, Joan being contented, as we have seen, with her pardon for the murder of her husband and the dispensation to marry her cousin, the point seems immaterial except that the motive of the chroniclers, one of whom must be departing from the truth, seems rather inscrutable.

In any case during the fourteenth and fifteenth centuries Avignon was a thriving—and indeed wonderful—centre for the plastic arts. It is not however until about 1444 that we have any financial accounts of the business done by the *Atelier d'Avignon*. What however is then certain is that not only did Avignon export pictures and altar-pieces all over France and Burgundy but that painters came from all over the Western world, except perhaps from England, to supply those masterpieces.

I was sitting yesterday up near the roof in a Fitzroy Street house, listening to a company of painters who were unanimously declaring that water and a misty climate were necessary concomitants of the art of the painter. They cited Dutch, Suabian, Norwich and North French painters; they extended themselves over Constable and Corot and Courbet whose subjects are so marshy that you feel as if you had wet feet whilst looking at his canvases . . . For some reason they forgot Cotman.

I mentioned him and then cordially agreed with their hydropathic assertions. How true it all was! Everyone knew that the Italian and French Primitives and the quattrocentists and El Greco and Velasquez and Zurbaran and Goya and Cézanne and Picasso all had to have umbrellas held over them whilst they painted in the rain that poured through their studio ceilings.

That silenced them for a minute, as when an owl flies over the frog's chorus in my irrigation cisterns, *là-bas*. But soon they were revived and proclaimed that Paris, in spite of the inartistic nature of the French, was the world's art-centre because of the dampness of the climate of its valley bottom . . . They were of course English painters . . . They said that the Italian Primitives were now exploded; that there never were any French Primitives and that, as for Velasquez, El Greco, Goya and Cézanne, every one of them there present had long since got beyond those aliens. They added however, modestly, that that was merely climatic. Those poor foreigners were quite able painters of course but how could you know anything, for instance, about delicacy of colour unless you had sat, say, in Kew Gardens on a misty day, with a south west wind over head and saw that the scarlet tulips across the water formed really a bistre mass with french-grey highlights in a grey-sage-green background with a white-sage-green tracery of boughs before them? . . . How, unless you had seen that, could you achieve delicacy? Those foreign fellows could not, merely geographically, know what that was. They could not escape from a world that was always too much with them. Wine bibbers and garlic-eaters, that was what they were: not such bad breeds, but without the Law. The Law said that the greatest of qualities is delicacy. You must be delicate. You could not be delicate without water. And so the one-sided battle raged. . . .

The crux of the matter is probably a matter of dietetics, dietetics being really a matter of vegetation. Where there is much moisture there will be quantities of green vegetable matter; where green vegetable matter is in profusion there will be cattle and so red meat in mountains in the market. Where meat has been produced there will be quantities of droppings and coarse vegetables. . . . I search the markets of London today in early spring and find, at prices suited for the pocket of the artist, nothing but frost-bitten turnips and carrots, a few, equally frost-bitten 'greens' and a profusion of Brussels Sprouts, which are the source of all evil. . . . In the market in my home town in Provence today I should find in profusion and at the cheapest rates, the tiniest of new carrots and turnips, peas, french beans, small new potatoes, tiny lettuce . . . But indeed, had I been down there all this time I should have had all those things in my own garden, raised by my own hands . . . And lemons and tangerines too! Not to mention cauliflowers. And then, strawberries! [1]

But the internal rumblings promoted by the home-products of the London markets call for "derivatives"—jerkings of the limbs or the befogged brain that shall take the mind off physical and mental discomforts. So, in moist green countries you have massacres, football matches, *noyades,* witch-drownings, puritanisms, flayings, drawings, quarterings, jew-baitings, Calvinisms and all the mediæval and modern Nordic horrors including *autos da fé* of books, street-shootings and Tariffs.

Below Valence, in the South, we lie in the shade of cypress screens, scratching with our toes the soil and dropping in the

---

[1] The reader should observe that I look at the world from the point of view of the poorer artist. I am quite aware that in Bond Street at this moment you can buy strawberries. But I should not like to be of the frame of mind of the person who would do it whilst there is left in the city one armless man selling plush monkeys from a tray in the rain. This is not politics. It is . . . delicacy.

seed that shall produce teeming crops of young vegetables. That you call 'going native' . . . But we shall meditatively digest an ortolan, a few green peas, a handful of grapes and let our thoughts wander in quiet scepticisms to the measure of an albade by Arnaut Daniel. We shall need neither the negroid jerkings of the jazz nor the sadic satisfactions of butchering a thousand driven pheasants to give our poor souls peace. Neither shall we need the æsthetic re-reactions of "delicacy" to show our penitence. We can look with equanimity at pink cliffs, a blaze of purple bougainvilleas, beneath an ultramarine sky, above a vivid emerald sea shot with myriads of scarlet fishes and bottomed with forests of magenta sea-weeds . . . And see nothing to be ashamed of. . . .

But any alienist will tell you that the first thing he does with a homicidal maniac after he gets him into an asylum is to deliver, with immense purges, his stomach from bull-beef and Brussels Sprouts and afterwards to keep him low, on a diet of pulses, salads, cooked fruits and now and then a little poultry . . .

(To the strains of "Lochaber no More," once more the three Highlanders who have for months been a torture to me, are playing in the rain in the street below. They are in the tartans of the Black Watch and the Royal Stewarts. They play remarkably well.)

A gentle critic who went away with me from that company of artists said, in the street:

"What is the matter with our fellows? What is the matter with our Art? . . ." The Royal Academy Exhibition of British old masters had lately closed and had left him in a state of ungovernable depression . . . I said I thought it was mostly a matter of diet—that and dampness. If you eat too much bleeding beef you become eventually ashamed of yourself. Then you yearn for 'delicacy'.

My friend said he wished I would sometimes be serious. He accompanied me back here, where I write, and, after he had drunk the cup of strong tea that I made him, sat desolate, his head hanging over his hands on the table.

To cheer him up I walked up and down behind his back, haranguing him. . . . After all, if I goaded him enough with the doctrines of the alien extremists that I share he might, in the end, react against me and take heart again for writing about the damp delicacies that seemed to have broken his back.

If, I said, you lived in Provence—even if you only came there as did Enguerrand Quarton, the Picard, or Pierre Villatte, the Limousin, or Flemings like Melchior Brederlam, or the Maître de Flémalle or Italians like Simone Martini—you could afford to look at life and make patterns out of it—as did Cézanne at Aix-en-Provence.

That was as true of Nice as of Avignon; in the fifteenth century as of today . . . The marvellous "Burning Bush" by Nicholas Fromentin, as the almost more marvellous picture by Quarton in the hospice of Villeneuve-lès-Avignon, or the frescoes in the little room through which the guide hurries you in the castle of the Popes were the products of the same spirit, of the same life, of the same digestions, of the same climate and of the same cosmopolitan spirit as the bathers of Cézanne or the glorious last ten years' work of Renoir. It was not for nothing that Cézanne stuck as obstinately to his Aix-en-Provence as Mistral did to his Maillanne; or that Gauguin and Van Gogh settled in Arles; or Monticelli remained faithful to Marseilles or Matisse and the Fauves live in the Provençal Riviera . . . Nor was it coincidence. It was the necessity for clear light, a life of dignity and a settlement in the only territory in the world where the tides of civilisation flow for ever backwards and forwards . . . Along the Great Trade Route that has been the main civilising factor of the world since the days when the merchant was sacred.

To be a great artist in any art, I went on, you must be content to look at and make your patterns from your own day. There was perhaps one English figure painter of whom one did not have to be ashamed when thinking of *any* meridional foreigner—the Hogarth of the "Shrimp Girl." And then Constable—whom the French discovered. And possibly Cotman—and just possibly my grandfather of "Work" and "The Last of England," pictures that at that moment were making their little sensation in London, eighty years after they had been painted.

Conditions of life had never been bearable for the Northern artist; could never be bearable. It took a Breughel to stand up against Northern rigours. . . . Paris was the world's art centre because it was the most Southerly of the world's great markets.

After it had reached the ford on the Seine which was the occasion for the existence of Paris, the Great Trade Route branched out, losing itself gradually in valley bottoms, swamps, heaths and damp nationalisms . . . And losing too its civilising mission. . . . I had been reading that afternoon in one of the "serious" magazines an article by a very cultured gentleman from Missouri who was of opinion that the art-hegemony of the world had passed from Lutetia into the hands of himself and his friends of Bloomsbury and Harvard. . . . It is early days to say that; gentlemen from Missouri are proverbially sanguine.

In arts, as in thought and as in statecraft, knowledge and ability have spread slowly with the slow spread of Latinity to the North and to the West, through Provence. To give us the Age of Dante it looped even back to Italy—who was the pupil of the Provençal poets.

I do not hold any special brief for Paris. She surely does not need it. She is impregnable just because she sits over that ford across the Seine. . . . I have written so much about that elsewhere that I cannot again take up the theme . . . It is sufficient here to say that Paris exists because the merchants of the Trade Route, finding the Seine and its marshes barring their progress to the North and West, had to find a ford across which to get themselves and their goods and that Paris is the first ford from the sea on the Seine—much as Kingston on Thames, being situate on the first ford on the Thames was, in the time of Cæsar, the capital of the Gauls of South Britain. It was not for nothing that the highest and most sacred official of Rome was the Pontifex Maximus, and until Paris can be divorced from her geographical position it is unlikely that she will cease to be the filter of civilisation.

And Paris, as should never be forgotten, is sufficiently far to the South for men to be able, most days of the year, to sit in companies out of doors and speculate aloud or think. That is a condition without which arts and civilisation are impossible. Thought or serious and speculative conversation are exhausting employments and call for the oxygen of the open air to aid in restoring wasted tissues. . . . Or if they are not impossible they are so difficult that few men can achieve them. That is why in London you may have a few great books but no literature; one or two great painters but no art-life.

In Avignon, on the other hand, almost all of life passes and has always passed in the open air. So you had the great school of Art in the time of the popes and the continued practice of the arts by almost the entire peasant population—a practice that has filled the churches of Provence with the thousands of little votive paintings that have had so great an influence on the living art of today. For, just as the writing of *conte-fables* has occupied the small trades- and craftsmen all over Provence ever since the days of the Troubadours, so painting, domestic architecture and sculpture in miniature have continued to be produced by small people in the small towns and hamlets all over Gallia Narbonensis, to this day.

That is a phenomenon very largely climatic; but it has also its social side. A peasantry that has seen its feudal lords engage in poetic contests and many of its sons ennobled because of their poetic gifts and that has seen painting and sculpture and painters and sculptors held in high honour in the courts of the sovereign spiritual director of the world will not look askance at the practitioners of those arts and so in Provence there arose and continued the tradition that occupation with one art or the other is a proper thing for sound men.

My house in Toulon has its rooms frescoed, very primitively, by the retired naval quartermaster who built it—himself and his wife, with their own hands, using a cement, said to be of their own manufacture, made from burning oyster-shells according to the Roman tradition and so hard that it will turn any cold chisel. How that may be—as far as the tradition of cement—I do not know—but there the pictures are: scenes of rural life, dovecotes, ponds, fish-stews, swans, wild-fowl, carp, small fish, men rowing boats, men fishing; all under the shadow of the great mountains that are in the Toulon hinterland and all amidst a profusion of leafage and flowers . . . And all a very charming decoration. . . .

Another room is decorated—I imagine by the wife alone, since the paintings are more traditional and she probably went to an art-school—with bouquets of flowers, only some of which are naïve, alive and charming, and all this having been done about 1890 or so.

But imagine an English retired naval quartermaster, in the suburbs of Portsmouth, building, along with his lady and with their own hands, a house of Roman cement, tiled with Roman-S shaped tiles . . . And then frescoing it! . . . Or, for the matter of that, what would be the emotion of an English or American ex-naval officer of high rank on learning that he had let one of his houses to a "poet"? Yet, as I have elsewhere related, the first emotion of my landlord here in Provence when he had that news was to get into his car and drive a hundred and fifty miles to fetch me a root of asphodel. Because all poets must have in their gardens that fabulous herb. . . .

And, if towards Christmas, I go out from my frescoed rooms, down into the town I shall pass near a village where they are performing their *pastorale* and at every street corner there will be booths where peasants will be offering for sale *saintons* such as their ancestors have made in these parts ever since the first

Attic-Boeotian colonists came to these parts from the Oropos three thousand years ago and moulded from the red clay their Tanagra figures. Today the little images are there manufactured in honour of the Saviour and represent every condition of man and every craft, so that all humanity may be shewn standing

The Rade, Toulon

before the *crêches* in the homes of the peasants and townsmen—fishermen with their nets, market-gardeners with their melons, vintners with their casks; white, yellow and black kings with their crowns to remind you of the Magi, and all standing or kneeling before the straw cradle of a little, pink, naked celluloid doll in a plaster of Paris stable. . . . You will not find the like of those *saintons* till you get to Mexico. There Indian peasant families have maintained the art for generations in their families and manufacture still such *saintons* as they learned to make at the points of the swords of the Conquistadores—the early Spaniards having brought the art from Barcelona and Aragon and

[229]

the Barcelonese and Aragonese having learnt the art from Provence at a time when Spain was part of Provence. Or Provence part of Spain, if you prefer it.

And if, on Christmas day, I go down to the harbour I shall see, lying in the sun beneath the exquisite caryatids of Puget on the Mairie and behind his incomparable "Navigator" an "oil-paintist." He will have ranged beside him along the Mairie wall ten or a dozen panel-paintings. Not deathless masterpieces of course for he will be neither a Monticelli nor a Douanier Rousseau. But like those two, and lying contentedly in the sun, he will earn his years' bed and board by those sincere crudenesses and neither you nor the burgesses of the city need feel disgraced at having paid twenty-five francs for one or the other of them.

And up in the town you will find one who will write for you your letters in verse—in classical Alexandrines at thirty lines per half hour for ten sous a line . . . But he will ask more if you want more tricky metres.

The point is that, in Provence, the arts live, if hidden from Missouri then in the hearts of the people. And you cannot call it either a proletariat art or one induced from above, since it is the product of peasant-proprietors—and not of peasant-proprietors only. The sons of not too rich newspaper proprietors paint pictures; those of millionaire tanners write epics; naval officers paint water-colours from Cap Sète to Annam . . . and proud of it! . . . That is the point.

I do not say that the production of masterpieces is enormous; but the presence of the celluloid doll before the three-thousand-year descended *saintons* is a proof of how intimately the native arts enter into the real life of the people even today. They are a part of life as unnoticed as the daily bread, the prayers, the games of boules, the furniture and the Sunday bull-fights.

The same tendency is to be found in the votive pictures. You will see a domestic scene rendered with all the sincerity and lack of tradition of any of the primitive schools—Sienese, French, South German, the pictures having that air of super-reality that marionnettes have. A man is knocked down by a carriage and six; a child is hauled head-downwards out of a fountain basin; a lady in ruffled skirts, carrying a parasol is in the jaws of a crocodile; an invalid is in extremis in a room full of Louis-Phillipard mahogany furniture, beneath a miraculous,

A Votive Picture
A Lady in ruffled Skirts in the Jaws of a Crocodile

oriental, bed-tester . . . In another part of the canvas or panel will appear the man erect and cured; the child eating soup; the lady, escaped from the crocodile promenading, her lap-dog behind her, stiffly beneath her parasol; the invalid will be sawing amazingly real logs with an enormous tenon-saw. And in the sky, between the representation of extremity and escape, will be the image of the saint or Holy Personage to whom the sufferer expressed vows or supplications in that moment of peril. . . .

That apparition will be within a wavy lozenge of light and

will be a copy or an inspiration from the most banal of devotional cards such as you see in the shops for *articles de religion* round St Sulpice or on stalls in the shadow of the spires of Cologne. It is the celluloid doll again; a proof that to the painter of the votive picture his art was a part of his daily life, like the seasonal greetings that the faithful of those parts exchange, at the great feasts, from four to ten times yearly.

And it is to be remembered that the motive of the artist was always sensual and never representational. He desired to give pleasure to the saint to whom his picture was addressed; to win with its prettiness one more smile from Ste Thérèse of the Roses in Heaven. It is unnecessary to record for her how the miraculous preservation looked. She was there. But you can add one more to her heavenly joys . . . and he, the painter, desired to add more beauties to the church in which his offering should be suspended.

It is that that has caused these works to have such a tremendous influence on the art of today.

Obviously the Avignon atelier drew inspiration from the Italian primitives of the fourteenth century so that they could continue and keep fresh a real art long after the gradually sophisticated Italians had abandoned the greatest of their traditions. For it was in the age of Raphael that the "easel-picture" was invented and the *image* reached its quintessence and evolved its stultifying conventions and the ateliers of Avignon and Nice were at their most flourishing just between 1480 and 1520.

Those earlier painters, whether of Siena or Avignon, painted to adorn spaces. If it was their aim to aid religion it was far more their aim to exalt the mind of the onlooker . . . to create in him a religious frame of mind by letting him see what good inventions of beauty they could see in the world of God. And the idea of making portrait-images of the Virgin and Child or journalistic records of the Crucifixion never entered their minds. They painted to make churches glow and tired eyes be rested by the assured beauty and movements of their designs. That was Art.

It was also an intellectual feat. The intellect of plastic art manifests itself not in portraits of thinkers or in the portrayals of the blessings conferred on humanity by the applied sciences. It expresses itself in design and pattern and in the movement of the eye running from place to place on painted walls.

Æsthetically speaking, movement in a picture has nothing to do with the correct anatomical representation of a javelin thrower in action or of a lion in mid air springing on its prey. It consists in such inspiration of line, colour and mass that the confiding eye, coerced by the art of the painter, can let its glance meet the surface of a painting and be conveyed unerringly from place to place on that surface. That ocular progress is what causes æsthetic pleasure and emotion.

The quattrocentists and their predecessors back to the Byzantines treated the subjects on their wall-spaces exactly as composers treat their themes in abstract music. The—literally and only literally—meaningless contrapuntal passages of Bach are infinitely emotional and the cause of emotion—and they are much more mystically so than the most realistic programme-music founded on the most earnest and ingenious renderings of the snortings of dragons, Valkyrs or serpents. So the Virgins and Children of the primitive Italians or French, like the mosaics of the Byzantines, are no more presentations of sacred individuals than Bach's "Matthew Passion" is a representation of divine searchings of the soul. They are, as I have said, abstract variations on an æsthetic, given theme.

And there is as much movement in a Byzantine mosaic, a design of Cimabue, Giotto, Simone Martini, Quarton, Clouet or Fromentin, or of the Master of Ste Anne, the Unknown Master of Cologne, Cranach, El Greco, Poussin, Cézanne or Matisse—to name the whole apostolic succession—as in any of Bach's fugal writings. And as much thought as in any of the writings of Einstein.

That narrow path is hard to keep in. In that late exhibition of British Art at Burlington House that you find so depressing . . . I am still addressing my appalled friend the Critic whose head remains between his hands . . . you had two excellent examples of my double theme. You had the mediæval, probably only so-called English, painted panels, retables and chests. Whoever produced them they were inspired through, and perhaps imported from, Avignon. Possibly some of them, like the painted rood-screens of Southwold and East Anglia in general . . . and it should be remembered that Constable and Cotman came from East Anglia and worshipped in those same churches—possibly, then, some of them came from Flanders. In that case the inspiration merely came, by a roundabout way from Avignon, passing through the territories of the Dukes of Burgundy in their court at Dijon—where I hope very soon now to be eating a *tournedos Meyerbeer*—and so to the Flemish provinces of that same sovereign. For when I get to Dijon, after having had my *tournedos* I shall go to the Ducal Palace and then see the works of Brederlam and Campin from Flanders, all painted in Dijon, and those of the painters of the Burgundian, Avignonnais and Sienese ateliers all equally painted there. And I shall see the great tomb of Philip the Bold which was begun by Jean de Marville, lent to the Duke by the anti-Pope Clement VII of Avignon, continued by the Fleming Claus Sluter, who was the Duke's favourite sculptor, and finished by Sluter's nephew, Claus Werve. . . . You could not have a better instance than that of how, along the Great Route, the streams of the Northern and Meridional Arts passed for ever backwards and forwards—through Provence. . . . And the other instance at Burlington House was that afforded by the works of the poor dear old pre-Raphaelites that the Royal Academicians so grudgingly exhibited. That these painters after barking up an astonishingly right tree should have gone off so wilfully and so soon after two hares as singularly wrong as the camera eye and the Great Moral Purpose, or that, after studying as well as they could, the decorative works of Giotto or Cimabue they should have so completely misunderstood their purpose—all that does not take away from the fact that the original impulse came from the Italian primitives, by way of those of Avignon. For I have already given sufficient proof of the fact that my grandfather who was, however ineffectually, their preceptor and precursor, went specially up the Rhone to see the Bastide at Tarascon, the Quar-

Good King René in his Cap of Vair
After Fromentin

ton at Villeneuve-lès-Avignon and the matchless Fromentin at Aix-en-Provence with the two wings, shewing as donors the Good King René in his cap of vair and his Queen in her steeple-crowned hat. . . .

It was at that point in my discourse that my silent listener cleared his throat.

The great woes, I went on, of the plastic arts arise from want of rational classification. Written works allow themselves to be contentedly sorted out into the creative and the factual—as fiction, non-fiction, poetry and journalism. Says the old lady in M. Béhaine's newest and most wonderful work—It was of course written in the hills of Provence—"Le Silence et la Solitude":

"*De mon temps les gens qui écrivaient se proposaient un de ces trois buts: toucher, instruire ou amuser*" . . . "In my day people who wrote set themselves one of three aims: they proposed to instruct, to move, or to divert." . . . It may be added that only those who sought to "move" the reader—the poets and novelists—were considered to be artists.

But every person who takes canvas, panel, carton, ivory, copper-plate, vellum or paper and on them makes marks, stains or incisions, in oils, tempera, gouache, charcoal, or with ink or acids, using brush, palette knife, pencil, graver or goose-quill becomes at once an "artist" not only in his own but in both popular and critical parlance.

("I suggest," my friend raised his head to say, "that you leave critics alone.")

Painters, etchers, draughtsmen, aquarellists have as such their labels—but only as such. A man might be a pointilliste, an imitator of Fantin-Latour, a disciple of Sam Prout, but as long as he used water-colour he would be for you a "water-colour painter." Yet no sane person would classify Homer and the minute-writer who condensed for the press the proceedings of the Versailles Congress as being both brothers of the pen. The one would be a poet, the other a practised stenographer. But, for you, both El Greco who imagined and designed the "View of Toledo" and the Westalls who with marvellous, photographic needles produced camera-eye topographical records of the Lake Country, to illustrate the works of Southey, Wordsworth, or Coleridge, must come under the heading of artists and you would say that "L'Estaque" of Cézanne is all one with a touched-up photograph of St Paul's Cathedral by Mr Coborn.

(My friend said: "Damn Cézanne!")

The issue, I went on, is really a great one. Art criticism would at last become enlightening and the painting world would be spared an infinite number of controversies and scandals once these classifications were fairly established in the painting mind. There can have been few greater real scandals than Zola's treatment of Cézanne or, in its smaller way, Ruskin's of Whistler. Zola was a worthy if unimaginative citizen; Ruskin, if he looked, as my grandfather said, like a cross between a fiend and a tallow-chandler, was probably on the side of one cohort or another of the angels. Yet both must for ever pass for fool-villains for want of perception of the fact that plastic poets, preachers, historians and journalists cannot be classified under the same heading and that yet none of them need interfere or compete with any of the others.

We writers of every genre get along very well, category beside category. What rifts and quarrels there are go on internecinely, not camp against camp. Journalists never envy poets, statisticians do not sigh for the laurels of the novelist. Why should they? Even the most pestilential of moral writers never league themselves professionally against imaginative writers and, when necessary, can amiably associate themselves in private with sporting journalists. It is only the plastic artist and the art critic who never learn. The arts suffer.

They suffer in two ways. The engrossed designer, the follower of Cézanne whose major pre-occupation is not with records but with the "look" of his pictures, with design and its movement, is continually persecuted by all his recording rivals whose profession is in reality quite another one and whose emoluments are so much greater that you would think that there could be no cause for jealousy. What is worse, the issue is apt to be obscured for the engrossed designer. Shaken by mob clamour and the obloquy of the word 'decorative'—which should be the highest guerdon of the artist—he is apt to be driven, like the poor dear pre-Raphaelites under the bullying of the atrocious half-fiend, half-tallow-chandler, out of the right way—the only right way consisting in the knowledge that the highest function of the brush is to beautify some building.

Without Ruskin it is possible that we might have had some real art in England and, but for the quality of indifference to the crowd that was displayed by Cézanne, Manet and Renoir, Zola might well have wrecked the Impressionists. But they at least stood firm and gave us the only great and only significant art movement that there has been since the days of El Greco.

My tortured friend stood up and exclaimed: What about Reynolds . . . and Gainsborough . . . and Raeburn . . . and . . . and . . . Raeburn . . . and Romney? . . . He was ready to grant that the English painter was too apt to take refuge from the sordidness of modern life and to seek oblivion in an attempt at a delicacy that only too often ended in weakness or even nullity . . . But he was tired of hearing for ever of these garlic-stinking Dagoes . . . What, after all, was Cézanne?

Cézanne? . . . An obscure Dago of whom hardly anyone in London had ever heard.

That, I said, was probably true.

The words excited in him an emotion that, if he had not been the gentlest and indeed the most delicate of men would admirably have simulated epilepsy. What did I want, he exclaimed? . . . That English painters should pass their time painting like the Fauves? Imitating Utrillo in Paris suburbs? Or Friesz in some Mediterranean harbour? Or Matisse amongst the obese odalisques, peaches, wine-bottles and pink table-cloths of Montparnasse? . . . Cézanne was no doubt the father of those fellows. But what had he got to say to the modern world? A fellow who hid himself away in some obscure provincial town and, as astigmatic as El Greco, added to his imitations of Monet a touch of decorative weakness by blurring outlines that his eyes did not properly see . . . Damn . . . no, hang . . . it all, weren't we white men? *Hadn't* we got a little beyond those coarse naïvetés? Were we to abandon, as you might say, the motor-cultivator for the wooden plough-share? If I wanted it I could see them ploughing with oxen in Sussex. But was *that* the way to obtain salvation? . . . He broke off to say that of course he was only talking figuratively.

I said that he might as well be talking literally for all I was concerned. I was on the side of the Dagoes all the time. They used, still, wooden ploughs drawn by oxen; they painted still in the tradition of the days before the Van Eycks invented oil paints; they lived as they had lived for three thousand years and only they could save a world ruined by, precisely, the motor-cultivator . . . He wouldn't deny, would he? that the world *had* been ruined by the motor-cultivator in the hands of the financier?

He said that no one denied that. But the remedy. . . .

A sudden spasm shook him; he threw up his hands towards the low, dark ceiling, muttered: "Insupportable." And rushed from the room leaving behind him a catalogue of the exhibition of Unit One and those of nine other exhibitions that he had visited that afternoon.

I said to the accompaniment of his footsteps that I was on the side of the Dagoes all the time. I would dig with a wooden spade; I would look at the world as Nicholas Fromentin looked at the court of King René at Tarascon. His crowd, as far as was consistent with delicacy, had discovered that the Machine was a fit motive for expression in modern art—five years after the crisis had struck the deathblow to the machine and fifteen after M Leger in paint and Mr Pound with photographs had bored the world stiff with representations of cogs and spanners and fly-wheel forms. DECORATION, I shouted, as the patter of his descending footsteps died, IS THE SOLE . . . REASON . . . FOR . . . ALL . . . THE ARTS . . . LET YOUR LIFE BE DECORATED BY CEZANNE . . . AND BACH . . . AND MR POUND and you will be all right.

The heavy reverberations of the slammed front door shook the house. That poor, gentle devil hated Mr Pound with a virulence you could hardly conceive of. Mr Pound is wanting in delicacy. He wrote such things to the editor of the *Daily Chron-*

icle! No gentleman would write such things. Yet Mr Pound is the mirror and form of the English gentleman!

I don't know what made me so intolerably loquacious . . . Or I do. It is because I smell freedom.

A few more days; several hours of grubbing for dates in the Reading Room and then Eastward Ho for the Great Route. We shall see Bignor with its Roman villa and Chichester of the Butter Cross which was the something or other of the Romans. And we shall see Lutetia and eat tournedos in Dijon where in princely wise the Dukes of Burgundy patronised painters whether from Flanders or Florence or the roads in between . . . And we shall wander about the night roads at Orange in search of something to eat, for as soon as you are in Provence the feeding is not so good. And we shall see the Roman theatre and all the Roman villas and walls at Vaison. . . .

I yelled:

"Come on, you miserable Huron from the Bronx where the ladies send up their maids from floor to floor with the message: Mrs Murphy's compliments and she'll trouble you for the butter . . . Let's go to the Museum and get our Reading Room tickets . . . There's spring in the air!"

My friend, ascending the stair, said it couldn't be done. . . .

"I look like a tramp; they'll never give me a ticket. . . ."

I pointed out that he was in a civilised city, the last stronghold of Christism and of Democracy. Here at least the poor dare plead . . . We walked by side streets to Gower Street. I was shocked to see that Shoolbed's seemed to have disappeared. That surely for London and Anglo-Saxondom must be the writing on the wall. You might as well expect to see the Galeries Lafayette fallen down or Macy's stock seized for rent . . . But my New York friend was unsympathetic and I went back to the subject of the London Museums.

In Gower Street we seemed to be in your true Academe— the dim light, the dim perspective . . . What other landscape would you choose for scholars? . . . Even for thinkers? . . .

And to that region, into that pocket, for hundreds, for thousands of ineffably tranquil years, gradually there had poured all the rarest treasures of the great Route. Where else, outside Egypt, would you see such decorative painting; where else, outside Greece, statuary so melting into buildings; where else outside Provence such evidence of the splendours that were Rome? There you had the tributes down the ages of Cathay, of Memphis, of Palmyra, of Nineveh. There you had the supremest beauties of Crete and a million statuettes from Tanagra. . . .

My friend said timidly:

"Surely not a *million*."

I ejaculated fiercely:

"Mornamillion. . . ."

And consider, I said, the accessibility of all these objects. Here was the British Museum in a position so central that it was proposed to pull it down and build a tea-shop in its place—or so I had been told. And it was but a step to the National Gallery where you could see the best El Greco, the best Renoir, the best Manet, the best Cézanne . . . The best because you could really see them, and without walking for miles or cricking your neck looking up to near the ceiling . . . And consider the excellent wall of Matisses, Cézannes, Picassos at the Tate . . . Our poor dear old ragbag of a city might not be able to produce art but it put into the display of its treasures all the genius that other cities lavished on their shop-window dressing.

We climbed the steps of the Museum. It astonished me to see beneath the portico happy scholars lounging . . . and pouring out clouds of smoke what time the top-hatted beadles chased crowds of tiny children who stood on each other's shoulders to reach the drinking fountains . . . I devoted a little shudder to the shade of Panizzi. The new Authorities of that Institution must have made it free not merely for heroes and democracy but also for infants, so that the Portico had a faint shade of the air of a Whitsun Bank Holiday.

And I reflected sadly that, had those conditions prevailed,

Planco consule, I might well, long before today have become, if not a gentleman, then at least a scholar.

For the great hindrance to my education used to be that, not long after I had been in the dim Paradise of the Reading Room, I should be assailed by a certain impatience. I would get through looking up the numbers and press-letters of my books in the catalogue and deposit them in the baskets round the central counter; I would consult all the works of reference round the outer walls and would return to my seat with perfect sheaves of notes. Then a miraculously silent-footed individual would deposit three quarto books on the desk in front of me; another after a minute would place there five works of atlas size, another, six folios, a fourth, an armful of sedecimos . . . So there with my rampart before me I would sit impregnable against the assaults of the world, Time and the Foul Fiend . . . Alas . . . No sooner had I opened Froissart or Hakluyt or the "Calendar of State Papers Foreign and Domestic; Henry VIII, Volume Nine," than unease would overcome me . . . I would fidget and fidget; my left hand would furtively seek my right, inner breast pocket . . . Alas, again. . . .

In illo die, to smoke, one had to go all the way to the front gates, pass the cerberus-eyed beadles who must have been the largest men in the world . . . And then, in great Russell Street, whilst one leaned on the railings that are decorated by Stevens' beautiful and demure little lions, Mr Edward Garnett would drift along with his peculiar lounging stride of the slow bowler and, taking me by the elbow would lead me to the Vienna Café where, in those days met all the youthful intelligentsia, and would lecture me on the Social Revolution. Or, if it was Thursday, I would go to Mrs Garnett's tea behind the windows that you can see at the end of the East Wing. And there Mr Gosse would trumpet the latest news from literary Scandinavia; and Mr Sidney Colvin, keeper of Prints, would drop in from next door, and tell us how, in the latest letter from poor dear Robert Louis, that exiled invalid would talk minutely about his health in Samoa; and Samuel Butler would relate the latest fluctuations in the four per cents. And I would be kept in a corner by Mr Robert Garnett who would tell me the latest eccentricities of his extraordinarily eccentric clients; or by Miss Olive Garnett who wrote some very admirable stories about St Petersburg and would tell me that I ought to become a Nihilist. And at last Dr Garnett would come in from behind his book-wall in the Museum, and Mrs Constance Garnett whose beautiful translation of Turgenev was then being a revelation to the world of the Intelligentsia would look in for a minute and beam absently with her blue eyes through her spectacles for a minute or two and it all became much nicer. I will even confess that I popped her as heroine into the novel I was then writing. . . .

And I would approach Dr Garnett and reproach him with the fact that the Museum's veto against smoking in the Portico interfered with my higher education; and, head on one side, he would regard me as if he were a deaf, smiling and august cat and go on lending all his ears to Mrs Garnett's amazing account of the astounding, Irish, day that she would have passed between the Museum Gates and Covent Garden . . . Alas, Who now sits in her familiar seat?

So my poor New Yorker and I ascended the steps and decided to take a look at the Egyptian paintings that were only a step away, before going to ask for our tickets. We ascended several hundred more steps and walked several miles between the showcases of the Tanagra figures, every one of which, like syrens, demanded our attention. So, in a couple of hours we reached a barrier that bore the inscription: CLOSED FOR REPAIRS. It was in front of the Egyptian Rooms. I nevertheless, I think, succeeded in persuading my patient friend that, except for Luxor—which was relatively inaccessible—behind that barrier were such specimens of the Art that, by way of the Fauves in Provence, had revolutionised the vision of the modern world— specimens so wonderful as could nowhere else in the world be seen. . . .

"That Art," I said, my words echoing along the gallery of Tanagra terracotta and awakening a slumbering guardian, ". . . and that of the painters of votive pictures in Provence." And as we passed back by the Etruscan ladies and their husbands reclining jocularly on their tombs, I told how, four years ago, in front of the Coq d'Or in the town below my home, I had heard MM Othon Friesz and Matisse exchange reminiscences as to their climbs into the Provençal hinterlands in search of churches that should contain votive pictures, say, to St Christopher who, if they travel by automobile will save travellers from crocodiles . . . But of course, if you are going to be knocked down by a plough, a carriage and six or a thirty CV it is to Notre Dame of Laghet, behind Nice, that you must address your promise of a picture . . . And at that reunion there had been poor Juan Gris passing the last days of his life, and other painters, and I think Colette and Cocteau and Max Jacob on their way to convents . . . Stirring days those in the town below my home!

So we went and looked at the bas-reliefs in clay of Sardanapalus hunting . . . Sardanapalus builded seven cities in a day; let us eat drink and sleep for tomorrow we die . . . Tomorrow we should jolly well have to get to work in the Reading Room . . . It was, too, just on closing time. . . .

We approached the little door beyond the end of the gallery where you see the head of Cæsar looking like a convict and those of all the other gangsters who were the Roman Emperors. Pleasure arose at the thought that behind that door I should find a suave official who would ask, Sirs, if we wished to have our tickets at once . . . It is never safe to indulge in patriotic elation. I placed my hand on the ormolu handle of the kingwood door.

An enormous voice bellowed:

"Ware the ell juthinkuregoin?"

My friend reminded me that he had said we looked like tramps.

I said: No, the poor fellow with his bottlenose and medal

[244]

ribbons wanted to get to his tea. It wanted only three minutes of closing-time.

We were nearly knocked down by a gentleman who burst hurriedly out of that closed doorway. No doubt he was hastening to *his* tea. He left the door open, so I dragged the unwilling Transatlantic into the holy of holies.

In a dim glass case a pale young man was just putting on his overcoat. He sank back with distaste into a chair behind an official table and brought out the word:

"Wajjerwant?"

My poor friend explained that I wrote books. It would perhaps have been better if he had not.

When, holding a number of forms, I rejoined him in the atrium outside I found him standing in the shadows looking expressionlessly at the bust of Caracalla, son of Septimius Severus. I handed him his share of the formulæ that the clerk had given me. I assured him that he had only to write to the Principal Librarian to be treated with the most exquisite politeness . . . I have only one passionate pre-occupation of a patriotic order—that England should appear in a favourable light to distinguished foreigners.

That New Yorker slowly tore those printed slips into minute fragments, looked round for a waste-paper receptacle and dropped the pieces into his pocket. He said:

"I have come to the conclusion that the Cockney accent is really responsible for the perpetuation of the class-system in this country. It would be otherwise incomprehensible."

I repeated:

"I assure you, the most *exquisite*. . . ."

"Other accents," he went on, "are merely local. There is a Virginian accent which I find disagreeable, a Cantonese, a Pekin, Lyons, Strasburg or Viennese accent. But to have the Cockney accent is not only evidence of low birth and probably defective education, it at once ensures that such an individual will never climb any social ladder at all and paralyses him in his efforts to that end. . . ."

I said that my friend had no idea of what his tea is to the Englishman. We should not have gone in just on closing time.

He continued:

Did I remember a chap we had met about a month before, sitting alone in a corner at some reception? He proved to be intelligent, instructed and gave evidence of a fertile and refined imagination. But he turned all his "a's" into "aï's" so that it had been impossible even for my friend to believe in his culture . . . That must be souring—and paralysing.

To the Englishman, I went on, his tea was the sacred episode of the day. It was at once his dope, his ruin and his badge of freedom. It spoilt his digestion, let him believe that he was not one of the lesser breeds who need apéritifs or cocktails before lunch and established an intolerable craving in the name of which he will commit any crime . . . Our men in the trenches were admirable soldiers. But if they did not get their morning tea they would refuse duty. Even if the refusal jeopardised the safety of the whole army . . . And to be kept from your tea by a septuagenarian and loquacious bore who belonged to the lowest social class of the community. . . .

That New Yorker brought out, regrettably:

"Shucks! . . . I am neither a writer, nor septuagenarian nor loquacious at the wrong moment."

That of course was true. At the interview that had so irritated him all that poor Septentrional from across the world had got out had been the inopportune information that Mr Ford wrote books.

I said:

"If the British soldier will jeopardise. . . ."

My friend span irritably round on me and brought out:

"The Hell he will . . . I've been rude to by functionaries in every language between Vladivostok and Portland, Oregon. That's nothing. It wasn't even merely the fellow's rudeness to

you that makes me determined to shake the mud-plus-gasoline
of this burg for ever from my Stetson . . ." A Stetson is a hat.
"It is," he finished, "that you should have been deprived of your
poor old patriotic demonstration . . . For a bum display it *was*
a bum display. And I wanted Ulysses to get something out of
the suitors. After twenty years of wandering." I have, you see,
my friends.

But I was appalled to the point of tears.

Was it I, I exclaimed, that had said that the inhabitants of
this city were the gentlest and kindest people you could find the
world over? Was it I that had said that poor old London was the
last stronghold of Christism? . . . No, *Sir!*

For what had most struck that ingenuous Occidental in
London—but most of all—after of course the evidences of shock-
ing indigestions, insomnias and mendicancies, had been the extraordinary part that Christ seemed to take in the affairs and
imagination of the City. You went to Hyde Park expecting to
see red flags and hear Communists. You saw, instead, nothing
but banners, waving to the skies in the insupportable north-east
wind the words: JESUS; JESUS CHRIST; CHRIST JESUS; COME TO
THE SAVIOUR; THE BLOOD OF THE LAMB; CHRISTIAN EVIDENCE;
CHRISTIAN ENDEAVOUR; and all that you could hear was the sound
of brass bands who invited you as Christians militant to go onwards . . . You went to see the Tower. On the hill above it
were assemblages of men with banners proclaiming: JESUS;
JESUS CHRIST; CHRIST JESUS . . . with tonsured monks, laymen
looking like pickpockets; laymen looking like cheesemongers;
clerics with purple peeping above their waistcoats; clerics lam-
entably threadbare and rednosed in the biting breezes . . . All
proclaiming the virtues of the Saving Name in the heart of the
business quarter of the city . . . At tea-time!

It had of course been really in the lunch-hour.

And, according to the testimony of that witness, there had
been no end to it. If you paused in the Strand for a moment you
would be jostled by an individual with the aspect of a city

merchant, smiling inwardly and at intervals shouting: Read the GOS . . . PELS; you passed elderly gentlemen with hatbands inscribed in golden letters ARE YOU SAVED. On the very walls of half the houses in the city you read, scrawled in purple and white chalks: COME TO JESUS.

And there were even more significant things. In the United States if you read a thin volume of new poetry you were astonished at the intimacy with Death that the young poet would display . . . All the young poets! They seemed to take their stands on hills beside that awful potentate; they interpreted for Him; they despised you, the reader, because you were neither dead nor personally acquainted with His ways . . . It was the Mode—and the expression of a defeatism that saw no way out for the world save in negation.

In London, if you took up such a booklet, you found the figure of the Redeemer substituted for that of Him whom the Saviour overcame. Otherwise it was the same thing. The poet represented himself as knowing what Christ would have done; would have thought; what he would recommend and how he would have viewed the poet's unblest and inferior contemporaries. On Christ these young men moulded themselves and their minds. You seemed to see them, with arms outstretched, cross-fashion; kneeling on the Mount or with slightly lunatic, Oxford Movement eyes, agonising in the Garden. The garden would most usually be in Sussex . . . In this case too it was an expression of defeatism. Only, in London where they had the faculty of not knowing when they were beaten it was not annihilation that they saw as the solution—it was calling in the aid of the Supernatural. . . .

But all this would have to be seriously discounted if, as I appeared to imply, all these—writers, poets, preachers, ranters and scrawlers on walls would become gnashing Hatheists if they were kept ten minutes waiting for their nice cupsertea.

It is difficult to explain the nuances of national traits to foreigners. And the more intelligent they are the more difficult it is. They will observe too much.

I tried still, if faint-heartedly, to bolster up the institutions of my country. I recommended my friend to take a hold of himself. The American is particularly prone—*too* prone—to take offence at the British official manner. He will submit unprotestingly to the physical brutalities of his own functionaries and to the moral insolence of those of every other nation. The English official drives him off his head. It was the Boston tea-party over again . . . When one has jeered as much as I have in a long life at German-descended scholarship it is only reasonable that the clerk to the Grand Master of that Teutonic Order should order one to provide him with the assurance that one will not use the fane over which he pontifies for support in one's, to him, pestilential and Gallic Heresies . . . and to get the assurance backed up by a Judge of the High Court, the chairman of a leading firm of stockbrokers or an Admiral of the Blue . . . And I pointed out to that by now cachinnating New Yorker that it was not fitting that a writer of a certain age and industry, with fifty odd entries in, and items covering seven or so pages, in the British Museum Library Catalogue, should be mocked by an immature non-Anglo-Saxon from the East Side.

He said:

"Cheese, *vieille fève*, it's useless your trying to promote international cordialities and understandings in the very shadows of your national institutions . . . Besides, you'll get in ten minutes at the Bibliothèque Nationale all the incorrect dates you need" . . . Since I had to leave Town next day but one that was what I resigned myself to doing.

. . . Patriotism is the meanest of all the virtues and an alcoholism to which one succumbs at one's peril . . . I had wanted to prove to that Transatlantic how superior were I and mine to him and his—and heaven knows I have received almost unreasonable courtesies at *his* Public Library. Without that pot-valiant impulse I do not suppose I should have thought of going to the Museum. There are enough public libraries in Provence and filled with documents about that country. Just at the foot of the hill on which I live is a magnificent library, established before that of the British Museum, and full of just the material that I need. I can walk into it,—my secretary has done it for me again and again—ask for priceless first editions and receive them without any question at all. On the other hand the Museum Library is hopelessly overcrowded with poor devils who have nowhere else to go for warmth and shelter—and the nutriment of the book worm. So it was really wrong for me to ask for a ticket, besides which I am the holder of a life-ticket which, as far as I know, has never been rescinded. . . .

A mean vice. The gods who wish to destroy our civilisations invented it to drive us mad . . . I was at a party yesterday and happened to say to a very pleasant Englishman that it was impossible without unreasonable expenditure to get decent vegetables in London whilst in the South of France vegetables were so cheap that they could be sold in London for next to nothing; but they were kept out by the tariff.

He said that that was splendid. Thank God, the outrageous and unreasonable French swine were being taught a lesson. I said that nevertheless many Englishmen were being kept out of work by the quota tariff that the French had imposed in retaliation on our manufactured goods.

For that too, he thanked God. He said that the damned swine of English workmen damn well needed a lesson taught to them too. Let them starve, the brute beasts who asked nothing better than to live on the dole—let them starve the whole lot of them. And if the French were not careful one day the German army would be in Paris and what price their tariffs then . . . Not that he wanted war, God forbid. It would spread through the whole world.

There are high matters as to which I am hardly capable of forming an opinion. My friend was of great-public-school-Balliol-Inner-Temple distinction. He could no doubt speak with authority. But it seems to me that if you succeed in starving a proportion of the population of nation A whilst starving a portion of nation B for the sake of starving that proportion of nation A and making both nations go without, the one, food necessary to health and the other, tools that are helpful in producing food and if as a consequence you run the risk of plunging the two nations and in equally natural consequence the whole of the world into war—well, you seem to be indulging in some confusion of feeling when you ask the Almighty to protect you from the results of your actions . . .

Part Three

MISE A MORT

Entry of Corrida

CHAPTER I

THERE THE POOR DARE PLEAD

NEXT day we were in a train, going South.

I ask to be regarded, from this moment, not as Moralist; nor as Historian; but simply as prophet. I am going to point out to this world what will happen to it if it does not take Provence of the XIII century for its model. For there seems to be a general—and universal—impression that our Civilisation —if that is what you want to call it—is staggering to its end. And for the first time in my life I find myself in agreement with the world from China to Peru.

Do you happen to know Haydn's symphony? . . . It is a piece that begins with a full orchestra, each player having beside him a candle to light his score. They play that delicate cheerful-regretful music of an eighteenth century that was already certain of its doom . . . As they play on the contra-bassist takes his candle and on tiptoe steals out of the orchestra; then the flautist takes his candle and steals away . . . The music goes on—and the drum is gone, and the bassoon . . . and the hautbois, and the second . . . violin . . . Then they are all gone and it is dark. . . .

That is our Age . . . There have stolen away from us, unperceived, Faith and Courage; the belief in a sustaining Redeemer, in a sustaining anything; the Stage is gone, the Cinema is going, the belief in the Arts, in Altruism, in the Law of Supply and Demand, in Science, in the Destiny of our Races . . . In the machine itself . . . In Provence there is every Sunday a *mise à mort* that is responsible for the death of six bulls. In the world outside it one immense bull that bears our destiny is at every hour of every day slowly and blindly staggering to its end.

I may seem to have written disproportionately of Mrs Patrick Campbell and I may seem to be going disproportionately to write about bull-fighting. But that is of set purpose . . . Mrs Patrick Campbell represents—and who could do it more magniloquently—the Muses of our day that, in the general break up of our financial machinery, have to creep into the mouse-hole of a mechanical method of reproduction that is itself dying of commercial tuberculosis. In Provence—and of course in Spain—the bull-fight continues still its triumphant progress at the sword-ends of actors who alone today are as beloved as the boy who in Antipolis a couple of thousand years ago danced and gave pleasure. The bull-fight too may die out in the whole general collapse; it is an immensely expensive mass-art—though its essentials are neither the expense nor the immense crowds; its essentials are swiftness and skill in wielding a thin spike of steel against a furious and alert monster. For still today the most admired matadors are not those who offer the most display of agility. They are those who with the classic nonchalance of the hidalgos who first practised this art—and who alone have the right to the name *toreador*—stroll about the arena, their sword beneath the arm, or sit on a chair till the moment comes to deliver to the bull who has meanwhile been worked into position by the servants, the *coup de grâce*. For that no lists are needed; no tiers on tiers of humanity . . . no limelight, no publicity . . . Nothing but a smooth place, some shade-trees, the arms, the man and the bull.

Yes, the great, shining *corridas* whether of Nîmes or Pampeluna or Perpignan or Madrid and St Sebastian may go, though it seems unlikely since that art has lasted two thousand years in these places.

But the art will not go, the courage, the skill; the alertness.

In every village in Provence there is a bull-ring and on every Sunday of the year when the days are warm enough all the young men of courage face, without arms, the wild bulls of the Camargue doing nothing more deadly to them than affix rosettes beneath their horns or on each shoulder . . . And they face the charging bull, place a foot between the horns and spring right over the beast, or vault over him with a jumping pole, or catch him as he charges with their two hands on his horns and somersault across his back . . . It is just a sport, like cricket, but without advertisement, carried on so obscurely that you might well say it was secret . . . a sport in the blood of the people, carried on by the sons of the barbers, the furriers, the peasants, the bakers . . . It is as it were the *conte-fable* as against the high and renowned *gestes* of the troubadours. It is considered that, before a man should have wherewith to pay for his seat at the *mise à mort*, he must have worked bulls himself. . . .

It is that spirit—the tradition that a man should not eat high cooking till he can cook; shall not inhabit a house of his own till he can sweep the floor; shall not drink the juice of fabulous fruits brought from the Indies till he can grow the fruits of his own land; shall not go to the play till he has proved himself an actor who can improvise his part; shall not travel till he has made a home . . . and shall not wear a fine coat till he can grow the wool, card, spin and weave the cloth, cut out, baste, fit and sew an every-day one . . . It is that spirit that could yet save the Western World . . . But to do that it must be enjoined on the world that Mass and the Machine are the servants not the master of Man and a man must blush as if he were caught in a petty theft if a stranger coming into his house should find anything that was not made by the human hand or if a guest should find himself being offered food out of a can or unseasoned meat that should have been kept beyond its due season by preservatives. It is in that way and in that way only that an economic balance could be re-established,

a law of Supply and Demand be re-enacted and the Great
Trade Routes be restored to their beneficent function of dis-
tributing civilisation to the darkest ends of the earth . . . It
is that or extinction: the one or the other must come . . . It
does not take any great prophet to foresee that. . . .

As I sat in that train lumbering down through Sussex I
came to the conclusion that I would write no more of the
public history of Provence, for the real history of the country
went underground at the death of King René when Provence
fell to the King of France and the first Mass Product in the
way of modern nations was begun. It is—that public history—a
long, sad story of an attempt at standardisation foiled by secret
tenacities—by the bakers, the barbers, the blacksmiths, the cur-
riers, the gardeners' and peasants' sons who kept alive the sub-
terraneous flames of the poetry, the crafts, the pacificisms, the
dangerous sports, the theatrical entertainments and the great
passion for the beloved earth.

Francis I and several other kings decreed the death of the
Provençal language; Louis XIV robbed of its power the family
of Orange, the last of the independent sovereigns of the triangle
between the Rhone, the Alps and the sea. The Wars of Religion waged themselves in the religion-less country; the lawyers
of the Parlement at Aix fixed on Provence the gadfly yoke of
the armies of functionaries that have ever since bled and crippled not Provence alone but all the country of the Lilies—and
for myself I hardly ever go to Aix-en-Provence, birthplace
of Cézanne though it be, and though it be the gravest and most
stately eighteenth century town that you will find anywhere.
For though the *mistral* and the Durance may be the flails of
Provence the Parlement of Aix wrought so much the more and
the more lasting harm. . . .

And then the Revolution did away with the Papal State
of Avignon, and the Marseillais adopted the song of Rouget
de Lisle and marched to Paris and Marianne came and here
we are . . . But in the Sussex train I fell to thinking of the

whole stretch of the Provincia Romana as it is today—and of making a survey of it instead of a history . . . And, I don't know why, since it is rather topsy-turvy, I began to think of Provence of the other end, the beginnings of the angle of the triangle where the sea meets the Maritime Alps and Italy opposes at the Bridge of St Louis a *chevaux de frise* of bayonets and lethal instruments to the slumbering and corpulent figure in a deck chair that seems to be the sole protection of Provence. . . .

All that region must at that moment be lying still beneath the sunlight that seems unchangeable. When there are grey days the mind does not register them. Next day you swear there has never been anything but sun.

The whole stretch of coast is fretted with white—from the gates of Toulon to Rapallo, for here Italy begins to make herself felt. But the white fringe on the incredible blue is not that of surf. It is caused by the limbs of bathers, as if the syrens had never left those shores . . . And indeed the syrens have never left those shores.

When I was a boy these were rather chilly resorts for the opulent so that my first recollection of them is that of being in the august sitting-room of a more than opulent American uncle in the most opulent hotel of the then coast. I was, I suppose, seventeen or eighteen.

With every precaution against cold we sat, one on each side of the table, dozing, which was unusual . . . So that I felt only the mildest surprise. My uncle, a staid, clean-shaven, frock-coated lean giant had thrown the water-carafe through the window. He had known that fumes of carbon-monoxide were coming from the white porcelain stove. Zola and his wife had just died in that way in Paris . . . Shining and frenzied Monte Carlo *pompiers* burst in, in their gorgeous uniforms, strung from shoulder to shoulder with medals as large as the tops of meat-tins, smashing through our white-and-gold doors with axes that glittered like those of the Fascisti today. I hope they each got another medal. But for them I should not be writing here now.

I used to be given a sovereign a day to play with at the tables . . . and the food we ate! . . . I daresay that laid the foundation for my particularity about food today as I am sure the daily losing of the sovereign has made me never want to gamble from that time on.

But nowadays there is a summer season . . . and there the poor dare plead. The great financial director, Louis Blanc, has been ejected from the Casino; the rigorous sumptuary laws and the Grand Dukes are alike very faded; the Grimaldis whose ancestor rescued the territory from the Saracens are less absolute; they charge you a franc for a sheet of letter-paper in the Casino, six francs to feed the fish in the Oceanographic Museum and eight francs to go in . . . The Principality is said to be managed from New York.

Nevertheless the summer season is far gayer than the old winter one that used to be rather stiff and *renfrognée* . . . But the poor food!

. . . I sat in that rumbling train running down through Sussex and had no urge to uplift my poor New Yorker by communicating to him the literary ambience of that county. He had had enough of uplift at the British Museum . . . So instead I let my mind go, remembering the Riviera which is what France and the World of Big Business have made of that corner of Provence. . . . ·

There pursues itself there, on top of the lives of the ancient inhabitants, a sort of double, parasitic life. It is, as in the time of the Romans and who knows of how many previous races of conquerors, a life of rich villas and another life of transient visitors. These pacific conquerors come from all over the world, which makes Provence present to the outside world almost solely the aspect of a land of pleasure cities. You moved there till lately amidst the frou-frou of the skirts of the aristocracies and the financiers of the whole world. Latterly the aristocracies and financiers have appeared a little wilted—or perhaps it is only that numbers of individuals have disappeared from those *parages.*

I think I have a great many memories of the old and some at least of the New Dispensation in the stage that it has there reached—a stage now of a rather crumbling internationalism, without much of the tradition of ancient names and without much co-ordination . . . A preparation for extinction; the last creakings of a door.

A year or so ago I invited some lovely English friends from the hinterland of those regions—and by chance my long suffering New York friend, who is not unusually in these neighbourhoods and who is perhaps above all interested in my gastronomic adventures, to a dinner that I wished to make impressive in that romantic corner.

It was in a restaurant that was once one of the Meccas for the mixed gourmets of the world. We overlooked the Mediterranean and the ghosts of grand dukes, famous beauties, forgotten geniuses, and famous rastas lurked in the shadows of the less lit colonnades.

We had *Potage Grand Duc Alexandre; Turbot Poché Princesse de Galles, Sauce Escoffier.* We had *Civet de Lièvre à la Reine d'Angleterre,* the usual chicken with salad *des Quatre Saisons, pêche Melba, Petites Friandises Meyerbeer, Fromages Assortis.* It sounds good, doesn't it? And with the shades of Bernardo Grimaldi and the captain of the troops of Haroun Alraschid and of Sordello looking down on us!

My lovely English friends expressed themselves ravished and drove off into the blue night, romantically, along the Corniche . . . When we had done waving handkerchiefs we retired hastily to a solitary spot beside the Casino and, before the impassive bust of Saint Saëns, beneath the great white stars . . . shot our lunches . . . It had been London expressing itself; and it had been too much. We were neither of us up to food for several days.

The *Potage Grand Duc Alexandre* had been tepid, greenish bill-sticker's paste; the *Turbot Poché Princesse de Monaco*, tepid white blotting-paper drenched with white bill-sticker's paste; Queen Victoria's jugged hare had been tepid, black-brown dough drenched with mahogany-brown bill-sticker's paste; the salad had come from a barrow the day before and was dressed with an infinitesimal quantity of cotton-seed oil and no vinegar; the *pêche Melba* had been a gummy substance from a Californian can drenched with tepid, pink, bill-sticker's paste faintly perfumed with orange water.

It had been London calling indeed . . . But both branches of Anglo-Saxondom had had a voice in that atrocity of the corruption of the innocent. Is it to be wondered that Providence has set millstones round our necks and is casting us into the deep sea? . . . The very chicken had come out of a can!

Mind you, that had been a famous, an august restaurant in the days before Prosperity and Profiteering had set their heels on the necks of the Monégasques and when Dagoes, Polacks, Wops, Russians, Magyars and the very Ottomans had had some voice in the affairs of the Principality and the other cosmopolitan resorts of Provence . . . and had insisted on having food with some taste to it, if only *gulyaches* and *paprika-schnitzels* . . . And still, in spite of Crises, that region remains the playground of the enormously rich, the relatively cultured and the apparently idle. You sit there, on the edge of lawns, in the shadow of cypresses, drowsily gazing at the isles of the Lérins on the incredible blue of the Mediterranean. On the lawns lovely figures drift in and out of the cloistral shadows, lean graciously over the balustrades, gracefully drape themselves and talk finance . . . For all the world like the Courts of Love! Well, this is the civilisation that by grace of St Dominic, St Louis and Cotton Mather has displaced that of those fellows . . . Mr Otto Kahn and Mrs Patrick Campbell and Prince Roland de Bourbon and Lady Patricia This and the Infanta That, and Mr Henri Wertheimer and Mr Van Dongen and the Duke of Moët and Chandon and the Grand Duke and M Henri Matisse and Mr Chaplin and all the great names off cans and automobile publicities and packets and the frontals of department stores. They will all always be there and when one drops out someone of identical appearance will take his place . . . But their poor digestions! That was the ominous thought that the day after we had eaten that terrible meal came into my dozing head as I gazed at that sunlit scene. What goes on inside all those gorgeous, dainty and posturing rulers of the world?

I had reason to ask. Let alone the meal I have described I had in that region eaten others. Incredible meals. The sort of meals that are eaten by Royalty and Presidents. Off gold plates before cannon-ball piles of pink, flawless apples, pears, peaches, grapefruit, nectarines. And everything all tasteless!

How do they achieve that? . . . Even out of caviare their *chefs* can take all flavour and their gorgeous Virginia hams will taste only—and that so faintly!—of maple sugar. You would have thought that impossible. It isn't.

Nearly all nations can in their private houses concoct one or two local dishes that suit the climate, the resources and the habits of life of their countries. Even England has admirable plain or professed cooks ministering to the middle and upper middle classes, using pot-herbs and spices and the humbler condiments with taste and discretion, whipping with the touch of angels the cream for their brandied trifles. America in private has cooks of enthusiasm turning out pimented sea-foods, roasts of admirable succulence, pies fit to be offered in the streets of Cokayne where the little pigs run about roasted and beg you to partake of them . . . These cooks are mostly negresses, preferably from Martinique.

Then why, in public and semi-public, must these colossi among the nations profess their passion for, their supineness beneath the heel of . . . bill-sticker's paste? For that is the sad fact. You cannot today in London get food that has any flavour at all. Not in a chop house; not in Soho; particularly not in any of the immense, be-marbled Palaces. In New York you can find food with some taste if you take a long time in looking for it—at the restaurants of Italians, Greeks, Smyrniotes, Hungarians, for the expatriate French as a rule lack courage in face of want of appreciation and being cunning soon fall back on cold pork, shredded cereals and lettuce sparingly cotton-seed oiled. At any rate in what they offer their publics: at home they eat well enough. London however steam-rollers out the individualities of its aliens far more swiftly and inexorably than does New York and even on Saffron Hill which used to be the entrenched fortalice of the ice-cream man you are today more likely to be offered tepid, half raw beef than *risotto Milanese*.

In the corrupting era after the War when Prosperity broke the American tradition and Profiteering destroyed the English rich man's character, millions of our common countrymen poured all along the Great Trade Route and, having the cheque books, called the restaurateur's tunes . . . For a country to be civilised the traveller should be able to turn into any restaurant, bistrôt or wayside inn in any smallest village and be sure of finding at any time a meal—a meal at least adequate, often exquisite, without trace of 'roughage' and completely without influence of Anglo-Saxons. Those influences are waning at last, but even now the only districts at all attainable on the Great Route where the traveller is in that way safe are Burgundy and the Périgord. . . .

Nevertheless under all that *tohu-wa-bohu* of discordant Anglo-Saxon and international cat-calls and indigestions the native life astonishingly continues. . . .

Sitting in that Sussex train I had suddenly a memory of discomfort . . . I remembered passing two or three years ago through Mentone station. It is an unadorned building in ferroconcrete. I felt incomprehensible depression—unprepared and incomprehensible. I had been reading one of Georges Simenon's detective stories and had looked up quite unthinkingly. . . .

On the 2d February, 1917, I had stood on that platform. There had been an icy wind and snow falling. I had been going up into the line again. If you had asked me then whether I felt the depression that, mnemonically, visited me when passing later through that station I should probably have denied it—mildly. I had at the time only been conscious of being dull and numbed in a dull, numb station. All France up to Hazebrouck in Flanders was deep in snow. I was going to Hazebrouck in Flanders.

I had been seen off—I will interpolate this literary anecdote —by an antipodean major that we used to call "Horsetrileyer" who, because he was not very popular in that Red Cross station, had attached himself firmly to me. He had instructed me as to the glories of "down under" as against the squalors of this effete continent, had interrupted and contradicted me a good deal . . . Now he went, rolling like a porpoise, to the bookstall to buy me a *Vie Parisienne*—a periodical without which no British officer could travel. He came back to me, running, breathless, his eyes sticking out of his head. One of my books was in those days covering the whole of France. He squeezed my fingers into jam and shouted:

" 'Ooffer, hif ever hi'd known that you'd've written a book Hi'd never've spoken to you as I 'ave."

It was typical that the sincerest tribute to Literature that I ever heard should have come from an antipodean mouth in the shadows of the palms of these shores that have always been my spiritual, and generally, my physical home.

Ah, but we had lived like gentlemen in that Red Cross Hotel on Cap Martin. A peeress of untellable wealth and of inexhaustible benevolence had taken, for us chest sufferers of H.M. Army . . . for us alone all the Hôtel Cap Martin . . . One of those great, gilded caravanserais that of my own motion I should never have entered. We had at our disposal staff, kitchens, *chef* —and a great *chef* of before the days when Anglo-Saxondom had ruined these shores—wine-cellars, riding horses, golf-course, automobiles. . . .

We had sat at little tables in fantastically palmed and flowering rooms and looked from the shadows of marble walls over a Mediterranean that blazed in the winter sunlight. We ate *Tournedos Meyerbeer* and drank *Château Pavie* 1906 . . . *1906*, think of that.

We slept in royal suites; the most lovely ladies and the most nobly titled, elderly seigneurs walked with us on the terraces over the sea . . . Sometimes one looked round and remembered for a second that we were all being fattened for slaughter . . . But we had endless automobiles at our disposal and Monte Carlo was just round the corner . . . It was then that I tried out poor Marwood's system. . . .

I will here interpolate my reasons—they are two—for my poking continually contemptuous remarks at those who eat underdone roast beef. My as it were public reason is simply that underdone meat is extremely indigestible. The Anglo-Saxon—and the Anglomaniac French, alas—beginning, because of excesses, to suffer from indigestion is forced by crowd-hypnotism into giving up most of his cooked foods and eating, at first with repulsion, underdone meat from time to time. That gives him real indigestion. Filled with mob-panic he eats more and more and more and more bleeding gobbets of flesh. His digestion falls completely down under him and to those cannibal viands he adds foods out of packets and then more foods out of packets and more tepid blood . . . So the night-mare streets of London and all its tubes are covered with the horrifying announcements that you suffer from night-starvation or 'can't' . . . I have a poor French friend, lean as a rake, transparent as a leaf, who insists that no meat he eats shall roast for more than five minutes . . . The English have sense to know that mutton at least should be well done. But that poor Anglo-maniac insists that his gigots shall be as *saignants* as his *bifteks*.

But, though it depresses me to think of whole continents

between noon and one-thirty dripping with gore between
gnashing teeth, my private reason is even more imperative . . .
I like, as I have said, to go now and then to bull-fights . . .
And when I have seen a splendid bull, his tail lashing his magnificent flanks, his eyes seeing everything at once, fly round
the arena in search of more empires to conquer . . . Every time
I see this I renew my vow that I will never eat meat from the
equals, or the poor emasculated cousins, of this magnificent and
unparalleled tragedian . . . I would as soon eat a steak from a
relation of Mrs Patrick Campbell . . . Sooner!

If it were a matter of eating the bull himself it would, I
think, be different. One may eat the flesh of a god that died
in the sunlight . . . Humanity has been doing that for thousands of years and the bull was once the god of a magnificent
conquering race . . . But to eat flesh from the poor relation
of a god, murdered by a low assassin in a dim and horrescent
cellar . . . May the fellest days of indigestion and the most
hideous dreams of night-starvation be my lot for weeks after!
. . . And that I mean.

Well, then, one day I was put in charge of a detail of my
comrades at that Hotel . . . An incredibly inaccessible and
distant town in the hinterland of high mountains that there
press down on the sea had asked to be allowed to receive a
deputation of British officers. We were told that the town
would send conveyances. I was to make a speech in Provençal.
It sounded very nice and for a day or two having got hold
of a copy of the "Trésor du Félibrige" I worked at my
speech. . . .

. . . Before the marble steps and the scarlet carpet of the
Royal entrance of that hotel—It is only used for ambassadors or
for those going to state functions—waited six very small donkeys; behind each, a meagre and dishevelled peasant woman.
They were our Rolls-Royces and there was no avoiding them
. . . It was a military order. All the six of us were portly and
too weak to walk much more than a mile on the level.

We climbed the shuddering inaccessibilities on those valiant microcosms. On the hand-breadth paths we shut our eyes so as not to see the precipices below. The indefatigable, lean women ran behind our valiant mounts, brandishing immense cudgels. Every few steps my attendant brought hers down on the flanks of my poor donkey. Each time she cried:

"*Courage*, Montebello."

It was an allegory, as if poor Montebello, the microscopic donkey were poor humanity with Destiny at its back, climbing the inaccessible peaks with the whole load of the stupidity of its rulers in its saddle. . . .

That mountain fastness was a madhouse of militarism. Our arrival was beflagged; the miserable cowbyres that served for houses had bedspreads from every window-hole. Before our donkeys' feet they threw lavender and rosemary . . . Little boys and girls whilst they threw those herbs ran beside us and shouted to us exhortations to kill each one thousands and thousands more Huns . . . Their ancestors had no doubt done the same for Hannibal with his elephants, for Caesar, for Napoleon, all of whom with how many conquerors more, had passed that way. They cheered my twenty word speech to the echo. They gave us the flesh of new-born kids, the miserable 'greens' from their miserable patches of soil carried up from the plains to the pockets they scrape out of the rocks in the eternal glooms of the high mountains . . . They gave us wine that they swore was of the days of the Greeks. It was hundreds of years old— of the days of Hannibal. It was thick, golden, glutinous and perfumed—like an enchanted hair-oil . . . One understood why Horace diluted his wine with sea-water. . . .

And they invited us into their houses. Regarding them through the doorways, gingerly, we saw that they slept on mud-floors beside their miserable cattle and their starved goats, the meagre hens roosting overhead and covering them with their droppings. . . .

Those patriots lived a life of an incredible squalor—and of

infinite passion for their locality . . . On our return down the dizzy precipices we had to be medically examined. The Military Authority had heard that every inhabitant of that city suffered from a disease that was to them innocuous but that was extraordinarily malignant to any one else . . . I do not know if that is true. But they were said to be proud of it as an inheritance from Napoleon—or maybe from Hannibal. . . .

You understand that that was not Provence . . . and had never been Provence. It was of the North . . . from which comes all evil. It was the North, in climate, in squalor, in poverty, in pride . . . and in ferocious patriotism . . . Even at that exciting date the true Provence could not be flogged into ferocious patriotism. Only yesterday I read in our local paper that on the 20th August 1914 the Senator for one of the Provençaux departments had the day before delivered a philippic lashing Provence for its lack of enthusiasm for the War and the soldiers of the Midi for their lethargy at the Front. It is true that next day he was contradicted by a fiery letter, at any rate as to the troops, by a medical Lieutenant General who was shortly going to command the hospital service in one of the regions behind the Front.

As to the troops I think they just did their duty—but certainly with a certain lethargy. In the Somme we had behind us battery after battery of French 75's. Most of that artillery came from Marseilles and the districts between Marseilles and Tarascon and at times I had talks with men whose relations or friends I had known. They had no enthusiasms. Their fields, after all, had not been ravaged nor their villages destroyed like the villages and fields that we could see in front of us. They strolled about with their hands in their pockets when they could and seemed singularly detached from the Septentrional scene. But the fire of their particular guns was as continuous and uninterrupted as those of any others of the French of that particular and magnificent service. . . . You may put it that they had seen all the blood that they wanted to see shed in the *mises*

[269]

à mort. . . . And Spain, for the matter of that, that appanage of Provence, where alone outside the Rhone valley the *corrida* sparkles among the hills—Spain was the only one of the Great Nations that had no hand in our puttings to death. . . . Not of bulls, but none the less, sendings of our fellows before their Maker. . . . I am no pacifist. . . . This morning the clear bugles of infantry sounded the General Assembly from all the hills around my terrace. . . . And I half rose from my chair . . . But if one sins it is as well to know that one sins—otherwise one will commit cruelties from stupidity, from which may Heaven preserve us!

Nevertheless I am glad to be able to believe that Provence shewed no great enthusiasms for that or any other war and that yet the Provençaux did their duties. Until Christianity shall be finally dead it is as well to render his things unto Caesar. . . . But one should keep one's enthusiasms for God. . . .

And *Courage*, Montebello!

That was a score of years ago. . . . The gatherings from the Continents on those shores seemed tremendous in those days. We sat on those Mediterranean terraces discussing ceaselessly movements of troops from Europe, Asia, Africa, Canada and South America, Oceania. . . . Like chain-caterpillars they seemed to be converging upon us, engrossed, from every quarter of the Universe. Or so nearly upon us as made no difference. As if we had been the Magnetic Pole which is a little distant from the True one. . . . But indeed in that War, as in every other one, we were there to save from Northern races the Provence of all time—the frame of mind of Sappho and the poetry of the soul of Catullus which alone can save this world alive.

Today—fallaciously enough since that trouble remains sempiternal—all that bother seems negligible in those sunlights. You have stopped talking about it; you have stopped thinking about it. You sit in the shadows of verandahs on the foothills of that hinterland and with faded Grand Dukes, financiers, world-beauties, famous artists, all a little de-gilded and anxious, discuss the movements of Gold. . . . From all around you columns of gold are moving like blind maggots in a universe of cheese. You ought to be at the Magnetic Pole on which they converge. . . . But God knows you aren't. . . .

You all confess that you have a little gold. . . . Only a very little. . . . A few hundred, a few thousand, a few hundred thousand, a mere couple of million or so of gold—in dollars, reichsmarks; francs, groschen, lire. Coin; minted. . . . And I should advise you to jolly well. . . .

A lady, beautiful as a goddess and kind as the land-breeze interrupts the almost kinder Mr Otto Kahn to say that her baby Pekinese is ill. . . . It has never tasted raw milk in its life; nevertheless it is ill. . . . Kind Mr Kahn offers to send for his own man; by aeroplane from Vienna. . . . But Monte Rosso stocks are no longer quoted at all. . . .

Someone says that Wall Street has decided to buy England. . . . Yes. . . . to finance it. . . . Yes, sick of our Conti. . . .

Your mind misses a beat. Below, the Islands of the Lérins are pink heaps on the distant, incredible, blue. . . .

We passed Three Bridges in that Sussex train. . . . My poor New Yorker asked where the bridges were and went to sleep again. . . . I went on thinking about Provence. . . .

Two or three years ago I was dozing in the background of such a conversation as I have adumbrated. . . . Suddenly there came into my head the opening verses of the "Vision of Piers Plowman"—alliterative lines running, as far as I could remember:

> "In a summer season
> When soote was the weather,
> I schrope me into sheep-shrouds
> In habit as an eremite
> Holy of living

and going on to its vision of Heaven that culminates triumphantly

PROVENCE

"There the poor dare plead. . . ."

It was not such an arbitrary selection of the subconscious mind. . . . All along that Mediterranean strip there is today a summer season—and there the poor dare really plead. You meet there the amazingly poor. You may yourself be amazingly poor compared to what you were yet, hardly needing even to plead, you may spend days churning the sea along the warm sands into that white strip of foam that from above the aviators see stretching from Carqueiranne, next to Toulon, to Rapallo where Mr Pound sits brooding violent communications to the Anglo-Saxon press under the shadow of the monument to Columbus. . . .

But you might possess nothing but a skin that will brown, the thinnest coverings for your torso and thighs and no more sous, groschens, nickels or francs than you can hold in your hands. . . . And yet you can browbeat the lordliest archangel at the doors of any Palace. . . . Those fellows have got the fear of God in them. . . .

Probably the poorest creature—the most penniless class—in the world at the moment is the German youth who has just passed his university examinations. He has no chance of a job in which his erudition will help. If he is Prince Charming with the gifts of Fortunatus he may soon be sweeping a street in Aschaffenburg. . . . Otherwise nothing. No future. No outlet.

But, frank, engaging, bronzed high-yellow, in ten franc sweater and fifteen franc swimming pants, there he is in thousands on the Italian Riviera, in hundreds on the Côte d'Azur. His parents will have dug up a few twenty mark gold pieces from under the damson tree by the well in the courtyard. . . . For centuries the German parent has regarded these shores as a place where the poor Septentrional can dance or . . . do something or other with broom or sword. . . . So the blond boys without futures get the few gold-mark pieces and off to the *Land wo die Citronen bluehen*. They confront Cerberus on his marble steps.

"Your palace rooms," they say, "are empty. Spiders spin in your cupboards. Your *rosbif* has been in your refrigerators since 1929. Your cash registers have not clicked this year. We will at least clear the spiders from your cupboards and the *rosbif* from your larders." So they get board-lodging for a price that makes Cerberus weep into his black, buffalo-horn moustachios. . . . For a dollar, for half a crown, for ten francs. . . . But he should not have come to a land where the poor dare . . . bluster.

On a broiling afternoon in the palace-bar in Cannes where everybody meets anybody none of my party would take anything but iced-tea . . . at seven francs a glass. . . .

"*Seulement thé glacé?*" asked the waiter and there was still a good deal of the old cerberus-contempt in his voice. . . . Or it may have been despair. . . . But there is very little of that spirit left in that territory. And in the course of an amazingly cheap lounge across that territory we did not come across even the semblance of an attempt to brow-beat or overcharge us. . . . That seemed to me to be tragic when I considered what it meant in the way of bowed-down hearts in the bosoms of once stout, moustachioed fellows. . . .

My reminiscences in the train as we began to reach downland were of course two or three years old . . . But I revisited those shores before writing this and found conditions much the same. . . . There are just as many Germans and they are just as poor—but today they are mostly exiles . . . and more agreeable to meet. There are about as many poor English and Americans and rather fewer financiers—but not much fewer. . . .

It is necessary to know a countryside a little before you can get the most possible pleasure out of it—but the eruditions necessary for pleasure on these coasts are mostly material. There are very few memorable castles, churches or ruins. Except for the very battered arena at Fréjus, Roman, Greek or Phoenician remains are there mostly in very small fragments.

. . . There are the votive pictures in the shrine of Notre Dame de Laghet of which I have already written but almost no other pictures. . . . There is not one, at Nice, of the thirteenth century *atelier* that in its day was almost as famous as that of Avignon and supplied all the littoral—and even Toulon—with altarpieces, retables and saints with donors. . . . On the other

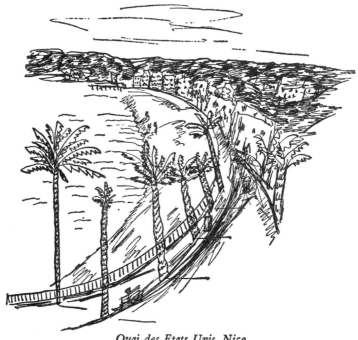

Quai des Etats Unis, Nice

hand I am anxious to record that when I had got well under way with an oration to the custodian of the Nice Museum—pointing out that we had come a thousand miles to search for Nice Primitives and now he had not got change for a hundred francs so that we could not go in . . . a little grimace came on to that functionary's moustached, cocked-hatted face and with a little motion of his hand like that of an aristocratic shopwalker inviting you to further regions of haberdashered glory he motioned us to go in without paying. . . . So that the Sodom of his class may yet be saved!

Literature and music pullulate on these shores. . . . But it is literature only of a sort. . . . The Anglo-Saxon novelist of immense popularity places his scenario in the Palace Hotels or the Casino of Monte Carlo or the now more fashionable Cannes. . . . In return when the mountains go a little back there are

Place Masséna, Nice

great numbers of French men of letters and painters in tiny villas, old farms . . . or even tents. . . . And it is great pleasure to me to think that in a little house built by his own super-royalist hands, my friend M. René Béhaine, whom M. Léon Daudet and I and a dozen others consider to be the greatest living novelist of any country, continues on a hill, the marvellous sequel to "La Solitude et le Silence."

With a little erudition and a knowledge of back streets you may even eat well in, say, Nice, though it is true that the usual foods of the dago populations is too compounded of macaronis and tomatoes and white haricots. . . . But even in Ventimiglia where we were delayed by the Customs and had to lunch, the waiter with his Brooklyn accent smiled ingratiatingly and said:

"We will cook-a you, especialmente, a nice-a leetle slice of bleedin-a bif". . . .

But the official classes—and Nice is a great official city—the officers, the lawyers, the judges and the retired French bourgeoise of the city, and the peasants from the hills on market days, see to it that they get inexpensively fed . . . and tastefully!

I will cite for you a few *menus:*

One I ate in the "Boeuf à la Mode," in a back street. . . . Here I used to eat almost daily, ten years ago, at a cost of twelve francs fifty—then two shillings, or half a dollar. The same meal now—August 1934—costs ten francs or three shillings or sixty-six cents. . . . Our fellow diners were all of the official or professional classes. We chose for *hors d'oeuvres*, *Salade Niçoise* and *Aubergines à la Turque;* grey—not red—mullet, grilled with a mustard-mixed-with-white wine sauce; *poulet chasseur;* ices and fruit. . . . Except for the ices everything was admirable. . . . And French-admirable. . . .

The other day—there is a Crisis—we ate in a garden of the same back street amongst mostly rich peasants and poor medicos—a meal for seven francs . . . An enormous meal. . . . Unlimited *hors d'oeuvres;* the best *jambon madère* I have ever eaten; *agneau printanière; tomates farcies; haricots verts au lard.* . . . And drank an interesting little thin, local white wine with a pronounced flavour of *pierre à fusil*—gun flint—and had unlimited soda water and ice with which to dilute it on the hottest day of the year. . . . And unlimited melons and pears. . . . The service was naturally rather slow—but if you are going to eat such a meal on a hot day it is as well to eat it slowly. . . . For myself I shall eat there again whenever I go to Nice—and take the same menu with one *plat* less—for five francs, which I suppose will then represent a dollar or four and twopence. . . .

The Surf of Bathers, Juan les Pins

PROVENCE

This region in fact, which is hardly real Provence, goes on much as it always did—if you care to take the trouble to find the places of those goings-on. The rest of France is as shaken by uncertainties as any other part of the overshadowed world.[1] But the real under-current of Niçois and Nicéens—who are families who have lived in Nice for generations—continues very undisturbed. The tax-collectors are perhaps a little more ubiquitous than they were in the days of the Greeks, the Phoenicians and the Romans; and, as in those days, every monticule behind the narrow strip of littoral is crowned with an agreeable villa, having shady and brilliant-flowered gardens. . . . All these are now more de-gilded than they were ten years ago but no doubt they will again be rejuvenated.

On the shores, the surf of bathers is so thick that swift mo-

---

[1] I append some menus of pre-ordered meals in this region.

At the RESTAURANT FRANÇAIS in the corner of the Place Masséna that is furthest removed from Anglo-Saxondom:

LUNCH: *Jambon de Parme* in place of *hors d'oeuvres*. *Pièce de résistance* a *Loup poché* with *aïoli*. I have already annoyed the Scots by saying that the *loup* is like a sublimised brook trout without the muddy flavour. This and the ham were lovely. The *aïoli* was really too strong for the fish; it is more suitable for conger eel, octopus, haddock and the like. But I had ordered it because I wanted my Anglo-Saxon guest to know what *aïoli* is like when superfinely prepared. And then *pêches Melba*—perfect peaches on a bed of whipped fresh cream, frozen stiff and dashed with a tiny flavour of *cassis* and a tinier of maraschino. The bill for all this was 67 francs which included a bottle of vintage *Bellet* that is the *vin du pays* of the mountains behind Nice. The franc was then at twenty-five to the dollar and 125 to the pound, so that the charge was less than three dollars or ten shillings. The same meal would cost today fifty francs—say, momentarily, three dollars thirty or twelve and six. And you have to remember that this was as perfect cooking as you could get in the world. I don't say more perfect, but as perfect.

LUNCH again for two . . . in a back street in Monte Carlo—as far back from Anglo-Saxondom as you can get in a principality that is the size of a pocket-handkerchief . . . in a restaurant kept by the famous former chef of the place where we consumed bill-sticker's paste, the meal being ordered beforehand: Eggs *en gelée* flavoured with *estragon*—with a *shade* too little estragon, the chef fearing Anglo-Saxon puritanism; admirable *sôles meunière* with amazing *pommes à l'anglaise*—for it *is* amazing what a real *chef* can do with that dish. . . . And then a masterly *soufflé* just touched with kirsch. An admirable and delicate hot weather meal. . . . Price with a half bottle 1914 Riesling, half bottle of Vichy, coffee, luxury tax and cover charges and tip frs 62, say $2.50 or ten shillings. Today 25% more.

tion, whether in automobiles or speed-boats is impracticable. In between somewhere are the natives, the farmers, wine-growers, market-women, lace-makers, naval and military officers and the world of functionaries—these being eternal and watching the ever-dying, daily-restored tides of ephemerides. So it was in the beginning and so no doubt it will be for ever. . . .

I had arrived at that point in my reflections when the train entered Pulborough station. . . .

CHAPTER 11

PARIS–DIJON–MÉDITERRANÉE

W^E were sitting outside the Café de Paris, at Tarascon, on Pentecost Sunday in mid-May which is the month of Mary and the first communions, eight days later. We

First Communicants, Tarascon

had been, as per programme, in Bignor where the Roman villa is; in Chichester which was the Roman something or other; in Paris which was the Roman Lutetia; in Dijon, the Castrum Divionense of Aurelian in the third century; in Orange where the Roman monuments begin with the Theatre and the triumphal arch, and which was called Arausia; in Vaison, the Vasio of the Romans and perhaps the most Roman of all the towns of Provence. . . . And now the City of the Good King, which is over against Beaucaire, the Erraginum of the Romans and one of the greatest fair grounds of the Great Trade Route. So we had followed, inversely, the current of Latin civilisation and there we sat on a Sunday, drinking our after-lunch coffee.

We had entertained languidly the idea of seeing a bullfight in the Roman arena of the ancient Nemausis, but strictly speaking Nîmes was outside the Provincia Romana. Besides, everyone in Tarascon told us that there was no bullfight that day in Nîmes. The bull-fighting company had failed; there would never be another *mise à mort;* the Roman arena was to be pulled down because the bull-fighting company had failed. . . . That was patriotism. One seemed to hear them say, in every undertone, "*Sac.r.r.é R.R.Royaume*". . . . The Tarasconnais never go to the movies in Beaucaire; the Beaucairois never cross the bridge to seek a night's entertainment in the city of St Martha and the Tarasque.

And it was hot! . . . I like the great heats when they gradually settle down on me and seem to hold me in an iron grasp. . . . But to come straight from London into the full glare of 101° in the shade has a little the effect of a plunge into icy water. The shadows of the planes in the avenue were lampblack; the sun on the house-fronts blazed ivory white; the automobiles that passed ceaselessly appeared to be on fire. . . . An immense autobus, labelled 'Nîmes' drew up, since our tables were off the side-walk, almost on our feet. Our faithful waiter —and in the end, perhaps, it shall be the waiters who shall save our Sodoms—hurried up and said:

"There is a *mise à mort* at Nîmes. . . . Hurry yourselves." He was from Perpignan. We said that it was perhaps not a good bullfight. He said: "Lalanda . . . Chicuelo . . . Dominguez. . . . An ace, he too." We said that it was too late. . . .

He said: "*Ces messieurs-dames seront à Nîmes à deux heures
. . .*" The *mise à mort* would not begin until three thirty. . . .
There would be plenty tickets. He would telephone to reserve
seats. . . . If these ladies-gentlemen wanted seats they could
have good ones in the sun for five francs; in the shade for
twenty. . . . That too was patriotism! The prices of the seats
proved to be considerably higher. . . . Nevertheless we found
ourselves in the immense, nearly empty autobus. . . . Though
it was a Sunday few people in the Empire could be found to
cross the long, swaying bridge into the Kingdom!

The Roman villa we had seen four days before at Bignor is
a small collection of thatched huts, like a cowlick on an Anglo-
Saxon skull, on the skyline of a spur of the Southdowns. The
huts contain some tesselated pavements, and, according to the
Guide "innumerable tiles and enormous burnt clay slabs for
floors, hypocausts, and roofing"—about as much trace of the
villa being left as of Roman culture in our civilisation.

Stane Street ran at perhaps a quarter of a mile to the East
of the villa. Stane Street is the great Roman road that ran from
Chichester harbour by Bignor to Dorking and then somewhere
else. Mr Belloc says it went to London; other authorities trace
its course to other places in the Midlands. I should myself
have thought it would have gone to the ford at Kingston and
across it to the North. Chichester was a Roman port and a
station on the great trade route for long before London was
anything than a cluster of marsh-dwellings. In making their
road the Romans would have had no reason for deviating from
their penetration into the interior by taking their great trunk
way towards an unknown spot. . . . See, again, how patriotism
will keep creeping in. . . . I used to live for years near poor,
depressed "Chi" or in its neighbourhood, so, though I have
no authority at all in these matters, I desire to impress you with
the fact that that poor city was a great place long before
London emerged sufficiently from the mists of barbarism to

become a Roman port of no great importance. . . . And so, to carry the local patriot strain a little further, as a Londoner I will curl a contemptuous lip at the mention of Edgbaston, a wealthy suburb of Birmingham claiming to be a patroness of the arts—as compared with Putney a poorish suburb of the metropolis but once the home of Swinburne and my guardian, Mr Watts-Dunton. And indeed wasn't I myself born within a couple of miles of Putney in a village celebrated as the home of the loves of Nelson and Lady Hamilton? . . .

In any case Stane Street, the great Roman artery, ran north from Chichester. . . . But Chichester was on the Great Trade Route that existed thousands of years before Remus jumped over the walls of Rome. . . . For the honest merchant coming to the Channel somewhere near Boulogne and impelled by just such a desire for precious metals as caused the gold-rushes to California or the Klondyke—the honest merchant faced by that strip of ruffled sea got himself and his wares somehow across in primitive craft. He would land in England, say at Dungeness or Rye Harbour. . . . I lived for long next door to Rye and, for other years, with Dungeness always under my eyes on the horizon of the Marsh. . . . Or, if you like, say they landed at Newhaven, since in following the Route I shall go back that way and you may be patriotic for me. In any case the sunken road that was once the Route runs all the way from about Rye, along the South Coast of England, to the Land's End. . . . Those traders went, not in search of gold which was then relatively useless, but of bronze which would help its purchasers to overcome savages armed only with flint-axe-heads—as surely as the Mark IV of the British Tommies at Tel-el-Kebir permitted them to mow down naked savages armed with spears.

Bronze, however, is made of copper and tin and copper and tin are found together in only two spots in the world known to the ancients—in Cornwall and the Straits Settlements. So from Pekin the honest merchants made for the Land's End and, returning, helped the Greeks to take Troy. And with the wealth of commodity they paid for Cornish bronze they enabled Arthur to set up his court and the splendours of the East blazed in Camelot and Lyonesse and with their wisdom, Merlin, the wisest of the wise, was filled.

And all along that South Coast of England, just off that sunken road—notably at Winchelsea where I once had a house—digging in the fields you will find traces of Bronze Age Settlements, armourers' shops and broken spear-heads and daggers that were brought to the craftsmen to repair. They will be decorated with concentric circles such as should at once beautify and ensure for their wearers such love of the gods and envy of their fellow men as come to those who lavishly patronise great armament firms. So true it is that the first uses to which men put the dubious benefits of Science are the destruction of their fellows—then as today.

In any case the culture that flowed like a tide back and forth along the Route ended in Cornwall and the legends of Arthur; and the glory and traditions of Rome, as far as England was concerned, landed in Chichester Harbour, swept with the legions up Stane Street, dropped a connecting link in the Roman Villa at Bignor, crossed the Thames were you will—and so spread out fanwise like water that you distribute in soil-pipes till its fertilising influences at last are lost. . . . That sparse civilisation the Romans had to fence in with the great wall that runs along the dreary uplands spreading from Carlisle to Newcastle, a region never meant for human habitation just as all this land probably was not meant for humanity to shiver and have damp feet, rheumy noses and floating kidneys in. At any rate all that is clean, sound, a little beautiful, frugal, equitable and beneficent in our civilisation came along that Route or up that Street. . . .

And let not the West be discouraged. Mr Allen Tate, the beautiful poet, shewed me in the Museum of Nashville, Tennessee when I was last there, a Roman short sword that had been dug up whilst laying the foundations of the Millionaires' Sports and Country Club, near that city.

But there is more to it than that. Mr Tate did me the honour to accompany me to the rehearsal in the Calanques of the pastorale of which I have already written, he going as poet, not as *chef*. That rehearsal was accompanied by a Homeric banquet, which, having previously caught the fish for the bouillabaisse, we cooked in immense cauldrons, on the beach, over leaping fires of dead wood from trees and drift wood from the water.

The place was unimaginable unless you had seen it. Try then to figure for yourself blood-red cliffs into which a blue, shining mirror should have introduced itself for miles—a fjord of the Mediterranean, a beach only to be approached in boats, with the dark-green, red trunked stone- and umbrella-pines, the multicoloured boats grouped at the landing, the incredible blue of the sky, the incredible whiteness of the light, the ten-foot flames beneath the cauldrons but pale beneath the sun. And, beneath the surface of the mirror, shoals of vermilion, of ultramarine, of amethyst fishes—and octopuses darting, like closed parasols, through the waving groves of the algae. . . .

Sixty-one bottles of wine were consumed by sixteen adults and a shoal of children that ran incessantly round the table, made from the bottom boards of the boats. They snatched a bite here, a mouthful of wine there, the banquet lasting four hours. . . . In the full sunlight, above the scorching rocks and shale, continuous songs and the speeches of the Blessed Virgin and the Holy Kings and the Jews and Saracens and Prussians of 1870. And the *chef*, obviously a baritone from the Scala at Milan, taking the part of St Joseph and swearing that with his voice he would make every one at the table cry. . . . And doing it. . . . And the tenor, a throaty blond-moustached shoe-merchant —but merely a son-in-law from Marseilles, and as such never allowed to get his part listened to. . . . And half a hundred weight of bouillabaisse. . . .

And twelve cocks stewed in wine with innumerable savoury herbs.

And a salad in a dish as large as a cart-wheel. And sweet-cream cheese with a sauce made of marc and other sweet herbs. And a pile, large enough to bury a man in, of apples, peaches, figs, grapes. . . . And the wives, dark, roguish-eyed, luscious, reclining on their elbows like the dark, roguish-eyed and luscious women on the Etruscan tombs.

And the wicked, little, eighty-two year old peasant—for all the world too like another Etruscan on another tomb. . . . He had brought down the precipitous goat-paths of the un-climbable mountain behind us the eighty bottles of forty-eight, twenty-eight and twenty-year-old wine of his own growing. . . . He sat at the head of the table and slapped always more, and always more enormous, fish from the *bouillabaisse*, onto the American ladies' plates; he interpolated perfectly outrageous songs into the pastorale, swam in the cove to shew what he could do at eighty-two and as a final demonstration—for all the world like a Roman of old in Sabina—seized one of the American ladies, threw her over his shoulder and danced round the long table with her there. . . .

"And no," said he to the black-avised wives who had been discussing, with side glances at the Marseilles son-in-law, the wickedness of two cities to which they never went, "Marseilles and Toulon are not such sinks of iniquity as all that. At Toulon you cannot get anything decent to eat." But he never went there. . . . But to Marseilles he went once a month and, having marketed his products, went to a famous restaurant and ate a two to three hundred franc lunch. . . . And, in a place where it costs you ten francs to look into a mirror, with the Prefect of the Bouches du Rhône and the Admiral Commanding the station at other tables, he would still, little old Etruscan though he was, be the guest most carefully cooked for and waited on and the most to the manner born. So at least it is related of him. I cannot say how it was as to the restaurant for it is a couple of decades and more since I could afford there to so much as look in a mirror. But why should it not be so since his ancestors, coming originally from Sidon, had been in that place for three thousand years? . . . Nevertheless those wives, looking sideways at the son-in-law, declared that never would they let *their* husbands set foot in Marseilles or Toulon. . . .

And what made it all the more to the manner born and touching was that, when it came to the song of Mary in Bethlehem we could remember that, coming to that little town the night before, all the beds had been filled by travellers, as it might have been in the year o of our era, it being the feast of that traveller's Assumption. . . . So we had slept, not in a stable it is true, but on stretchers, under pine trees, over the great drifts of shale on the mountain behind. . . .

What brings it into the story here is this: Mr Tate being at that banquet on the shore of the sea of Virgil, went home and wrote his noble poem having for its inspiration how the Trojans, landing on those shores, feasted, beside the sea. In just such a way, off just such viands—for we ate nothing there that the pious Aeneas could not have eaten, cooked in just the way his cooks prepared his viands. And if we did not eat our platters we certainly ate great manchets of bread that had been soaked in that sauce of the bouillabaisse or had lain under the twelve *coqs au vin* in their cauldrons.

quem das finem, rex magne, dolorem?

Where we went in the boat was a long bay
A sling-shot wide, walled in by towering stone,
Cracked margin of antiquity's decay—
And we went there out of Time's monotone. . . .

Where we went in the small ship the sea-weed
Parted and gave to us the murmuring shore
And we made feast and in our secret need
Devoured the very plates Anchises bore.

Where we feasted and caroused on the sandless
Pebbles, affecting our day of piracy,

PROVENCE

What prophecy of eaten plates could landless
Wanderers fulfil by the ancient sea?

When derelict you see through the low twilight
The green coast that you, thunder-tossed, would win
Drop sail, as hastening to drink all night,
Eat dish and bowl to take that sweet land in.[1]

And—this is what makes the coincidence so singular—the
first thing that the unfortunate and homesick New Yorker,
homesick not for New York but for Provence, must find on the
study table of our kind host in Bignor, which is in Sussex by the
Roman road, was the poem that Mr Tate had written after the
pastorale-rehearsal on the feast of the Assumption, in Provence
—and that he had sent from Nashville, Tennessee, where the
Roman sword is, to London, to be printed and lie on that table.
At Bignor where the Roman villa is. . . . I tell you that gave
that New Yorker some emotion—the only thing that had given
him an emotion since he had been in that island. . . . Except
of course for things in museums.

The sunlight lay for three days on Sussex. On the old
thatched houses with their pebble-work decoration; on the
beds of perennials, the heavy, still-bare ploughlands, the corru-
gated iron pig-pounds à la Denmark, the morris dancers, the
territory that, to the resounding lamentations of the neighbourhood, a whiskey-baron has got away from the hunt of 'Is Real
Lordship up to Petworth where Turner painted . . . and on
the little bathing places that beneath the bleak skies and beside
the cold sea all along that coast imitate Nice and Cannes and
St Tropez. . . . And on Arundel Castle, and Hurstmonceaux
and Bodiam, the sunlight fell, and on the chalk downs of Good-
wood and Chichester spire and the cap-touching yokels for
ever exclaiming "Sir" and all the threatened relics of the age
of homes of ancient peace. . . . And mightily that New Yorker

[1] "The Mediterranean" by Allen Tate from *New Verse*, Vol. 1. No. 5.
London, Oct. 1933.

took it all in and enjoyed it and proposed to hire thatched cottages and sit in ingle-nooks and interview yokels beside inn-fires and drive plough-teams of red Sussex oxen and hang nesting-boxes on apple-trees. . . . New Yorkers are like that—even quite sophisticated ones. . . .

As for me I had the sudden sense that I was in an island. . . . And the moment that I am in an armchair or on an island or far from the sea or near an intervening sea I am at once attacked by claustrophobia. . . . Violent claustrophobia. . . . Of course in London you do not feel that you are on an island. . . . It is the whole "b——y world" of Mr Morley's Cockney. It is true that London is the city of that most dreadful of all arm-chairs—the club one. It encircles you, the air puffs out when you sink down in it, it confines your arms, your hips, your very mind. But of course you need not go to clubs. . . . Neverthe-less, once I am outside London, I feel the island-claustrophobia. The dreadful greennesses of the countrysides frighten me. I imagine I am going to be buried in the emerald-plush sofa of a third-class Sussex pub-parlour. I feel that my thoughts are going to turn into glue; my brain into curds. I feel that if one more yokel touches his hat to me and calls me "Father" in a French-derived locution I shall scream. . . . My chest will burst. I shall suffocate if I cannot get to a hard, hot stone, flat on an iron, parched hillside, looking, between olive, almond and mulberry trunks, over the Mediterranean and over the trunks of the gum-trees from Australia and the oaks from the Teuto-burger Wald—poor expatriates introduced into a pacifist land by conquerors armed whether with the Teutonic spear or the colonial cheque-book. . . . I shall suffocate. . . . But there, on those stern, baked cliffs I might have a chance of sitting, leaned on my elbow, with leering eyes, sneering at you, the museum visitor, like the very young American poets that know all about Death . . . from on top of my baked clay tomb. . . .

Mr Tate, on the other hand, in Tennessee, knows all about Provence. . . . I can't imagine how the Roman sword got into

his museum and no one in proud Nashville would afford me
any explanation. It was perhaps dropped by a strolling company,
playing "Coriolanus." . . . So you would have had Shakespeare
in London, lapped in the tepid tide that passed by Provence, and
passing on the lore of the Romans and of the Volsces whose
capital was at Narbonne. Passing it on against the current of
the Gulf Stream to the capital of Tennessee. . . . And, even
if "Coriolanus" was never played, say by the students of Van-
derbilt University, and the mysterious sword which is worthy
to rank with Excalibur, the sword of Mercy and the other
famous swords of the world, was only the forgotten gift of
some former Nashville magnate-traveller . . . nevertheless its
existence there, like a piece of jetsam, is demonstration enough
that the civilisation of the Caesars has passed in a warm tide to
regions with which no Caesar was ever acquainted. . . . And in
the same way, Mr Tate's white colonial house with the Roman-
fashion portico giving on the Cumberland River, has its little
corner for Provence.

Certainly to come on his poem in Sussex was as startling
to me as it was to the New Yorker. It was like seeing a green
bough of almonds flower on a tree killed by ivy. . . .

For Sussex—that part of Sussex—is the Greenwich village of
London or the *Hôtel des Négociants* on the *rade* at Toulon for
those Occidental peasants. At any rate a young woman from,
I think, Poughkeepsie—or perhaps Rochester, N. Y.—told me
the other day that unless she spent several nights in that hotel
at the foot of my hill she could never be taken seriously as a
literary aspirant on Michigan Avenue—which again shews you
the influence of the warm current still mounting against the
Gulf Stream, to the shores of the Great Lakes. . . . So in
London, unless you pass your Saturday evenings in some Sussex
inn-parlour throwing darts at a paper target to the applause of
thatched-headed beings drinking beer of your providing, you
can be no London literary man. I know because once again
I can say:

[290]

"*Atque ego in Arcadia vixi.*" . . . And do not believe that my Latin ends there, for without looking at any book I can quote:

"*Valle sub umbrosa locus est aspergine multa,*

Uvidus ex alto desilientis aquae" . . . lines of the "Persephone Rapta" which would seem to counsel young women to live rather in Provence than in Sussex dampnesses. . . . And maybe young poets too. . . .

Yes, the aspiring Londoner must have his thatched cottage, his tangled, plaguily weed-filled beds of perennials, his cask of cyder, his records of patronising intimacies with the aborigines. . . . Above all that! . . . He must learn not to write "thiccy" when he means "yon" or "be" when it should be "dü be." And he must have indispensably his personal and private collection of Sussex labourers' wise-cracks. Don't again believe that I haven't mine. I could quote a hundred. I have in my day been much admired for my Sussex anecdotes. . . . Why, when I came out of Pulborough Station I ran, in the doorway, right into my old bailiff. Just standing there to see the trains come in he was. *Cela vous change un peu les idées*, they say in France. . . . Once he was actually in a train . . . with an excursion 'Is Lordship sent up to London to see the coronation. . . . Powerful big place, London. . . . Make a note of the fact that if it had been Kent he would have said . . . "Terr'ble big place London." And that fellow is a perfect mine of *obiter dicta* that in my day I could quote to Bloomsbury applause. . . . Have you the toothache, straight he will provide you with a picture of dentistry on the Western Front. . . .

"Hup you goes; down you sits; hout it goes. . . . And when you go away 'tis like walkin' on 'ail-stones. . . ."

Or of course, as I have elsewhere quoted, *ref. Provence*, it was he who said: "Wonderful country that there South of France they dü say. . . . I dü hear the bees do work there all the yeer round." Or—*philological motive*—. "Here in th' winter they do go and *dorm* (E.fr.) in theer *hames*. (E.ger.)" . . .

A little baggage like that is as necessary to the London literary aspirant as a dress-suit. It so gives you the County Family air. . . .

And there is undoubtedly sometimes sunshine in Sussex—in much the same proportion to the sunlight of Provence as is the feathered dart you throw at a cardboard target to the banderillos of Lalanda. I daresay it was that that contributed, along with Mr Tate's poems to my lamentable *bévue* of the feast of St Joan of Arc. . . .

It was one of those *erreurs grossières* that awaken you in cold sweats at night; that remain with one to the end of one's life; that are one's ruin here in earth, and that no doubt in the end the Recording Angel will tally against you far more heavily than your weightiest sins of commission. . . . As when in 1916 I asked the French foreign minister for ferrets for my battalion instead of a decoration for myself. . . . That is really a champion instance of the bévue. . . . For, if I had asked for a decoration M. Delcassé would have been pleased and I could have proceeded to ask for ferrets and got them. As it was I offended his Excellency who thought I was drunk—or perhaps even in the clutches of delirium tremens.

For what could he know about ferrets? The French soldier is rat-proof. Whereas my poor comrades in arms having lost all their ferrets by influenza missed their most congenial form of sport and passed sleepless nights with the rats trying to pull out from under their heads the knapsacks containing stolen ducks or mutton bones. . . . I have already told that story somewhere. But it continues to grow and grow on me and recurs whenever I eat beef at night. . . .

So I was walking in the Sussex sunlight with my kind host between the church with its Roman-Saxon remains and its black churchyard yews and the Southdowns—and the thatched Roman villa and the thatched cottages. . . . If I were American—or he—I might well tell you his name: but I was brought up in a great English public school. . . . I suppose it was the downs that did it. . . . They were perhaps nine hundred yards off and so looked like the Alpilles seen from nine, or the mountain behind Toulon from nineteen, miles. The effect was nostalgically similar. . . . In Provence the atmosphere has no obstacle to offer to the eye. In the bright sunshine your sight travels as far as it can carry. On my terrace looking over the sea I can see across the bay the windows in the chapel of the miraculous Virgin on top of Cap Cepet which is twenty miles away—and on the slopes of the mountain the shadows of the umbrella pines. —The young as a rule do not see so well.

In Sussex the effect is reversed. Between you and the downs in the brightest sunlight there is the curtain of moist particles, bluish, drawn up by the sun. . . . The effect, to the eye used to Provence is to throw the downs back four or five miles— and then the tufts of small firs and the little, paintbrush yews, each throwing its defined shadow, exactly resemble the umbrella pines and tufts of lavender, thyme and rosemary of the Alpines. . . . You might indeed call that part of Sussex the Provence of England—but a Provence so fugitive. For this is a country where you are for ever, mechanically, cocking one eye at the sky and, in spite of yourself, your subconsciousness whispers inside you: "It can't last!" . . . Always!

It seems absurd to call Sussex fragile. Her emblem, as I have reminded the reader, is a hog and her proud motto: "Wunt be druv." But set against the permanencies of Provence one has the dreadful feeling that, very shortly, it will all be packed up and put back in its box—the morris dancers and the thatched roofs and the aged yokels balanced on sticks and touching their hats and the whiskey barons and the Real Lordships and the literary gentlemen and the two or three spans of plough-oxen and the Roman villa. . . . For this is as far as the Romans ought to have penetrated; penetrating further they jeopardised their empire and ruined the World. But as far as here you can still feel, however feebly, the warm pulse of civilisation. One imagines the Roman equivalent of the whiskey

baron, bolting here from Rome, towards the end of May,
snatching a catchcrop or two of cabbages that the Romans in-
ordinately loved; of broad beans, field peas, watching the poor
centurions who pass half a mile from the house on Stane Street
to guard the North Wall. . . . And then, shiveringly, bolting
back, with a hundred barrels of Chichester deep-sea oysters, a
hundred crates of fowls and a hundred tanks of red mullet and a
thousand of sauer kraut, to his winter villa in the triangle of
land called *Petite Afrique* just where the Maritime Alps come
down to the sea—where the purple of bougainvillea covers the
cliffs and the banana palms droop in the tropical heat. And
there, to the grunting of the drove of Sussex hogs that he will
have sent before him by road so that they may fatten against
his arrival, he will boast of the adventures and splendours of
his sojourn amongst the lesser breeds without the Law. . . .
And will make arrangements to let or sell his Sussex estate,
before next season, to some other nitwit. . . .

   And all the while, gazing perpetually to the North from the
Great Wall, the poor centurions with red dripping noses will
be thinking the thoughts of the Bowmen of Shu in Mr Pound's
"Cathay":

"Here we are, picking the first fern-shoots
And saying: When shall we get back to our country?
. . . We have no comfort because of these Mongols.
We grub the soft fern-shoots.
When anyone says: "Return," the others are filled with sorrow.
Sorrowful minds, sorrow is strong, we are hungry and thirsty.
Our defence is not made sure, no one can let his friend return.
We grub the old fern-stalks.
We say: Will we be let back in October? . . .

   The Bowmen of Shu were of course, at the other end of the
Great Trade Route, venturing from China out amongst other
lesser breeds three centuries before the birth of Christ. . . .
They built a North Wall too. . . . But it was all one. Those
that survived returned to draw threads of water over the red

soil to their plant roots. . . . In a climate meant for occupation by human beings. . . . For we may say of civilisation, amending a little the plaint of James of Scotland about his dynasty . . . it came from a little plot of irrigated ground and in such a plot it will finish. . . .

It must there finish. . . .

I have never felt so distinctly and so terribly the earthquake tremors that run ceaselessly under our *ersatz*-civilisation as when on the feast of St Joan of Arc I went walking with my kind host along the road north of the downs and talking tranquilly of pig-breeding in the Danish fashion. I seemed literally to feel beneath my feet the stealthy snake movements of that flint road. It was time that I got back to permanencies.

In that Roman villa up the hill there are those traces of the blackmail that a civilisation in decay pays to the forces of barbarism. That Roman of the Decline had plumbing and steam-heating. A civilisation that cannot do without those things is doomed . . . is already half way back to the igloo of the Esquimau whose heating and water-supply are near perfection.

I confess that I had a sudden premonition of doom years ago in New York when all was still prosperity and no Crisis appeared to loom. . . . Not even the smallest cloud was seemingly on the horizon.

And a controversy arose in the New York papers as to at what heat a banker should keep his office if he wanted to get full work out of the unfortunate wretches that filled the space behind its counters. Apparently if it was too cold the mind worked slowly even at the mechanical work that was demanded of those hirelings. If it were too hot the brains slowed and even—horrible to relate—might grow mutinous. A touch of the comic was imported into the discussion by one financial magnate who declared that on a very hot day the sleuth of his establishment had found one of the clerks employed by the magnate actually writing poetry in office hours . . . on a very hot day. . . . Poetry addressed to one of his female fellow labourers. . . .

What was finally decided to be the right temperature at which to conserve the poor wretches already devitalised by a diet completely out of cans and so internally disinfected by the boric acids and other chemical preservatives. . . . I do not remember. Let us put it about 69° Fahrenheit; the air to be dried and devitalised by filtering through medicated cotton wool.

I confess, as I have said, to being horrified at that discussion . . . and to have felt a premonition of coming doom. Humanity, it seemed to me, ought not to be treated like that. The proceeding aroused in me feelings analogous to those that I used to feel in Lady Michelham's Red Cross Hospital at Mentone during the war. By her ladyship's generosity we were treated with a lavishness that I have never seen equalled and we were surrounded by doctors whose concern for our health and well-being exceeded that of our mothers. . . . And then, looking round the gay throngs in the magnificent rooms and on the terraces over the suave Mediterranean. . . . Suddenly one had the grisly thought that we were just being fattened to go as soon as possible back to the slaughter-house . . . as cattle are humanely treated by sagacious breeders.

This sort of matter is of course profoundly controversialist. When I see my friend Dr Lake at his devoted labours in the hospital on top of Macy's, I am lost in admiration for the industry, learning and application of that scientist bending over his charts. By the aid of science he will tell you exactly how many hours employees can work so as to shew the greatest margin of profit; in the basement, on the first floor—where there are of course drafts—on the second floor where there are fewer drafts and on the other floors where there are none. At the slightest sign of recurrent illness in any given location he will have alterations made in that location; he will work out exactly how many minutes employees must have for their lunches so as most actively and intelligently to do their afternoon's work. Macy's employees are therefore treated with all the consideration possible in a great department store. Humanity, as you might say, is the best policy. . . .

I, however, with my eyes—my incredibly presbytic eyes—fixed on a distant future when all of humanity that is healthy and capable of innocuous pleasures shall be settled on little plots of ground on the shores of the Mediterranean—and if necessary on those of the American Coasts south of the fortieth parallel—I wish Dr Lake and the benefactor who worked out the exact temperature at which bank employees must be kept would. . . . Well, I don't exactly know what I want them to do. If they should cease from their labours the lot of the employees of Macy's and the Banks would be heavily deteriorated—which I should deplore. If they continue, those immensenesses, the end of which I ardently desire, must to some extent be perpetuated. . . . With their artificial Provençal climates, their devitalised milk, vegetables, meats, fruit juices and lives.

I don't, you understand, speak as a politician but merely as an observer of life. I don't care a bit whether Fascism or Communism of the Russian type eventually prevail in the Western World. But if Lenin had preferred to establish agricultural rather than industrial communities I should have been wholeheartedly in favour of them. The curses of humanity are not property but the sense of property, not War but the ill-nature and ignorance that lead to Wars. Both these evils would have been swept away by Christianity, that tide that, sweeping from the extreme eastern shores of the Mediterranean, carried along the great Trade Route the stream of Graeco-Jewish altruism. . . . To the extreme limits of the habitable globe. Even Prussia was temporarily Christianised towards the end of the XVIIIth century. . . .

You cannot however have vast organisations without Faith—and Christianity as a faith died a few days after the 4th of August 1914 . . . the only sign of protest against that reign of crime and assassination having been the death, as soon as the effects of war manifested themselves, of Benedict X. . . . Of a

broken heart on the 19th August, 1914. . . . I like to think
that the poor old Church, thus before our common Faith died,
should, alone of all its derivatives, have achieved that tribute
to the Saviour. . . .

And so the whole Western world once the war was finished
plunged into a sort of Albigensism. . . . What else could it
do, the parallel being so very exact? . . . For the appalled
soldiery saw all the Churches of the world plunge into that
hellish struggle with the enthusiasm of schoolboys at a rat hunt.
Not a pulpit thundered that if you slay your fellow man your
forehead will bear the brand of Cain. Great lights of the
Churches plunged into the whirlpool itself—and not armed only
with maces, either. . . . I saw, in 1917, a Northern Angli-
can dignitary emerging in Rouen from the street in which was
the house presided over by Mlle Suzanne. With a revolver at
his belt and the full insignia of an infantry field officer—Not of
a chaplain!—At dawn! I was marching a number of men to re-
lieve guards. . . . I said to him in mess afterwards that he had
been very matútinal. . . . He said: "You mean, ah, matutaïnal.
. . . All Latin-derived words with the termination *inal* are pronounced *aïnal*," in his best Balliol voice. I said: As for instance
uraïnal! . . . which even deans pronounce otherwise and he
cursed me up and down, using language that would have shocked
the regimental sergeant major. . . .

I don't of course blame him. . . . Why shouldn't the clergy
of a National church be Englishmen too? . . . But I had been
marching over a hundred men—most of them non-conformists
of his battalion to whom he was well known. So that his having
been seen in a questionable neighbourhood so matutaïnally had
not been conducive to the religious discipline of H.M.'s Fourth
Army.

And there is worse than that. I mean the performance of
their sacred duties by the clergy on the battlefield. . . . Before
the great attack on Wytschaete in the Salient I was given, along
with such Catholics as there were in my battalion, the holy

communion by Father Butler, our admirable, cultured and heroic chaplain. It was a touching and primitive ceremony, we kneeling in the straw of a barn whilst the pigs moved among our feet, the shells went overhead and Father Butler preached a sermon on the more abstruse aspects of the doctrine of the Immaculate Conception. He did that very properly and humanely so that our minds should be taken off our surroundings. . . . Or there is the story, that in those days the French found touching, of the Jewish rabbi who was killed in No Man's Land whilst holding a crucifix before the eyes of dying men—incurring no doubt damnation for himself. . . . The dead however were buried as having died duly fortified by the sacraments of the Church of Rome. . . .

But even whilst we were taking the communion the thought occurred to me that it would have been better for the poor reeling world if the Church of which Father Butler was the servant had ordered him to refuse to us the sacred elements since we knelt there with the purpose of murder in our hearts . . . and better if those poor French dead had been refused admission to holy ground. . . . Those of us who came back would have come back to a world with a living Faith, a living Church, a surviving propulsion towards the example of the Founder of the Church. . . . And for the poor dead. . . . Is it not as true here and now, as it was in Provence in the XIIIth century, that God will know His own?

As it is we are in a world of Albigenses. I do not think it is exaggerating to say that the proper man today—the man of some culture and reflection believes that there are two first principles, forgets the Divine Birth of the Saviour, regards the rest of the Christian Creeds, if with affection, yet as legends having no relation with the life of the day. He believes in the necessity for personal and mental purity, like the Cathares; in the necessity for the reduction of the population; in the absolute sinfulness of wars and in the right to suicide. . . . His religion in fact, like that of the gentle people who were destroyed at the battle of Muret is rather one of negation than one of any positiveness at all. It is a product of doubt coming after immense public catastrophe in which, as he sees it, all his leaders have been found wanting—of a doubt and languor that distinguish at once the populations of London as of New York. The population of Paris itself is touched by the same spirit of hesitation as is that of North France. In the South the tendency is less marked partly because this people is inured to public catastrophe and, being almost entirely peasant, is much less affected by the present industrial Crisis. There were last month one man unemployed in the Department of the Alpes Maritimes; seven in that of the Var; under a thousand in the Bouches du Rhône which takes in the great City of Marseilles and ninety-seven in the Vaucluse. Thus the Provençal, though passing through relatively lean years on account of the imbecilities of the Tariff Wars waged for the profit of the industrialist has always been so wealthy and in addition so frugal that he cannot by any means be said to suffer more than enough to become a little more cynical than he has always been. Mildly royalist as often as not, sometimes even Bonapartist, and usually mildly Catholic he has no illusions as to the advent of a Henri V heralding the millennium or that the fact that an Emperor sat on the throne of France would cover him personally with glory. . . . As to the priest, the Provençal keeps *his* nose tenaciously out of his affairs and even out of his house. He permits his women and his children to go to mass regularly; attends as a rule the chief feasts in his church because it suits his regulated taste for festivals to go, if he is young as a bullfighter or attired in green velvet as a member of the bodyguard of St Hubert, to meet the procession accompanying Our Lady of the Castle from St Etienne des Grès to pay her yearly visit of six weeks to St Martha. He will fire off his gun with enthusiasm and with equal enthusiasm will play the trombone part in the version of the Toreador music from "Carmen" that on that great day will accompany the canon of the holy office. Or if he is old he will listen decorously to those sounds, dreaming meanwhile of the time when he too used with even more spirit to make those joyful noises. . . . But, young or old, he will vote for the election of the atheist negro mayor who will prohibit processions in his town. . . . So the Virgin, coming with Her bright, beflagged procession over the shining fields [1] is stopped at the town limits,

[1] Our Lady of the Castle used to cause me great searchings of the—aesthetic—heart. The image was made by a shepherd lad whilst keeping his flocks in the Alpilles. He was chiselling a rock when Our Lady graciously appeared and sat to him for Her portrait. When it was done She expressed Her complete satisfaction with the statue both as a portrait and as a work of art.—I particularly asked the Bishop about that last point.—There at once was presented to the world the final canon of aesthetics. There are as many schools of thought in the arts as there are rivers in Mesopotamia with the addition of those of North and South America—and there is no touchstone by which you may tell which is finally right though one and only one must so be. If then, it seemed to me, one had an authentic object that had earned the approval of the Mother of God the matter would be solved for ever. In England the approval of the Royal Family is the hall-mark of taste: if the President of the United States has his portrait painted the fortunate artist finds his prices soar to unimaginable figures and so with other Royal and chief-magistrates' families through the world. It is true that people can be found sufficiently temerarious to differ from the Royal or semi-Royal tastes. But here the Highest Royalty of all had sat. The matter thus seemed to be settled. One had only to see that statue. . . .

An obstacle however intervened. The miraculous image in its chapel does not, like the Muttergottes zu Kevelaer, wear its best clothes, those being reserved for Her visit to St Martha. Nevertheless it is so covered with lace robes, veils, crowns, wax flowers and the offerings of the simple faithful that it is impossible to see through them the slightest trace of figure or countenance. And the guardian of the chapel is incorruptible. You may not by so little as the hundredth of an inch move that priceless and sacred lace.

On a day, after a procession one year, I went into the church in the hope of really seeing. I chanced on the venerable and beloved Bishop of the place. His first words to me were: "Have you seen our beautiful Madonna?" My heart beat so that I was nearly suffocated.

I imagined his Eminence to point a venerable finger towards a perfect conflagration of candles before a pink and blue statue on the other side. . . . It was one of those objects that before the war used to be supplied wholesale by a Cologne firm that advertised that all its wares of devotion were designed by the personal sculptor to the All Highest and so might be supposed to have the sanction of the All Highest himself. . . . The All Highest of Germany, of course, not of Heaven. So also they might be expected to have the approval of our own admirable Royal Family. My heart sank in my side. Tears were almost in my eyes as I began to address the venerable churchman who now had his back to me and was pointing down a long aisle. . . . And at the same moment my eye caught the inscription shewing that statue

her great, pure gold crown is taken off Her and She is packed
into a fiacre and driven to the Place de la Concorde.

The Place de la Concorde surrounding the church is under
the control, not of the chocolate, atheist mayor but of the ivory
and silver Christian bishop. So there, to the strains of the "Toreador" march and the firing of the guns of the *chasseurs de
St Hubert* in their green velvet costumes of state that shepherd's rock is again dressed in its great crown, its gown upon
gown of priceless lace; its diamond earrings; its English twenty-
four-carat full-hunter watch, the gift of a great landowner saved
from an avalanche in the High Alps. . . . And the sun shines,
and the bells ring out and the mistral carries the sound of the
chorales away over the Rhone which is swollen because of the
heat over the snows in High Savoy and Switzerland. . . .

But, at rising from lunch, passing the time of day with one
of those fierce, half lunatic, wild-eyed missionaries that come
from time to time from Africa to preach mission-sermons in a
cooler land, I happened to say, politely, that I wondered that
one so eminent as his Eminence should waste his precious time
on us of that region. Weren't we all Catholic, there?

His Eminence grinned—rather like a tiger that, already sati-
was the image of Notre Dame de Bon Secours—who will help you whatever
your taste in art.

At the end of the long dim aisle I saw a great crown of gold on a rush-
bottomed chair and billows of white lace covering another. And two beetle-
like old ladies washing something in a pewter receptacle. . . . Our Lady
of the Castle was being given Her bath. . . .

And that image was a rude, carved piece of reddish rock. It might have
been carved by Gaudier Brzeska of Marseilles himself . . . or by the sculptors
of the cloisters at Nîmes or the façade of St Gilles. . . . Or by Mycenaeans
or North Africans, it was so simple . . . and you might say divine.

And indeed how could it be otherwise? Was not She Who sat for it
and approved of it a peasant girl with aesthetically innocent eyes, the wife—
as poor Brzeska was the son—of a carpenter, or Pierre Puget, also of Marseilles, of a jeweller, or Mistral, of a farmer, or Peire Vidal, of a furrier. . . .
Or the painters of the votive pictures themselves weavers, blacksmiths, wine-
pressers, chefs in hostelries, shepherds.

So, confident that that Tower of Ivory was, as you might say, on the
side of the angels, I installed myself art-critic to the extent of a chapter I hope
you have read.

ated, should contemplate a chicken. He said: No! Catholic! Decidedly no! . . . We were like Madame, the King's sister, who said that she had a *petite religion* of her own. . . . A little religion that did not tie us down. . . . Like the former inhabitants of that region. . . . But the word 'religion' means precisely a tying down. . . .

"You are all the same," he said, "you pick what you want when I, your servant, offer you the dish!" And he patted me ferociously on the shoulder and told me one of those piquant stories that eminent religious love to tell. . . . About a late sovereign of an adjoining country and a frail lady who had written on her photograph that was on the king's table: *"Laura, toujours à Votre Majesté"* and of how the king was appalled to find that one day the queen had added to that inscription the words: *"Et à tout le monde!"* . . . His Eminence said he had had the story from the late Lord Halifax, the President of the English High Church Union, the *brave homme* who had so laboured to re-unite England to Rome. . . . High dignitaries, you see, amuse themselves too, in the pauses between good works. . . .

But his Eminence had said it. That was ten minutes before we took the autobus to Nîmes and all the way there, whilst the bus threw us about and peasant after peasant climbed in and exclaimed joyously: *Vé . . . la mise à mort. Té, la mise à mort. . . . Fen de brut* . . . and whilst the Americans of the party were wondering how they were *really* going to like it. . . . For, having been told that the bullfighting company had failed and the Nîmes arena was to be torn down, we had not even speculated on the nature and morality of giving a bull a chance for his life instead of pole-axing him tied up in a stable. . . . Because you must not believe, though you will be told so over and over again, that the bull has *no* chance at all. It is a small one. . . . Otherwise, why is it set in all matador's contracts that they must not be asked to fight a bull that has already fought. . . . The classic instance within my recollection is that of the great animal that, I think, Joselito—or it may have been Chicuelo—and afterwards the great Maera and a substitute, all failed to kill and who still lives as a stud-bull on the Camargue. . . . In any case my companions had had no opportunity for the endless discussions that Anglo-Saxons indulge in before seeing the *corrida* and, in the bus itself, had no chance to do more than wonder what their sensations would be at the sight of blood. So that they came to it with comparatively virgin minds. . . .

But all the time I was thinking of that missionary's declaration that all that countryside had fallen back practically on its old heresies. . . . We stopped before a grim, incredibly ancient *mas*—a bare, baked farm-house that seems for ever to slide off a small pinnacle of rock more bare and more baked. . . . And, as long as I can remember, I have wanted to own, or at least to live in, that grim *bastidon*.

I suddenly imagined a crowd of Albigenses of the XIIIth century issuing, as they probably did, from those very doors, armed with cross-bows, hatchets and partisans, rushing to the attack, hoods flying, of a detachment of Simon de Montfort's. . . . And then I considered, the bus having stopped within a hundred yards of it, that there was no particular reason why I should not at least try to secure that desirable residence. It had used to be twenty miles from anywhere. But now that it was at a bus stop there was no reason, even if there were no local drinking water, why one should not get filled tanks from Nîmes or nearer . . . or why one should not live in contact with. . . . Upon my word, I had almost written "civilisation." . . .

CHAPTER III

ANIMAM NON COELUM MUTARE

I DON'T know—I have indeed been worrying a good deal lately
—about what will happen to Paris under the New Dispensation. . . .

We have agreed that the habitable world ends at Valence,
going North. . . . And indeed immediately after Valence you
come to Lyons which city, to give you a foretaste of what you
may expect, has I again say a worse climate than any of the
great industrial towns of the rest of the world—worse than that
of London or that of Manchester. Because of that, cooking there
begins to be excellent and so continues until it reaches its Mecca
in Dijon, deteriorating gradually until in London it reaches its
unspeakable Nadir. . . .

But Paris is another matter. Until you reach it the climate
is bearable, and even useful, for a climate that will produce the
great wines of Burgundy cannot be wholly condemned. It must
have a share of sunlight. On the other hand it will not produce
the olive and no country can be wholly blest that will not give
you the most beneficent of all fluids. . . . But as soon as you
reach the depths of the valley of the Seine you are in a region
with a climate that is more than dubious, edging on territories
that are definitely Northern and only to be visited in snatches
when the barometer is at set fair.

So that at first sight one would say that all that is left for
Paris is to decline into a summer resort, Dijon becoming the
world centre of cookery, Avignon that for the Arts, and the

financiers, touts, Members of both Chambers and their hangers on who together fill all the atrocious Haussmannised Quarters being painlessly—but not *too* painlessly, exterminated.

They might perhaps, as was done with the dogs of Constantinople, be set on an island off the Atlantic shores, and there left until they had devoured each other until only a couple or two were left. Then that residue might be kept at the Vincennes open air zoo as a horrible reminder of humanity to remain civilised!

And Paris could then serve as a pleasure-cum-night-life city for those not inclined to face too bad climatic conditions—for it is to be remembered that in Paris on most days between March and September you can sit outside the cafés. In the meanwhile those who were not too *frileux* could, as people today tour the fjords to see the midnight sun, make short dashes into Sussex, as far as Chichester . . . to see where the Great Route died away. . . .

But obviously that fate would be too ignominious for a city that—patriotism whispers, "next to Nîmes"!—is the most beautiful in the world and the most sacred to the humanities. . . . And immediately the solution comes. The function of Paris would be that of educating the world as to life.

You would pull down everything on the right bank except the fringe of buildings along the Seine, leaving no stone upon another. You would clear out and afterwards fiercely disinfect all the buildings on the North side of the Place de la Concorde. You would export to Alaska where they could be kept in cold storage about seven hundred acres of Old Masters from the Louvre leaving only the Primitives, the Impressionists and their successors, the Brueghels, the Poussins and a few works of the contemporaries of Poussin. . . . And think of the pure joy of going to the Louvre intending to see a Clouet, a Kranach and a couple of Cézannes and to be able to do it without having to traverse seven acres of Titians, twenty-five of Rubens's and the *Gioconda!* The rest of the Louvre you would give to a vast school of cookery and domestic lore, with the proviso that anyone found guilty of trying to enter that sacred fane with any boric acid, pheno-phenyl or other food preservative, implement for pasteurising milk or labour-saving device should be instantly shot as a traitor to the New Dispensation. . . .

And that at once brings one to the contemplation of the case of Science. . . . What could you do with Science in a new world founded on Provence and the laws of the Great Trade Routes? . . . Science has done more than anything—more than the Churches themselves—to break the faith in its imperial destinies, of humanity. . . . For a generation before 1914 we were deafened by assertions of the benign services that Science would render to humanity . . . and then when came the day of humanity on its trial, just as the Albigenses saw that the first use to which Christianity was put was their extermination, so the first use of Science in the mass was to put an end to infinite millions of human lives. . . . And indeed, sitting as I am writing on my iron hillside looking over the Mediterranean and the bay in which Ulysses once slept, I am deafened by the roar of six squadrons of hydroplanes of six each, passing just over my roof; and the Port Extérieur is whitened as if by the fiercest mistral by the bombs that they are dropping. Each bomb purports to contain sufficient gas invented by a Heidelberg scientist to impart glanders to a thousand human beings. . . . And drifting across the roads comes the artificial mist that will soon blot out all the visible world.

I do not pretend to all knowledge or to a brain that can solve all problems, but for the moment I wish that Raleigh had never seen his kettle lid moved by steam, that Newton had been killed by his apple, that Lord Lister had died in his mother's womb and Archimedes of pneumonia caused by wetting his feet before ever that washing had inspired him to discover his Principle and to cry *Eureka!*

Obviously I am not the one to deprive an anxious mother at the bedside of her sick child of the services of a doctor. . . .

But the whole affair is so paradoxical that I hardly dare write
even as much as that. . . . Science at once evolves the principles
of eugenics, preserves the lives of infinite millions of the mentally and physically defective and enables millions of men to
move about the world carrying cans of explosives and bacteria
and other cans containing inferior, scientifically preserved foods,
and so to destroy other millions of their fellows. In the meantime with those same preserved, pasteurised, refrigerated, chem-
icalised and *ersatz* foods it lowers the vital and intellectual forces
of whole continents and at the same time throws into hopeless
confusion the markets of the universe. . . .

So, if it were left to me I should give to physicians the
Jeu de Paume, to surgeons the Ministry of Marine, to herbalists
the rue Royale—with, to encourage them, the death penalty if
discovered in possession of any apparatus for producing synthetic products; to surgical, medical and obstetric nurses I would
give the south side of the Rue St Honoré as far as the Café
de la Régence and to electricians the whole of the North side
of that street. The whole of the Latin Quarter and the Rue de
l'Ecole de Médecine I should devote to the theoretic education
of market gardeners, giving them the destroyed Haussmann
Quarters for putting their theories to the proof and giving to
the students of the Fine and Applied Arts, of the humaner Letters, of Abstract Thought the whole of the rest of the Sorbonne
buildings and of the only Quarter that matters. . . . As for
Night Life in its reduced and atrophied condition it could do
very well with a couple of streets in an expurgated Montmartre.

Faith, in short, died after the war—every sort of Faith and
it is time to get back to life. . . . And Paris, curiously enough,
is the one of the great cities—the one tract of land outside
Provence and Burgundy which is her appanage—where close-
ness to life has been most tenaciously maintained. You get there
the most and the best manual domesticity; the most tolerable
cooking; the fewest canned goods and departmental stores; the
most *petites industries* and non-machine craftsmanship. And

above all—of course once more outside Provence and Burgundy —the most amazingly efficient market-gardening—which is the only way of innocently getting something for nothing, or for so little as makes no difference. . . . And considering the difficulties of her climate you might well say that that is the proudest feat of no mean city. . . .

Indeed all that the New Dispensation would do to the capital of the Ile de France would be to change the proportions of her employment of time and to disturb the order of her hierarchies. . . . Even today she is a city of a constantly fluid population, the far greater proportion of Parisians consisting of provincials who come to her in order to gain sufficient to return as soon as possible to the tending of their gardens in their *pays* and *patelins*. And, because of that she is, amazingly, a city of market-gardeners. For miles and miles outside that city, far into Normandy, into Burgundy, into Picardy, into Champagne, you see the little boxes, little cabanons, little cottages in which the Paris shopkeeper lives for his Saturday afternoons and Sundays and where unceasingly he plies trowel, hoe, secateur and spade. . . .

And all, as I have said, that the New Dispensation would do to him, as for all humanity, would be to change the proportion of his hours. He would be for five and a half days in his garden and one and a half per week behind his counter. . . . And he would be a radiantly happy man with a continually smiling wife and two indefatigably healthy children . . . all of them taking a weekly day off to go to the *mises à mort* at Chartres or Vernon or Crécy-en-Brie.

And the same with all the other avocations or professions. The question of the fate of the Machine is probably what bulks largest in the human mind at this date. The psychology of the Roman Empire was probably the largest factor in the decision of human destinies for many hundreds of years—for a couple of thousand if we include its influence on the Empires that succeeded. The Empire of the machine, gradually and fatally coming into its own, has lasted since soft iron came into general circulation—say since the last two decades of the eighteenth century. It has long been obvious to a number of minds—I prophesied as much thirty years ago—that the unreined Machine and man could not exist for long in the same universe. And today unbounded faith in the Machine, as in Science and as in the Churches and, as amongst thinkers, in Nationalisms, is a thing of the past.

The one thing that remains stable is the land in a dry, temperate-to-hot climate—and along with the land, the Arts in all their branches whether called Fine or Domestic. For it should be kept for ever in the forefront of the mind that who sweeps a room or sows seeds or plays the pear-drum in the name of humanity makes that and the action fine.

The land should be in a dry, temperate-to-hot climate because the rigors that that may present can be mitigated by skilful irrigation; but nothing can remedy damp with its attendant coldness—and there is no sense in cultivating unprofitable land when the land between the fortieth and twentieth parallels of the globe can supply unlaboriously all the vegetable food needed for the human race. . . . But I will undertake, reaching my own couple of acres on the Mediterranean on the 16th May, to be able to keep in food my own family and guests entirely by the labours of my own hands—except of course for wheat and dairy products and sugar which I could perfectly well produce if I were in the mood. . . . And that by the 15th July.

I am aware that there will be protests. But I am not preaching a back-to-the-land crusade. I am merely prophesying. To that condition the world must inevitably come and it is as well to prepare oneself in time. I am aware that I shall be told that I make enough money by books to pay for my bread, butter, tea, sugar and clothes. That is true. . . . But the publishing of books is drying up, like every other branch of trade, commerce and industry. In the middle ages, as I am never tired of reminding you, they used to say that when land is gone and money spent then learning is most excellent just as they used to say that literature is a good stick but a bad crutch. But learning is no longer a safe way to earn one's bread and there is just one stick left that can if necessary become a perfectly good pair of crutches. . . . So as long as trades and industries remain I should recommend you to support yourself sparingly by them and to trust to your little plot of ground to provide you with luxuries. For there is no grape sweeter than that which you pluck from your own vine nor, unless you have been raised in Putney or the Bronx, is there any sweeter occupation.

It is the strong conviction of that fact that makes France in general and Provence in particular the only stable and prosperous states in the world. But the inhabitants of Putney and the Oranges immensely outnumber all the thinking men of the world and it is the occupations of their spare times that is the real difficulty in front of us. . . . You will suggest to one of them that the ideal—as well as the only practicable—state is one of very small communities belonging to hundreds of little nations each not much larger than, say, Monte Carlo; without rigid boundaries, violently settled codes of manners, without lethally supported senses of property. . . . And imagine his guffaws! . . .

You will point out to him that he will work only for one day and a half a week at whatever his avocation may be. . . . For he may be a cobbler, a silk-embroiderer, a miner, an electrician, a motor-mechanic, a strolling player, an aviator. . . . In that case, if he is a handicraftsman he will work at home. If his vocation makes him occupy himself with machines he will be flown to Paris for his thirty-six hours of employment; or to his mine; or to the Camargue to tend the bulls; or to his farm in the wheat-belt . . . and flown back on the conclusion of his turn of duty.

That won't seem so bad to him. . . . But then he will ask you what he will do with his leisure. . . . You will say that he will take a hand in the garden. Then he will help the silk-embroiderer; write songs for the strolling players; paint frescoes on the house-fronts; rehearse in the *conte-fables;* practise the art of the matador; cook on feast-days for the Viscount; command the body-guard of the Count, or of the Exarch, or the President, or the Commissar, according to the form of government of the community that he shall choose to honour with his residence. And he will play *boules,* or go to the movies, or fly to Marseilles to see if he cannot pick up some cinnamon or spices, or command a corporal's guard in the war against the next village, or go to see Mrs Patrick Campbell play her new part when, having strolled along the Great Route, she arrives at his little fortified town. . . . Or contest in the combat of *tenzones* in the local Court of Love. . . .

So he will yell: "Me live in a backwoods town! . . . Me never eat canned goods again! . . . Me go native! . . . Me live with Dagoes! . . . Me eat things out of a garden! . . . Me wear home-made pants! I *don't* think! . . . What a hope! . . . Oh . . . *hell!*"

It will however come to that after the world has passed through the preparatory stages of Fascism or Communism of the Russian variety or the mutually exterminating contests of those two opposed world tendencies. . . . We must go back to the Dark Ages. . . . For if we do not go back to the Provençal Dark Ages we shall go back to those of the Teutoburger Wald with the poison-gas clouds for ever above the appalled tree-tops. . . .

I do not suppose we shall get rid of—or even that it would be desirable entirely to get rid of—the Machine. I do not suppose that we shall ever not have War with us, or rid ourselves entirely of the sense of property, or of Churches, or of Science or even of Law which, ever since the Evil side of the Dual First principle put a *tabu* on the *pamplemousse* and Eve ate the first brussels sprout, has been the primary curse of humanity. And it would be hopeless to think of ever being relieved of the final curse, national patriotism.

But all these things must—they will inevitably—be made little. They will be reduced to their proper status either because the armament firms and scientists will blot out almost the entire populations of the world, leaving here and there mere pockets of men. Or else by a change of heart in humanity!

One way or another the number of machines and of machine hours worked must be reduced to a minimum. The wars of the nations must be little wars of little nations brought about by local jeers; the religions must be little religions; the churches without temporal powers; the leisure enjoyments be individual enjoyments. The glorification of Mass must disappear. You will talk of the largest pumpkin in the village as a glory, not of the largest armament-factory in the world. There must be the change of heart—the progression.

Christianity, the distillation of the Mediterranean spirits of Judaism and Hellenism, gave us the injunction that we must love our neighbours as ourselves. The Boston tea-party led to the declaration that all men—except niggers, Jews and Catholics —are born free and equal and that every man is as good as his neighbours—and better.

The maxim that will save the world will—if the world is to be saved—be found in the ultimate discovery that you must love your neighbour better than yourself and that, all men being born free and equal, every man's neighbour—and in particular niggers and the Mediterranean races—is as good as oneself . . . and better.

That is what is meant by the Latin schoolboy tag that I have chosen as epigraph for the conclusion of this book. . . . You must, when you travel lay more stress on changing your soul and your cuisine than on covering the roads of the world beneath the skies. . . . I met an upper-form boy from a great English Public School the other day. . . . A superior classic, not modern, wallah. Someone in the company, appositely enough, mentioned the late *corrida* at Nîmes. . . . That English schoolboy exclaimed:

[313]

"What *damnable* cruelty. . . . The stinking French!" He added that a Frenchman in the train had given him a great sandwich that so stank of garlic that he had been inclined to throw it at the fellow's head. . . . As however he had had not enough French to venture to go into the restaurant car he had decided to eat the sandwich. . . .

So little will the humaner letters do for amenities between nations! Truly, unless the watchmen watch the gate the labourers labour in vain. . . . I am thinking of that unfortunate boy's classic masters who should surely have told him that since he was going to the Provincia Romana, the very home and centre of such lore as he and they had, and the very region of a three-thousand-year-old, unchanged civilisation, it might be as well if he tried to improve himself according to that model. . . . After all the Athenians *did* fight one of their bloodiest wars in defence of their garlic fields. . . .

Or again the Romans except for their armament lords and fascist Imperators lived almost entirely on, and had a passion for, a purely vegetable diet with a little fish thrown in now and then. The most impassioned writing of the grave censor of life that was Cato is contained in his treatise on the varieties, the varieties of flavour and the methods of cultivation of no—not of the red mullet which fetched its weight in gold—but of the cabbage. He devoted to the production of that simple vegetable the same passion that he gave to the destruction of Carthage. And an almost purely vegetable diet varied with a little fish still characterises the tables of the inhabitants of Provence today. So that their cuisine is rather picturesque than plutocratic; [1]

[1] One of the most distinguished of gastronomes of the last century has written as follows about the cookery of Provence. As he was a Northern Frenchman I quote him rather than lay myself open to the suspicion of local patriotism. . . . Says then Désiré Louis:

"Les Provençaux semblent avoir hérité du goût des Grecs et Romains pour la bonne cuisine. Ils savent la faire abondante, pleine d'ingéniosité et avec le degré d'excitation voulue pour l'appétit et pour les sens. Sous le ciel bleu, au milieu d'une nature gaie et fleurie, remplie de parfums et de couleurs, le Provençal s'exerce en toutes choses, d'une façon amusante et joyeuse pour les convives.

and, as I have said, if you want real succulencies it is to the damper regions of the Bourgogne, north of Lyons that you must go. . . . Nevertheless the real Provençal cuisine is exactly suited to the Provençal climate and, at any rate during the heats of summer, you are apt to have to pay for it if—as I myself seldom do—you go outside it. It has for me the defect that it is rather bulky, which is of necessity the case with a largely vege-tarian diet, and there is nothing I dislike so much as a feeling of distension after a meal. So that when I am at home I eat astonishingly little—so little that the Septentrional would hardly believe that on it I can get through a fairly gruelling day of writing and gardening. . . . For breakfast at seven-thirty some coffee and a couple of slices of bread and butter; for lunch at one a salad and, very, very rarely, a little goat's milk cheese; for dinner about two ounces of veal or mutton—never beef— or in the shooting season, an ortolan, a grive, a little pheasant, venison or wild boar; one vegetable from the garden—tomatoes, egg plants, *petits pois*, *pois-mangetout*, string-beans or sorrel and some stewed fruit or jam, of which I make great quantities; and sometimes some junket. Occasionally instead of the meat or game I have two or three grilled, fresh sardines or anchovies, or a grilled *mulet*—a Mediterranean fish that is nearly as good as the *loup* and a tenth of the price of that gift from the gods. . . . Nevertheless I do not lose weight—which I put down to the olive oil and *fines herbes* which accompany or assist at that cuisine. For olive oil alone is a sufficient nutriment and *fines herbes* assist in the digestion of other foods. And your weight is not a question of the quantity of food you put into your mouth but of how much you digest.

Now then my nearest neighbours are, on the one hand, a

Je me souviens d'un excellent chou farci préparé à notre intention avec toutes les règles de l'art culinaire. Nous étions dix à table. La délicatesse, la juste mesure des produits composant cet inoubliable chou farci me firent désireux d'avoir son importante recette. . . ."

He gets the receipt—which I will spare you—and judging as well as I can by the ingredients and method of cooking it must have given exactly the flavour that Cato ascribes to his favourite Milan cabbage.

French seigneur of the *ancien régime* who is an Anglo-maniac, as it were perforce because he cannot approve of anything that has happened in France since 1792 and, on the left, a really scintillating American of about the rank of Duchess and of German extraction. The French gentleman in consequence lives entirely on underdone, rare, *saignant*—which means bleeding —*rosbif;* my charming American friend—who, *more suo* is an admirable cook—provides for her family nothing but the cuisine of Mecklenburg-Schwerin—*apfel-strudel; eisbein mit sauerkraut; gedaempfte-kalbs-hachse mit erbsen; sauer-braten mit schmier-kaese; ochs-zunge mit eingemachte-pflaum-soze* — all viands admirably calculated to produce the mediaeval frame of mind in a Nordic climate and all, as far as possible coming out of cans or otherwise sterilised.

And both my friends—the lady when she has occasion to pick at somebody and the gentleman when his car has broken down—use my garden-path as a short cut to the high-road and come upon me at my irrigation in the attire of the gone native. So I shall hear a gentle sigh and at my back will be the French nobleman.

He will say: "*Mon cher ami . . .*" and indeed he has the right to. He will explain that he and his wife have been lying awake all night thinking of my terrible case. . . . The food I eat! The way I work in the garden! . . . No human being could stand it. . . . The Provençal cooking and life are those of savages. . . . Let me take example by him and eat nothing but *boeuf saignant* without condiments and play a round of golf every morning. . . . I suggest that he come and eat with me. . . . We have today *chou farci* à la Provençale—as eaten by Cato. . . . He shudders and says: "If I thought I should have to work in a garden at sixty". . . . His tone has real pathos in it—and compassion . . . I should die, now. At the fear" . . . And if he had to eat anything à la Provençale. . . . He breaks off to ask if it isn't the bleeding beef and the beer and 'th'black'n-white' that have made England what she is? He says that that is therefore his sole diet. Thus he will probably never at sixty come down to eating à la Provençale, or to labouring the distasteful soil. He will never reach sixty. His digestion is completely destroyed; he has hardly even now the energy to drag himself along. But for the English *frootsells* he would never leave his bed.

Out of the corners of his fine, melancholy and poetic eyes he catches the flutter of a skirt down between the clipped hedges. He takes the time to express his regret that an appointment with his stomach-specialist will preclude his availing himself of my so amiable invitation and hurries away. . . . I shout after him the information that Provençal stuffed cabbage was the favourite dish of the great Cato, the Censor who never ended a speech in the Senate without throwing a bunch of figs into the House and saying: "These figs were gathered this morning in Carthage. . . . *Ceterum, censeo Carthaginem esse delendam*" as if he were Mr Hitler speaking in the Reichstag about France. . . . That Frenchman however has disappeared. . . . The Duchess is coming up the garden.

Those two unfortunately can never meet. The American lady has been taught never to speak to Dagoes; moreover France by not paying her war-indemnity debts has disgraced herself in the sight of all civilised nations. . . . The French gentleman of the *Ancien Régime* will never speak to an American. Americans live under a Republic. Moreover America by devaluating her currency has committed an act of repudiation—he himself being a very heavy sufferer—and is therefore outside the pale of civilised nations. . . .

I return to my occupation of, with my hoe, leading the irrigation water from the melons to the *petits pois*. I hear a gentle sigh. Her charming Grace is behind me. She says with breathless animation:

"Why don't you leave this *dreadful* place? . . . With your poor heart you will one day drop dead on these terrible hills"

. . . The path is of course a little steep. . . . Her eyes assume a dreamy look. . . . She says contemplatively:

"Isn't it *wrong* to water in the sunlight?"

I don't answer that in Grand Concourse they can water their window-boxes when they like with fluid from the tap and they have the idea that, if you water when the sun is on, the aspidistras, as if they had gone out without their undervests, will get inflammation of the sinus. . . . I answer instead:

"Of course it is *better* to water at dusk and dawn. The water does not dry up so quickly so the plants benefit more. . . . But it isn't *wrong* to water in the sunlight; it is only not so good. . . . And in this country we have to take our share of irrigation water when it is allotted to us. . . ."

She says:

"Of course no one but a *lunatic* would think of gardening in the South of France. . . . This *dreadful* country is tropical: that's what it is. . . . It ought to be *abolished*. . . ."

I say:

"Have a fig, Duchess. . . ."

She looks at my peas:

"I should have thought it was *wrong* to have peas so late in the year. . . . I had some beans from the market yesterday. . . . We almost *live* on beans at home. . . . They were as hard as buckshot and with a *horrible* taste. . . . But come and try my *canned* peas. . . ."

I do not say that there is a difference between vegetables cooked five minutes after they are picked and the beans that in the market they reserve for foreigners—a fortnight old and preserved with a variety of phenacitin. . . . I say:

"Take some figs, Duchess, dear. . . . The *figues blanches* on that tree are delicious. . . ."

She gives a little scream:

"Eat fresh figs from the *tree* . . . ," she exclaims, "I'd as soon think of drinking raw milk. . . ."

I say:

"I didn't of course mean you to *eat* the figs. . . ."

She interrupts with an earnest mien:

"My dear Ford," she says, "I want to speak to you very seriously. . . . Your life has, well . . . a *certain* value. . . ." And she goes on to tell me that the other day she nearly died. She had seen me eating junket. . . . Made by adding rennet to tepid, Non-Pasteurised, RAW . . . M.I.L.K!.!.!.

She herself had only drunk *raw* milk three times in her life and beside the fact that it had each time made her vomit it had had a most *horrible* taste. She attributed the serious illness of one of her children to the fact that, in a private hospital, she strongly suspected it had been given raw milk. . . . And she would as soon think of drinking that poison as eating fruit straight from the tree. . . . Without even washing it with a diluted disinfectant. . . . No, she seriously begged me to give up my dreadful habits. After all, there were *some* people still who wanted to read my books. I wasn't *quite* written out. I was too *old* to work in the garden in the hot sun. Let me take example by her husband. Would he think of gardening? Never. . . . And in this pernicious climate. . . . He had his work for the enlightening of the world as to the *real* position of the German Empire to think about and to work at, night and day. And this dreadful affectation of going native here. . . . What was it Mr Kipling had called these people? . . . Lawless degenerates? . . . Something like that.

These people ought to be rooted out. . . . You couldn't get so much as breakfast cereals in their shops. . . . And the filthy *fines herbes* and condiments that I used. . . . Didn't I know that they burned the lining of the stomach *completely* out. . . . She begged me, she really begged me, to eat more often with them. . . . To eat that very night with them. . . . She knew that I was a strict chop-for-chop man. . . . But I couldn't *expect* her and her husband and children to eat with me. . . . With all their ruined digestions! . . . Yes, to come tonight. . . . There would be Hamburger buecklinge; erbsen suppe mit nudeln; sauer bohnen—from Boston itself; gaenser-brust pastete mit sauerkraut; herring-salat; kreppeln. . . .

I did not interrupt her rapturous catalogue by reminding her that it was then the middle of the dog-days in the South of France. I merely accepted with rapture her kindly invitation. She said with gentle reproach. . . .

"And you asked me to eat fruit fresh from the *tree!*"

I exclaimed with indignation:

"I *never* asked you to eat fruit from a tree. . . . I would as soon think of offering you tripe from an umbrella-stand." . . . You could, I went on, make umbrella-stands into tripe. It was one of the wonders of science. . . . Mr Wells had told me all about it—years ago, in his Utopian phase. Utopia, he had said would be here when all humanity carried its week's supply of food in its waistcoat pocket. . . . In little tabloids manufactured synthetically out of wood so as to provide all the real nourishment you needed. . . . Then you would fill yourself with some prepared wood-fibre which would pass through you without being digested. . . . You would do that so as to give yourself the agreeable distention of the stomach that, said Mr Wells, is the chief pleasure of eating. . . . In Germany, even now, there was a scientist who could so manipulate wood-shavings that he could give to the finished product the aspect, consistency and flavour of any meat from goose-breast to stuffed breast of veal. . . . The process was at present rather costly but, when it was commercialised wouldn't it be the saving of the World? . . . But figs fresh from the tree? . . . Never. . . . What I had meant was that her Grace should pluck a branch of the *figue blanche* and send it in her private plane to General von Goebbelings—if that was the name. . . . Then he could throw it on the floor of the appalled Reichstag and say: "These figs were picked in Provence this morning. . . . *Ceterum, censeo Provinciam esse delendam. . . . Ubrigens meine ich dass Provenz zerstoert sein darf. . . .*" . . . I said that those were the words of the other great Censor. . . .

The lady looked at me curiously. . . .

"I wish you would tell me, Ford," she said, "whether you really *know* Latin or whether you do as other writers do—look up some quotations and write your story up to them. . . ."

And, remembering how often the part of me that now is on a hard rock, had stung as the penalty for writing a false quantity in Latin verse, I began:

"*Infandum Duchesa jubes. . . .*"

Her charming face lit up with a certain kindly contempt. She exclaimed:

"Oh, *that* . . ." and catching out of the corner of her charming and satirical eyes the form of my French friend re-descending the hill with a gadget for his invalided 16cv, she tripped lightly back the way she had come.

Alas, it *was* in the middle of the dogdays. I had been up at five and dug till seven when I had had my coffee; I had irrigated till nine when those two martyrs to indigestion had come upon me. . . . After that I had written till one—which is too long; had lunched off a tomato salad; taken my siesta; set out some romaine plants—and a hell of a lot of watering they would need if they were to come to anything. . . . And I will confess that very few of them have. Still they will give us a salad or two. . . . Then, having no cooking either to think of or suggest, I wrote from five till seven—which is too long. . . .

And suddenly I came to the conclusion that must have been lurking all day in my craven heart. . . . I couldn't face it. . . . I can normally digest a keg of nails. . . . But not when I have written too long—as I had been doing daily for some time. . . . I would have attempted *Hamburger buecklinge;* or Boston beans; or goose-breast *en paté;* or pea-soup with noodles. . . . Any one of them. . . . But all of them—with trimmings and makeweights. . . . Ah, *mais non.* . . . In Mecklenburg-Schwerin in December, perhaps. . . . But not looking out on the moonlit island where the syrens sang . . . in the full glare of the immense dog-star. . . .

I was suddenly reminded of a novel—I think by the Freiherr von Ompteda that I had read during the war. . . . Its heroine came in one day from a glorious ride on the moors in the stinging breath of the October wind. She threw her reins to the butler, sprang from her horse and exclaimed: Bring me a snack. . . . Bring me five poached eggs, a liver sausage and a quart of beer. . . . After that she had lunch. . . . And, says the author, that is the way our glorious German women are brought up so as to give to the Empire its incomparable millions of soldiers. . . .

And for the first time in my life I failed to take up a challenge. I must have been ageing. I sent the rest of my family to partake of that banquet, telling them to say, for the pleasure of my really amiable and distinguished friend, that I was suffering from a touch of sunstroke and indigestion. . . . There is no pleasure so great as being able to say "I told you so." . . . And that enthusiastic controversialist availed herself of that opportunity for a couple of hours. . . . As for me I dined off a soft-boiled egg taken in a glass *more Americano* and afterwards did some more irrigation by the light of the moon and the dog-star. . . .

And—curious detail and one that I cannot explain—when my family came back from that banquet they smelt so strong of garlic that I had to implore them to keep their distances. It appeared that her kind Grace, determined that for once in my life I should have enough food to eat had had a couple of capons cooked and had them stuffed each with twenty-five cloves. . . . She was under the impression that she would thus be giving me *poulet béarnais* but she was a little mistaken. The dish of Henri Quatre has the garlic stewed under the fowl and you—though *I* don't—eat the garlic-cloves as if they were haricots blancs. . . . Boston beans. . . . I may be a hero but I am not such a one as the *roi bon enfant*. . . .

And I will here again take occasion to emphasise that the real function of the condiment is not to be tasted but to be just merely suspected and to clean your tongue so that you may appreciate the flavour. . . . A *chef* whose dishes leave you certain of the ingredients he has used is not a good *chef*. . . . You should be left in the condition of thinking that you catch fleetingly the perfume of garlic, thyme, absinthia officinalis, nutmeg, clove or anything but perhaps taragon or basil of which certain quantities may on special occasions be used. Such regional cooking as the *poulet béarnais* is suited for the regions in which it is cooked, by reason of climate, occupation or for other local reasons . . . or of course for Protestant Kings who are above the law. . . . So that in one region of France you should never eat the *plats régionaux* of another region . . . except in Paris which has no *plats* of its own.

. . . ANY MORE THAN IF YOU COME FROM PUTNEY OR THE BRONX YOU SHOULD ASK IN PROVENCE FOR YOUR NATIVE FOODS AND AMUSEMENTS OR THAN I IF I VISITED YOU OUGHT TO BE OFFENSIVE IF YOU FAILED TO PROVIDE ME WITH BOUILLABAISSE BOURIDOU OR BULLFIGHTS. . . .

To that—which is the final moral of this work about what Mr Allen Tate calls "the sweet land" of Provence—I will return. . . . For the moment I am still intrigued by the case of the Duchess and the cloves of garlic. . . . I cannot feel sure why she did it. . . .

It may well be that, having so efficiently roasted me with her tongue in the morning, she thought she ought to make it up to me by succulent viands. That would be in tune with her kind nature. Or she may have thought that such an excess of what she took to be my favourite and unspeakable condiment might disgust and so uplift me. . . . Or it may be that, being German, she did not flinch from *knoblauch*—And I will here insert the statement that outside Burgundy, Paris and such regions of France as no Anglo-Saxon ever visited—the general run of German cookery is certainly the best and the best-adapted to its climate of any that I know. . . . I mean not merely the cooking in private houses but the public foods of restaurants. Except for

[323]

rare mediæval survivals like smoked tongue with plum sauce and assafœtida, you will get in almost any German restaurant—and in quite cheap ones—good meats, really cooked and prepared with properly balanced condiments. . . . So obviously, as a German, she would not shrink from the indispensable accompaniment to all meat dishes. . . . But as an American? . . .

Is it then possible that the impossible has been accomplished and that one Anglo-Saxon traveller's mind has at last been opened? For a convert may be pardoned for zeal; to employ twenty-five cloves of garlic when three would have been more than sufficient is wrong. But what would that be as against the glorious fact of a turn in the tide of international pickings? For one of the greatest dangers to the peace of the world is the Anglo-Saxon, of whichever branch of that great sister-cousinhood—who, travelling for pleasure, rings the welkin with complaints at not finding in the more civilised countries that he visits his own special home nastinesses.

The first thing that the traveller of any nationality must learn is that the habits of the country that he visits are infinitely more adapted to the leading of a reasoned and harmonious life there than are those of his own country. Then, after long travel, he may find some sense of international proportions and may venture to criticise the foreigner and even to spend some praise on his own country. As an expatriate I may properly praise in England the admirable nature of her constitution, of her public services and institutions. I am entitled to praise also the kindliness of her population or the incomparable traditions of her judiciary. I may even go so far as to palliate the atrocities of her *cuisine* and the complete absence of æsthetico-critical alertness of her peoples by laying them to the account of her lamentable climate and her imbecile tariffs which occasion the permanent, brain-numbing, indigestion in her inhabitants. . . . But I must not, if I am a public-schoolboy paying my first week-end visit to Paris and being asked ten sous for a postage stamp, yell out at the top of my voice that all Frenchmen are robbers because I receive only fifty centimes change for the franc that I have tendered. I must wait to form a judgment until I have discovered that a sou is five centimes.

I hate Germany, her constitution, the rigidity of her scholastic thought, her heroic traditions and every side of her public life and manifestations and all her inhabitants north of a line drawn from Hamburg to Frankfort on the Oder—a territory that with the exception of Nietszche—and what an exception!—has produced no single artist or thinker since the world began. I hope that the end of Mr Hitler—and soon—may be a long stay in a cage in the Tiergarten of some small South German town. But I hate Germany only as a disturber of the world and I am ready to assert that the South and Middle German is a man of infinite conscientiousness, kindliness, love for the arts, domestic self-respect and dignity who contrives, even in a Northern climate, to make his territory flow with music, poetry and simple, innocent, kindly and deeply pacific merriment—and all this to a degree unknown outside Provence and the Mediterranean littoral. If, in short, you could transfuse into Germany the public psychology of England, into England the spirit of the private life of the Germans, into North France some of the spirit of the public services of England and some of the personal kindliness of manner of the German of the South—and of course the Austrian! . . . And if you could take the fine flower of the resultant population and settle them alongside the Provençaux "between the Durance and the sea." . . . And if you could let all the remaining populations of those other regions blissfully fall asleep and never re-awaken (And of course you would have to apply a similar process to the mixed populations of the North American Republic, settling them on the Atlantic and Pacific littorals below the fortieth parallel where Florida, Louisiana and Mexico supply a good flow of the Latin tradition). . . . Why then the Western World could, without shame, and in perpetual peace, face the rest of Civilisation.

Until the traveller can voyage with that end in his mind

there will be no hope for humanity. That day must eventually arrive for the end of humanity is not yet and in no other way can it logically be preserved. . . . Let us then go to the bull-fight, leaving Paris and taking the spectacle of the exploits of Lalanda, Chicuelo and Dominguez en route for the pleasures of the Riviera and the great view into Italy from Provence, that

The Great View into Italy from Provence

singular eastern frontier at the Pont St Louis where as I have said the traveller finds himself faced by a minatory array of fixed bayonets, machine-guns, uniforms and arresting fists. . . . Looking back into Provence he sees, as if symbolically, that that country is guarded by a man lolling in a deck chair, a Stetson hat well down over his closed eyes, waving to the passing trav-eller a negligent hand that tells him to put back his extended passport. I do not say that the frontier of Provence is not as efficiently guarded as that of the outside world: it is no doubt even more efficiently attended to. But as an international gesture the dozing guardian is more satisfactory. . . . Manners after all makyth Nations.

A single day in Paris is a bewildering experience. It is as if the film of your life had been hastened up rather than slowed down. You arrive at the Gare St Lazare at an hour you don't know because you are allowed to sleep in the train till about eight. . . . Your last previous sensation has been that of a sudden feeling of liberation at arriving in black Dieppe in the smallest hours.

And that reminds me that I have never recounted the *bévue* that I made in Sussex on my way to Paris and the South. I was walking along the quasi-sunlit road of Sussex with my kind host between the yews of the Anglo-Saxon churchyard and the little yews that cast shadows on the downs. There burst suddenly from my lips the words:

"My God! Am I really going to be out of this prison to-morrow?"

I do not apologise for the sentiment. It has been that that has built up our Sister-Cousin Empires—the adventurous lads sighing to be out of sound of Bow Bells or sight of Manhattan Island. But it was not a sentiment to give vent to in the hearing of a kind, cultured and admirable host who over shining naperies in venerable manorial rooms, had dispensed cyder fit for heroes and dishes almost too good for the Gods. . . .

At any rate, arrived at Dieppe and once in the train, though still filled with English comestibles. . . . No, no—that is not the way to put it; nor is it even yet the truth. . . . Because then, the cuisine of our kind host had been most admirably cosmopolitan we knew no longer the terrors of Night Starvation, Insomnia, Bile Trouble and the rest of the nightmares that for months had attended on our couches. . . . "As per advt.", is I believe the phrase. . . . But no sooner were we in the train than deep

sleep sealed our eyelids and we were being awakened at the
Gare St Lazare and I found myself saying: "It's the fifteenth of
May, the feast of St Boniface . . . no, of Ste Denise. . . .
There ought to be a *mise à mort* at Nîmes to celebrate Pente-
cost. And on the way we will eat *tournedos-foie-gras* and drink
one of the noblest of vintages at Dijon. . . . At Dijon which is
in Burgundy where grew the finest of all Primitives except for
Avignon. . . . Think, amiable transfuge from the Bowery. . . .
Tomorrow we shall be seeing the *Adoration des Bergers* of
Robert Campin and the *Annunciation* of Melchior Brederlamm.
. . . And next day the Roman Theatre at Orange. . . . And
next day the Roman villas, hundreds and hundreds of them at
Vaison. . . . And next day the Fromentins and the Unknown
Masters of Avignon and the marvellous Quarton at Villeneuve-
lès-Avignon. . . . And next day the Only Bastide, confronting
the white tower of Aucassin across the Rhone. . . . And next
day, if the Gods are kind on the Feast of Tongues, in the arena
that the Romans built. . . ."

My New York friend shivered and muttered:
"You are mixing your theology. . . . The Feast of Tongues
is a Christian festival. . . . Christians are monotheists. . . . The
Gods on the other hand. . . ."

I said: "*Connu; connu, aimable pédant Occidental.* . . .
Nevertheless the Universe is very large and in it there is room
for an infinite number of Deities. . . ."

He said: "Where did you pick that up?" . . . I answered:
"From one of my own books that you have never read, old
bean."

I don't know how my soul had leisure to appreciate the
ESCARGOTS DE BOURGOGNE; the TOURNEDOS FOIE GRAS; the CLOS
ROMANEE that passed at Dijon our enchanted lips. . . . By an
amiable remains of the Trans-Atlantic barbaric that poor fellow
took hors d'œuvres instead of snails . . . and admirable the hors
d'œuvres of Dijon are. But you should have seen his face when
he smelt the perfume across the table, from my snails. . . .

Hors d'œuvres—the very best of hors d'œuvres are lamentable things intended by their exaggerated flavourings to blind your tongue to the defects of the meats that follow. . . . And when he tasted the sauce from the shell. . . .

He forgot entirely to discuss the morality of witnessing bull-fights, a topic that he had saved up for that repast. . . . And indeed he never did get an opportunity to discuss that subject.

The rush in Paris had been so incredible. . . . They will tell you that Paris is empty of English and Americans. . . . I only know that we moved about in troops of them. . . . And of Russians and Palestinians and Poles. . . . And we ate in Russian, in Armenian, in Greek, in Belgian, bistrots and bought peanuts from an Abyssinian Jew who—black as the Shulamite—was descended from king Solomon and spoke the dialect of Sullivan Street. . . . How, in the ten minutes prescribed by my friend, I got together the dates for this book and for the "History of Our Own Times" that I am writing not even the omniscient Principal Librarian of the British Museum could tell you. . . . The most I know is that you have seen some of the results here. . . .

And the trouble for that over-seas hesitator as to the morality of bull-fights was that, as always happens when one passes through Paris, troops of candidates for expatriation detached themselves from that capital and decided to have the benefit of my guidance through Provence. . . . That has always been my agreeable destiny. . . . And there is really nothing I like better than pointing out Birthplaces to enthusiastic searchers into the associations of Lafayette—who was born at Chavagnac on the Haute Loire. . . . Nevertheless it is not always all beer and skittles. . . . Champagne will come creeping in. . . .

I see that my time has come to talk about wine.

There is one only course to pursue if you wish to taste the best wines of France. I have drunk French wines ever since I was eight and ought therefore to know all about it. . . . It is to ask the proprietor of any restaurant in which you may eat, what wines he suggests should go with the dishes you have ordered. Do not ask the maître d'hôtel who will have an interest in telling you to take the most expensive wines on his list. If the proprietor is out ask the sommelier—the wine waiter—and tell him you do not want to pay more than seven or twelve or twenty francs a bottle. . . . No one should want to drink wine costing more than twenty francs a bottle. . . . And the proprietor—to whom you may leave the question of price altogether—will tell you the best wine to take with your food. It will be the best and, as a rule, the cheapest. . . . A good restaurant proprietor is as a rule an artist and desires to retain your custom—and the great majority of the proprietors in modest restaurants are good men and true. . . . Of course if you go to gilded and famous palaces you will get your deserts as a fool. . . . Nevertheless, wanting one day to impress a publisher, I took him to a famous place on the Quais and gave him *caneton Rouennais au sang*—a gross dish whose distensive powers I detest. And I asked the proprietor what wine to order with that horror. He said: You will take my *vin d'Arbois* 1929. . . . According to the wine-publicity-agents *vin d'Arbois* is a third or fourth grade wine. I have known really great connoisseurs who have never tasted it. . . . Even Mr Shand confesses to that. . . .

I looked then at the wine-card and finding that that wine cost only seven francs I asked that proprietor if he could not make it something a little more expensive. He said:

"You will take my *vin d'Arbois* 1929."

I explained that my fortune for the next year or so depended on my giving my friend either something out of a gilded bottle or the disgusting treacle they call *Château Yquem*. I said I knew it was a shame to disgrace his restaurant in the eyes of the connoisseurs who were dining all round us. I apologised from the depths of my heart but he could see my predicament. He said:

"You will take my *vin d'Arbois* 1929. . . . Or a carafe of my *vin ordinaire*. . . ."

[330]

The contract that that publisher offered me was so derisory that my income ever since has been much reduced. . . . But as against that I have still in my mouth the taste of the three of four mouthsful of *caneton au sang* that I degusted with that wine. . . . It was almost as memorable as that of the *tournedos foie gras* with the bottle of Burgundy—which cost twelve francs fifty—that we had on the recommendation of the table-waiter at Dijon the other day. . . . In Dijon you may take the advice even of a table-waiter. . . .

I will not tell you the name of that restaurant on the Quais. . . . It is not the one you think. . . . Try nearer—a good deal nearer—the foundation of Cardinal Mazarin. . . . But, in return, I will tell you what Mr Belloc calls a Cautionary Tale that when you next visit France will be worth to you ten times the library subscription on which you have obtained this book. . . .

It was before the Crisis. . . . I was at Villeneuve-lès-Avignon with crowds of charming American friends settled around the immediate landscape. . . . There came down a lady almost *too* generous and almost *too* beautiful from the countryside where the Studebakers grow.

Nothing would content her but that she must take out and treat the whole crowd. . . . That was all right. . . . I led them to the Avignon tavern where you can get the best wine in all Provence. Then the disaster occurred. That lady who was beautiful enough to hold the eyes of everyone in that place of entertainment would have it that we must drink champagne. We must have champagne: she had never heard of anyone dining without champagne. Champagne it must be. . . .

You should have seen the incredulous faces of my Avignonnais friends sitting round. . . . Champagne may be all very well in its place—but I do not know what may be its place. . . . Perhaps at a very young child's birthday party with an iced cake or after two, at a dance, as a before-supper cocktail. . . .

But on the next day came the tragedy. . . . Wanting to be quiet after that whirlwind I lunched at the same place. It was a special occasion and I ordered—there were two of us—a famous Bordeaux, bottled at the Château in the year 1914. . . . I had eaten at that place often enough to know its wine card and the proprietor very well. The sommelier however was new.

Now mark. . . . That fellow brought the wine in its wicker carrier, already uncorked. He shewed me the cork which had the brand of the Château all right. He made to pour out the wine but as we were still eating an exquisite *soupe de poisson*—which is one of the specialties of Avignon—and drinking one of the little local white wines which goes very agreeably with fish and saffron, I told him I would pour the wine myself later.

Now listen very attentively. . . . When with reverential hand I tried to pour out that wine . . . *it would not pour.* . . . In the neck of the bottle was part of a perfectly new cork.

I called the proprietor who, as I have said, was a very old friend of mine and signed to him to pour out the wine, shewing him at the same time the Château cork and the date on the label of the bottle. . . . I did not say a word. . . . He peeped into the neck of the bottle.

I have never seen a man become so suddenly distracted or pallid. He caught at his throat. . . . He really caught at his throat. . . . When he was a little recovered he shouted at that sommelier in a voice of shaky thunder to fetch the cellarman.

That procession of two threaded its way between the tables of the appalled diners. And M. le Patron shouted:

"Take off your aprons. . . . There is the door!"

Then, as their crestfallen shades obscured the doorway, he went himself to his deep cellar and came back, bearing with his own hands a bottle of *Château Pavie* 1914.

I don't know if you see the point. Americans are said never to be able to see an Englishman's point and the English never to see the point of any story at all for a week, when they telegraph to the teller the two vocables "Ha! Ha!"

The point isn't merely that that sommelier, taking me for an ignorant Briton, had, with the connivance of the cellarman, poured a bottle of local wine at frs 1.90 into an empty *Château Pavie* bottle which he had re-corked with a *bouchon* so new that, unknown to him, half of it had remained, when he re-uncorked it, in the neck of the bottle. . . . *Château Pavie* is a very expensive wine when it is of the year 1914 so he and the cellarman would have made a handsome profit. . . . They would of course have reserved several authentic corks from real bottles previously opened. . . .

But you had seen that already. . . . There is of course the other point that the sommelier had never seen me before, being new, and had observed me the day before to drink champagne —but positively *champagne!* with a titianesque Bacchante from Studebakerville. So naturally he had taken me for one of those other Anglo-Saxon "brutes."

But even *that* is not the point. . . . *Je vous le donne en mille!* . . . The real point is that, if that bottle *had* poured I might have gone through all the ceremonies of turning the wine under my nose, swirling it round in the glass, regarding the light through, and finally sipping and respiring it. . . . And might quite possibly have been taken in and have lectured my unfortunate—for once Antipodean!—disciple as to its colour, bouquet, body and the rest. Do not think that that would have been the result merely of snobbishness. . . . I do really know something of Bordeaux and Mosel wines. I am not one of the great writers on wines, like Mr William Bird or Mr Shand or M. Monot. . . . But *Château Pavie* is my favourite wine and I ought to know something about it. And you have to consider that I was in a restaurant that I had known for years; that I was entirely convinced of the probity of the proprietor and the excellence of his kitchen and cellar. And who can really pledge his personal taste against such overwhelming things as the cork and bottle of the Château? Not I!

I should probably have smelt, tasted, and looked through that wine and have thought that there was something the matter with my liver and eyes. . . . And I should have delivered a perfectly correct lecture on *Château Pavie* to that disciple from down under . . . who perhaps would not have got any harm from it.

I once in a similar way unintentionally deceived one of the really great connoisseurs. He looked in on me one day and asked me to let him have a taste of my excellent Calvados. . . . I had had some really wonderful 1895 Apple Jack that came from a Princely cellar. It was rather unique because the Prince was selling his cellar as it were incognito and only to personal friends. The Calvados was in magnums with the princely seal very large on the bottles but the date written only on a paper label. So, that distillation being famous, I had a number of friends and my little lot had lasted only a year or so. . . . But at the same time as I had bought that lot I had bought a quantity of 1920 from the same cellar. It was a very good fluid but *not* 1895. If you tasted the 1920 alone it was excellent but if you did so after the 1895 it rather suggested spirits of wine in which you should have macerated some good apples.

My friend the connoisseur had come however so long after the 1895 had been exhausted that what I gave him, without after thought, was the 1920—from an exactly identical magnum, with the same princely seal and the paper with the date naturally gone.

My friend smelt it, tasted it; threw back his head, breathed out through his nose. And then said reverentially:

"Ah, nothing will ever beat your 1895."

There is however as much trickery in the wine trade as in that in secondhand automobiles. . . . And there *is* a great deal of snobbery. So that, if you are not an expert, or if you are an absolute novice, the best thing you can do is to provide yourself with Mr Shand's compendious book on French wines which you will read at home and with Mr Bird's really wonderful little pamphlet which you will carry around in your pocket. Then get a real connoisseur to give you some hints as to bouquet, body, colour, the *goût de pierre de fusil* and the rest of it. And after that try the proprietors of good, but unmarbled old restaurants. When they have recommended to you wines that you really like then ask them to order what supply you need of that vintage from their wholesale suppliers. You will thus build up a cellar. . . . But do not be lured by great names. There are little local vineyards producing wines just as good as all but the great classic vineyards in their best years. For myself I drink with perfect contentment year in year out a little domain wine grown not far away from where I live, it costing me, when I have bottled it, Frs 42 for a barrique of 25 bottles—or less than two francs the bottle. I could get it for less if I took larger barrels but I find them a nuisance to handle. And, just occasionally, I get, from a little vineyard in an adjacent village two or three barrels of a vin du pays which in a good year is as good as the wine of the best years of all but the most famous vineyards of the world. It is not famous because it is too small to pay for publicity. But when I get a little of that then I can call myself happy for as long as it lasts. I should of course like to drink Château Pavie—or even Château Mouton-Rothschild, once again. But I do not suppose I ever shall and I am perfectly contented with what I do drink.

About this bullfighting. . . . There are amazing—as you might call them—king-emotions that are available to one only once or twice in a life-time and that fate allows one only very rarely to renew.' . . . One of those came the other night at Dijon after we had had those snails and that tournedos and half a bottle each of that Burgundy. . . . Not a drop more liquor nor a bite more of food, for it would have been sacrilege to take any 'sweet' after that ineffable small steak. . . . And let that shew you that I travel in the proper spirit, since as a rule, as I have said, I never eat beef and I infinitely prefer claret to Burgundy and, as a rule I prefer snails *à l'Alsacienne* to those of the Bourgogne method of preparation. . . . But once in Burgundy, in Dijon, I knew that I had to put away all preconceptions. As a proud Provençal I despise those barbarous Northerners: they are North French crossed with German with a good dash of Flanders thrown in. They are not over-courteous. They eat too much; they drink too much; they walk about the world grossly blissful with too much eating. . . .

But that night in Dijon we knew that they would be real damn fools if they did not. For we staggered over the cobbles of the black, nearly midnight town, meeting no soul but in a state of bliss! And of such complete tranquillity and peace with all the world. . . . We lost ourselves amongst the fantastic, baroque buildings towering up into the black skies . . . buildings that normally I should find too ostentatious as against our classic severities. . . . What, I should say, is the Palace of the Dukes of Burgundy as against the Maison Carrée or even the Castle of the Popes? . . . The expression of a vaunting vulgarian! But that night it was all one supreme harmony—And one saw that to those despised savages was given knowledge and virtue that to us were unknown. We had eaten very little and drunk less. . . . And yet there was produced the effect of the tranquillity that, according to my friend Mr Wells, can only follow a large distension of the abdomen, and of a gaiety that, I have been told—in New York and by Omar Khayyám—can only follow the ingurgitation of a quart of synthetic gin . . . So those Northern barbarians had discovered the secret of how, with extreme frugality, one may know delights only elsewhere attainable at orgies of food and drink. We might well veil our proud glances . . .

And, listen. In the darkness there was music—coming from somewhere out of the Palace of the Dukes of Burgundy? But whence? . . . All that was needed was music . . . The waltzes of Strauss for preference . . . Where? . . . Not a soul in the black streets; not so much as a cat on the black roofs. . . .

Suddenly from the mouth of a *ruelle* blared some bars of the "Blue Danube" . . . And staggered . . . and stopped . . . And after maniacal yells, resumed. It was like being blissfully mad. We had asked for a Strauss waltz and there was the Strauss waltz of all waltzes . . . But as it were cut into sausage slices . . . And yells . . . And Yells! It was perhaps a patriotic or anti-Semitic demonstration . . . Against an Austro-Jewish composer?

Light was falling on one wall of the *ruelle*—the little blind alley. And on the heads and shoulders of a tip-toeing crowd. . .

Behind a barred window was a blond, stout lunatic in shirt-sleeves . . . Almost out of his shirt . . . Disgusting of the crowd to stare at the poor demented! . . . He had a short cane with which he menaced the world, and swung himself, and balanced on his toes and yelled. . . . Let us quit the distasteful spectacle. This will put the shutters on the enjoyment of our escargots . . .

There welled and blared out the twenty-seventh bar of the introduction to the "Blue Danube" . . . Sitting beneath that mad-man were men, blowing into trombones and hautbois; sawing at fiddles and double-basses . . . A crowd of sober men . . . The President of the Republic was coming in state to Dijon on Sunday—while we were going to be in the arena at Nîmes . . . And those were the elect of Dijon . . . The musically elect . . . And with their sweet strains they were going to make M. Lebrun forget the murder of M. Leprince . . . The candle-stick maker; the postman; the mustard maker's assistant; the blacksmith . . . They were valiantly taking up the task of making the Highest in the Land be for a moment oblivious of the knavery of the politicians that surrounded him . . . A task worthy of the minstrels that played to make the Good King forget the loss of Naples, Sicily and Anjou . . . And I do not believe that the fanfare plays better . . . even in Tarascon when the Queen of Heaven comes to pay her visit to Her old servant. . . .

I think the most atrocious emotion I have ever felt occurred to me when Chicuelo was working his second bull—the fourth of the afternoon, an ungainly red-Sussex sort of animal that should have been at the *Cat and Fiddle*—which comes from *Château Fidèle*, so does the language of the Gods become transmogrified as it goes along the Route—at the *Cat and Fiddle*, then, trying to jump over the moon. . . . Heaviness descended upon me; I thought the brilliant sun had struck my brain. I looked desperately round for exit . . . The red bull capered as if it were trying to jump over a churn. It ignored completely the scarlet cape of Chicuelo. It was no doubt trying to shake out the banderillos . . . That was fatality!

I go to bull-fights now and then because I like to go to bull-fights now and then . . . And that's that. . . . I do not profess to be an *aficionado* nor instantly to recall the Spanish for all the *suertes*. If I had Mr Hemingway's book by me I could, but I have not Mr Hemingway's book by me . . . And I have never before felt that heaviness at a bull-fight. It was the heaviness of nightmare . . . In the incredibly white light of the sun, hemmed in by crowds of silent people. Silent, you understand.

Yet before and beneath these tiers on tiers of parti-coloured humanity that mounted until it touched the blue sky was Chicuelo . . . The great Chicuelo, the darling of the city of Nîmes and of all Provence and the Narbonnais . . .

I began to think that I must be getting too old for these pleasures. One must learn to *vieillir avec dignité* . . . I should never again see Lalanda as I shall never, probably, again drink *Château Pavie* 1914 . . . The incomparable Lalanda who for me is greater even than was Maera . . . Yes, age was making my limbs leaden and my eyes avoid that clumsy russet beast and the motionless scarlet, blue and golden figure before him . . .

And then suddenly Biala, drawing engrossed, hissed violently.

Chicuelo, crouching forward had touched and held the right horn of that animal . . . whom by then I detested . . . Yes, you can detest a bull in the ring as you can feel intense friendship for another . . . That is why a bull now and then escapes death . . .

Suertes

But Chicuelo had performed that part of the ritual quite as well as it is practicable to do it . . . The matador, I mean, seems always so ready to jump away that, for my part I had rather see the ceremony omitted . . . he leaned forward holding the horn for far longer than seemed necessary.

The heaviness continued, drooping over all my limbs. Not a sound came from the vast audience—which usually calls for music in applause of that *suerte*. Biala hissed again. Venomously!

The Frenchman between my knees—a mustachioed Norman, a higher functionary, I believe at the Post Office—looked round, up at me and said:

"But one should not hiss . . . After all it is Chicuelo . . . We detest him. We have agreed not to applaud any of his actions. But not to *hiss* him. That is not done. . . . Besides he has been fighting magnificently. . . ."

So that that intense depression that I had felt had been the ambience of all those detestations falling through the air upon poor Chicuelo . . . I have seen enough dull bull-fights, but they were just boring as dull plays are boring with, however, always brilliant passages or riotously amusing exhibitions of cowardice. But this was something different . . . It appeared that in two successive *corridas* Chicuelo—who has his bad moments—had fought so negligently that he had earned inexpressibly bitter criticisms from the local bull-fighting press and on the second occasion had been almost continuously hissed. He was reported to have replied with something contemptuous of Nîmes audiences, comparing them, as far as I can remember, to a flock of ganders . . . Now he was attempting to stage a return. But in spite of the magnificence of his performance with the first bull, the audience would have nothing of him. And that Destiny should have given him for his second bull such an awkward animal that neither could nor would fight simply sealed the fate of his ever again appearing in Nîmes at all. . . . The curious thing was that I had had no idea of the state of mind of those thousands and did not hear the story until later at Tarascon—where of course it may have been patriotically distorted . . .

So that I paid relatively little attention to the entry of the fifth bull though it was to be worked by the incomparable Lalanda . . . I sat there still with the remains of that nightmare heaviness; still with that desire to escape . . . The sun glared, the people shouted and coloured things moved over the great oval of swept sand . . . For I find that when I am at a merely dull fight my mind wanders—to the international complications of the day; to the financial ones of the hour; to the subject of my next book; to the minute to spare with which we shall catch the fast train back to Tarascon—or, if one is in St Sebastian, to Hendaye . . . For I am one of those rare beings who prefer to sit in a nearly empty smooth-rolling train to being thrown to heaven in an autobus constructed to carry twenty-seven and carrying forty-two. . . .

And then suddenly my heaviness was gone—as if a crisis of indigestion had passed . . . Suddenly the movements below gave me pleasure . . . I had been on the point of saying: "Attending on bull-fights is a mug's game" . . . All of a sudden I felt that I could sit on that hard stone for ever . . . Lalanda with his mysterious dignity was making to a matador near him a little movement with his hand. I had so little attended that I did not know what it was about. . . . But Lalanda moves his field with the smallest movements of his wrist whilst he stands apart as if he were a mediæval Italian prince, communing with himself, his arms folded, leaning against a little pillar of a colonnade whilst his courtiers tremble. . . .

And suddenly . . . there again was bullfighting . . . You must repeat the word 'suddenly' all the time while you sit round the arena . . . But . . . Bullfighting . . . Your heart suddenly moves to a quicker beat; your pulse throbs . . . What a bull! What a devil . . . Black; light-footed as a cat . . . Hurling itself through the air . . . Weighing a ton of black iron; all of a piece and light as a feather; its tail swinging like the tail of

Lucifer; its eyes on everything in the arena at once . . . A
bull! . . . An animal that even Lalanda may be content to
work. . . .

You must remember than when such a matador—but indeed
you could almost call him a *toreador*—when such a matador
meets such a bull the interplay of the minds of beast and man is
as rapid and as much in sequence as when two matchless swords-
men make sword play . . . You say with your mind: It will be
now: tierce, tierce, quarte, tierce, quartequarte, quarte, tierce-
tiercequarte—touché! And your breathlessness comes from the
exact realisation of your prevision . . . It is logical . . . Why,
the chess played by two masters might be a very slowed-down
rendering of a bullfight!

For you have to remember that the whole encounter of bull
and man is a long programme of strategy from the moment
when the bull hurls himself into the arena to the moment when
the mules trot swiftly away with him, the bells a-jingle . . .
And with a royally right bull the matador knows just what is
passing through the animal's mind and what will pass through
it in five minutes or in seven and a half . . . Dull bullfighting
comes with a matador who cannot read the bull's mind—or with
a bull that does not run true to type . . . And here Lalanda
saw a master-animal—one that would furiously attack everything that it saw, so that he had to arrange everything that it saw
till the moment of the *volapié* . . . From the first lightning
entry of that ferocious devil—and it has always seemed curious
to me that the four fiercest of all animals—the bull, the stallion
that is more terrible than the bull, the rhinoceros that is a charging castle, and M. Hitler, should all be vegetarians—so from that
lightning entry one's breathless mind and that of the thousands
who also look on, is devoted to checking, not so much the perfection of bull and man—for when it is Lalanda and such a bull
your mind may be at rest about that—but whether the ritual
will exactly take place. Almost as it were you lose interest
in the living beings and fix your attention on the run of the

tragedy . . . I think that is why all idea of cruelty goes out of the affair in the minds even of men like myself who though my garden may be brought near to ruin by ants or snails cannot bring myself to kill either and who hate winning out in an argument . . . It is the intellectual character of the long duel that impresses you—the intellect of the bull with his immense

Bravo Toro

resources and tremendous strength against that of the man armed with a tiny, thin steel rod. Of course if a clumsy picador —and all picadors, because of the Trade Union rules of this occupation are clumsy—if the picador fails to defend his horse you feel a momentary and passing sensation that there is cruelty . . . But nowadays, with the mattresses all round the animal the horse, at any rate in appearance, is seldom injured more than by the shock of the bull's forehead . . . And for myself I have never felt the slightest anxiety about any of the human beings in the arena . . . I am perhaps callous but to see a man tossed or gored on the ground by the bull gives me almost no emotion at all . . . That may be because of 1914-1918 or perhaps it is because I have never seen a great matador killed . . . I remember that when I heard of the death of Maêra by tuberculosis I was more—and more prolongedly—grieved than at the death of any other being not a member of my family or a very intimate friend . . . And when, at the arrival of the time for the *véronique*, with a matchless bull and a Lalanda to go through it, that amazing and prolonged dance of butterflies was performed, impenetrably grave Lalanda with his back to his charging adversary, swinging the scarlet cape to right and left in his rear, with the rhythm of a flashing crinoline when a woman runs . . . why, that so passed out of the realm of human and animal possibilities that I felt that if Lalanda should slip and fall the bull would stand to attention, waving his *fleuret* and inviting his adversary to recover his feet. . . . And the knowledge that the bull wouldn't, only added to my breathlessness. . . . But that is the impression, that of two courteous and engrossed duellists functioning in a fairy tale.

It is the fantastic and the unthinkable . . . Lalanda walking towards where we sat, without looking at what was behind him, as if he were humming a tune with a straw between his teeth and thinking out the words of a lyric—and with such a smile on his classical features—why . . . it was as if he were walking, a marine deity, to his wedding, through scarlet foam with a black attendant dolphin gambolling around him . . . And the countless thousands, the whole parti-coloured lining of that immense Roman bowl, thinking as I thought, feeling as I felt—to give me the infection of all their minds and the infinite satisfaction of being at one with one's fellows over a supreme work of an incomparable art! . . . As if one should stand with a million of one's fellows all unanimously gasping with overwhelmed admiration at their first sight of Cézanne's "Baigneur." . . .

It is to have that feeling of unity in admiration that I go now and then to see a *mise à mort*—I a man who cannot bring myself to kill a snail and who when I have won out in an argument have a feeling of shame.

The rest of the afternoon was good enough. . . . When he had killed, Lalanda instead of proceeding round the ring and picking up the torrent of cigarettes, hats and fans, ran straight to the gate by which the bulls enter and came back, all flashing, with a large, black bird of a stocky fellow . . . Then you should have heard the applause—the crows flying overhead falling dead into the arena . . . Or they said in Nîmes that they did. I did not see it. It was the *gardian*—the trainer of that unparallelled black thunderbolt who was said to be the brother of Lalanda, though I fancy I was misinformed . . . I have never seen a man so applauded—not even the Abbé Liszt in St James's Hall had the equal of it . . .

It was certainly the greatest occasion that I ever saw of the sort. I suppose it was not so overwhelming a manifestation of admiration as that classic one which Mr Hemingway, I think, was privileged to be present at. Then Joselito—or I think it was Joselito for it was not in the *genre* of Maera—purposely manœuvred himself whilst using the banderillos so near the barriers that it seemed impossible that he could escape the bull's horns . . . and the whole audience unanimously stood up and shouted: "No; no! It is too dangerous" . . . But that display of Lalanda was good enough. My American companions were fortunate indeed to see it.

Dominguez, who killed the last bull, performed very soundly and satisfyingly. As a relative novice it was fitting that he should provide a sort of calm . . . And in it my New York friend explained to me the motive of Biala's eccentric hissing of Chicuelo—which had been repeated when Dominguez in his turn touched the horn of his bull, though that draughtsman had been silent when Lalanda had done it . . . You see, Biala had been so infused with the idea, like myself, that this was a duel between courteous opponents that when the matadors went through that prescribed *suerte* it had affected a gallant spirit as if the more skilled of two participants in a meeting with rapiers should have spat in the weaker fighter's face . . .

And curiously enough Dominguez was the only one of the three who killed his bull, dead, *sur le pied*, his sword going in as if effortlessly at the exact right spot and penetrating to the animal's heart so that it fell as if struck by lightning . . . It is now years since I saw that done and then it was done by a great Mexican bull-fighter who had at first, owing to stage fright at his first appearance in Europe, made a hopelessly clumsy display with his first bull on a great occasion with both Maera and Jose-lito in the ring. The audience was absolutely merciless to him and, when it came to the second *mise à mort*, they yelled at him that he should use his left hand since he had made such a mull with his right on the first occasion. He held up his bandaged left hand with an ineffable smile. Without any of us seeing it it had been transfixed by the first bull's horn. Then he threw his handkerchief in front of the bull's nose and slowly sat down on it with his back to the bull . . . To show that he was a brave man! In the position in which he had put himself—for though I have seen many matadors do the like never one so almost touched the animal's muzzle—he had about an eighty per cent chance of death. Nevertheless the bull backed and he escaped . . . He made his evocatory speech previous to the *mise à mort* —it is called I think the *brindis*—with his cap trembling in his hand through nervousness; put his sword under his armpit as used to be done by the *toreadors*—who were hidalgos—and with almost no preliminary sighting—whereas when he had sighted his first bull his sword had trembled with his stage fright so that it had been hideous to see—laid the bull stone dead . . . He got the Toreador March from "Carmen" and the muzzle and the tail and everything in the way of plaudits from the audience that he could get. . . .

I suppose that the matadors of today are so preoccupied with and so practice the muleta that they comparatively neglect the *mise à mort* itself. Or it may be that such a succession of *veron-*

icas as a great matador today puts up is too exhausting to let
them be at their best for, let us say, a *volapié*. In any case, today,
the thunderbolt death of the bull is rather rarely seen—and then
usually at the hands of no very notable matador. I think it is
rather regrettable. But of course the modern preliminaries to the
killing are of an almost incredible beauty. . . .

One of my American friends as we came away made under
the black outer walls of that Roman building a remark that,
curiously enough, exactly duplicated the remark by another
young American whom I had taken with a party to a *corrida*
some years ago. The one was from the neighbourhood of Washington Square, the other from Seattle . . . Each expelled the
air from his lungs, took a deep breath and exclaimed: "I feel a
better man." Of course it may have been no more than an
expression of relief that the utterer had not fainted during the
long afternoon . . . But I think not.

I am not going to discuss the morality of the *mise à mort*, but
I will tell three anecdotes and make a surmise. . . .

I listened some years ago to the excited denunciation of his
country delivered by two young men, the one English and the
other American, to an aged Spanish retired diplomat . . . They
said in effect "Stinking Spaniards," relieving each other in turn
for about a quarter of an hour.—We are of course the divinely
appointed Lords and Censors of the world. We are taught that
in our schools and believe it for the rest of our lives.—When
they were completely out of breath the old man—he had been
attached to the embassies both of the Court of St James's and of
Washington—bent a little deferentially and said:

"Yes, gentlemen, bull-fighting is a cruel sport. It is to be
regretted that its survival should be . . . necessitated. But
. . . " and he bowed to the English youth . . . "I read in your
papers that every year in your country there are two hundred
and fifty thousand prosecutions for cruelty to children and animals—but mostly to children. And," bowing to the representative of Old Glory, "in your great country there are . . . " (I do

not remember how many) "hundred thousand children of eight employed in coal mines." He bowed again to both and in his reedy voice added gently:

"Perhaps if in your great Empires you had bull-fighting those expressions of Sadism would not be . . . necessitated. For you will not find in my country from here in San Sebastian to where Spain ends in the territory of one of your nations, a man or woman who will raise a hand to a child. . . ."

"That," said the unbeaten Englishman, "is a fine lot of punk. Isn't it an acknowledged fact that you Dagoes and the South French sell all your girl children to brothels?"

Or again I happened one day to be talking about Maera to a mixed company in England. I was explaining that the most amazing dexterities of the bull-fighter are not the most spectacular ones. A man who stands the direct charge of an infuriated bull and, not moving his feet from the ground which they occupy, avoids the charge merely by inclining his body aside and at the same time plants a couple of banderillos within a prescribed space of about half a circular foot on each side of the charging animal's spine as it passes him—such a man will appear to be doing nothing spectacular. . . .

I was interrupted by a roar of "By God . . ." A magnificent blond colossus with a dragoon's moustache, a vast morning coat and a copper nose had sprung to his feet.

"By God," he said, "put the slinking coward on my huntsman's spare horse and send him over a line of country . . . But by God if I saw him in my field I would strip all the skin off his body with my whip . . . By God, I . . . Sticking children's skewers into drugged cows . . . And by God . . . The Horses . . . By God, when I think of the horses. . . ."

I will not discuss the morality of fox-hunting . . . I saw it described lately in a book—by I think a Hungarian—as the martyrdom of a small dog by two hundred and fifty drunkards filled to the teeth with brandy and forty couples of its brothers. But that gentleman is one of the finest masters of hounds that ever made a wide cast on a damp and foggy morning . . . And to avoid the accusation of Pharisaeism I will confess that I would give no little to be able once again to feel the glorious thrill of waiting, while the pheasants rocket overhead, outside a wood for his hounds to break cover . . . For undoubtedly fox-hunting is the sport of kings. . . .

So I did not reply to him that, his country being in one of the Home Counties and his field averaging maybe a couple of hundred, and he hunting every day of the season except Sundays, probably as many horses are impaled on stake and binder hedges, break their knees or legs or backs and are shot, sold to the knackers, fed to the hounds or sold to be exported and butchered for human food in Belgium—in his country alone and in one season—than are badly injured by bulls in ten years in the whole of Provence and the Narbonnais too—from Nice to the Spanish border. . . . So I asked him instead if he had ever faced an infuriated cow.

He said:

"By God, every day of my life . . . Thousands of them . . . Any English child could . . ."

I said:

"It's more than Maera would . . ." I felt I must get a little of my own back. He answered however:

"I told you the coward's cows are drugged, didn't I? . . ." and stumped off. So I didn't get much. . . .

The other day I was in a mixed company of French and Anglo-Saxons making a little picnic. It was in the paradisaic panorama of a little bay by Cap Banat where the stone pines bend right over the tideless water and the Golden Islands rise out of a sheet of sapphire . . . It was such a scene as you would have thought would have softened the heart of the chief torturer of Ivan the Cruel . . .

And suddenly the English youth of whom I have spoken as calling the French stinking swine because they go to bullfights and put garlic in their sandwiches and give them away—that representative of a proud and ancient civilisation uttered a violent and startled objurgation and, brushing something like a golden leaf out of his American aunt's hair, ground it violently with his heel into the sand. . . .

You should have heard the regret in all those French voices that exclaimed simultaneously:

"Un scarabée d'or . . . Mais c'est un scarabée d'or . . ."

The golden scarab is one of the most beautiful, rarest and most innocent of all the bright and innocent things that God has made. That boy's aunt wore a scarab on her finger—because even the ordinary scarab was venerated by the Egyptians as the symbol of Immortality. And this was the fabulous golden scarab that was one of the attributes of the God PHtah . . . Those poor bloody Wop-Dagoes, the Provençaux, must, in their corrupt blood, have a certain strain from the time when their ancestors, an effete fellaheen visited these shores, thousands of years ago, and worshipped beasts. . . .

At any rate it was under the gaze of veiled and reproachful eyes—for those people would almost as soon contemplate killing their only child as of killing a golden scarab—that that scion of world-conquerors exclaimed above the little corpse of the emblem of Immortality:

"Didn't know what it was . . . Haw . . . Always kill anything when you don't know what it is . . . Might sting . . . Only prudence. . . ."

It was of course a fine day and he had not yet sent the soul of anything before its Maker. . . .

And that boy was one of the ornaments . . . I mean really one of the ornaments . . . of a venerated educational establishment that for hundreds of years has taught youth the languages of Sappho and Catullus and—for hundreds and hundreds of years—manners . . . and the humanities! I have said that before. But I repeat it again. Some educationalist in England chancing on this book might dip into it and read a few words; so he has twice as many chances of coming across this suggestion for the avoidance of wars. . . .

Of course the instinct of cruelty that is so strong in children may become merely a rudimentary organ in them when they are adult. I knew in his boyhood a peer of the realm whose favourite and almost sole engrossing pursuit was roasting live sparrows in front of a slow fire. Today he is an admirable hereditary legislator and one of the best and most useful men in England—or indeed the world . . . But supposing a French littérateur had come upon him—as I once did—at his then favourite pursuit . . . and he the son of one of the most powerful and intelligent rulers of our country. . . .

So it is better to avoid discussions of international moralnesses and humanities for they above all our other miserable preoccupations conduce to World-Wars . . . World-Wars being things that should be avoided. I am not as I have said an anti-militarist. Mutual envies are things that are inevitable; property is a thing the sense of which cannot be got rid of . . . I shall be more embittered if you put your socks in my private collar drawer than if you take away my good name . . . But the thing to aim at is to limit the extents of wars and to confine the sense of property to your collar drawers . . . Obviously you must backbite your neighbours. That is part of the sadist desire for liberation that leads people to kill—and not for the pot—thousands of pheasants in an hour. But it is well to limit the scope of your libels to the inhabitants of your own town and to leave alone the lesser breeds who live a hundred miles and more away . . . For you might bring in the intervening cities. . . .

A war between Nîmes and Tarascon because the Tarasconnais said that the bull-fighting concern had failed and the Nîmois were pulling down their arena might be a jolly little affair, both sides to be armed with sharpened vine-stakes and

the inhabitants of Beaucaire refusing passage over the Rhone
. . . But a war of gas-bombs between the United States and
Great Britain because the nasty-tongued English said that the
United States had baths but used them for storing their coal
and onions . . . that would be almost a crime . . . Really
quite a crime . . . Or of course the cause of the war might
be Great Britain's putting an export embargo on tin, the United
States producing no tin, or the United States doing the same
thing for maple sugar which England cannot produce.

One must of course protect one's own countrymen . . . or
I suppose so. Because as I have explained before that is a queer
thing. My French friend despises nearly all his compatriots
because they connive at the existence of the French Republic;
my English friend of the other day expressed almost apoplectic
loathing of the majority of his fellow countrymen because he
said they wanted all to be on the dole. Yet if you tell M. X
that it is uneconomic for France to grow wheat and that
France should admit wheat from the United States, the
Argentines or the Soviet Republic he will denounce you to the
police as a foreign agent determined to starve the French wheat-
growers . . . whom he loathes because they will not pay him
his rents . . . And if you tell that Englishman that it is absurd
for England to grow vegetables, the soil and climate being
entirely unfitted for their economic production and that it
would be better to import vegetables from the South of France
turning the whole of England into an immense enterprise for
the production of pedigree stock, he will strike you to the
ground. And Mr S . . . will tell you that that is because you
are a stinking little Englander intent on breaking up the Empire. For, he will say, every one knows that the disgusting
Colonies—who insist on choosing the bowlers who are to play
against them in Test Matches—insist also, under threat of part-
ing from the Mother Country, on the introduction of their
wizened and uneatable store-stock alive, thus ruining the poor

dear British farmer who, anyhow, is rather a loathsome ignoramus.

And the worst of it is that, omitting the adjectives, the allegations in that last sentence are true enough. The only thing that Great Britain can produce better than any other country in the world is pedigree animals of all kinds. Her climate and the temperament of her people are alike exactly suited to that. Then she should think of producing nothing else—except perhaps potatoes, and pedigree potatoes for choice . . . But the colonies insist on the right of introducing their beasts on the foot, so that England can no longer give the foreign buyer the absolute guarantee that her livestock are protected against foot and mouth disease and swine fever . . . Without that the foreigner from the Spree to the Seine and the Paraguay may just as well buy his rams, bulls and boars at home, paying a fifth of the price that he used to pay for them in England. . . .

It is, you see, all very confusing. But the principle that each countryside should produce only that for which it is most fitted and that such products should circulate freely through the world—preferably by barter—that principle is so blindingly clear that no human being can miss it . . . And the putting into practise of that principle must of necessity abolish wars since no country could dispense with the products of any other country . . . And then we should be back again to the manner of the Great Trade Route with the sacred and honest merchants travelling with their wares from tabu ground to ground . . . and civilisations flowing backwards and forwards from China to Peru . . . And all of us sitting gasping with admiration for the tales of other races that they brought back and at the films that also they should bring shewing the marvellous accomplishments, virtues, frugality and beauty of all the foreign parts of the great world . . . For I think that civilisations are better things to exchange than bombs containing poison gases and loathsome infections. . . .

PROVENCE

After the bull-fight at Nîmes the crowd is so thick through-out the large and beautiful town that for minutes you cannot move. But after the matadors have passed from the arena gate to their *posada*, opposite, slowly and gravely, you are carried along the streets. We went, so pressed, down the broad, and as it were grandiloquent, avenue that leads from the Arena to the Bourse and the Theatre. It was impossible for any of us to converse . . . From time to time we could exchange a shouted word whilst all the time went up the words *mise à mort; mise à mort;* now no longer with the shouted gaiety of antici-pation of the autobus but with the grave, savouring softness of those criticising and assaying what has passed . . . So we progressed as it were ritually, like Spanish women in black mantillas pigeon-stepping along the Rambla. . . .

The whole crowd at one moment stopped still. And in the silence my New York friend said from behind me into my ear:

"By Jove I should not like to be the woman that Lalanda wanted to put the comether on" . . . and added: "But perhaps if I was a woman I *should.*" Then we all flowed on again. . . .

We were beneath and between trees and trees and trees and kiosques and shopfronts and sweet-stalls . . . And then slowly a large open space and, on high, in the centre of it . . . You know the tiny crescent of the moon, gleaming through a veil of orange, just born and wavering down to the horizon above the islands in a breathless night . . . It has that tranquillity . . . the *Maison Carrée* . . . That very tranquillity and the in-effable perfection of all the quiet words that were ever written by Sappho and Catullus. And whenever I see it I seem to be reading the words that seem to me the most beautiful in the world

ERAMEN MEN EGO SETHEN ATHI PALAI POTA

Or

TE SPECTEM SUPREMA MIHI QUUM VENERIT HORA

Or

Less than a God they said there could not dwell
Within the hollow of that shell
That spoke so sweetly and so well . . .

This is by way of being a testament and so, though I ask
pardon, I take pleasure as it were in laying before the most
beautiful building that was ever built what have all my life
been for me the most beautiful words that were ever written
or said.

And then the singular Destiny of Provence gave one of
her enigmatic smiles . . . An automobile coming from behind
our backs knocked down—before the very portals of that House
—just under our faces and so that he actually touched one of
our unfortunate American ladies, a poor old peasant. And there
he lay dead . . . And she had never seen either the Maison
Carrée or a dead man before . . . It was a queer way of what
we used to call coming to the end of a perfect day . . . Queer.
There is no other word for the destinies of this country and
the manifestations they choose. . . .

I went down just now to see that the irrigation was turned
on ready for the water when it comes. It is just after noon . . .
Pan's hour . . . One ought not to go into one's garden in Pan's
hour. On these absolutely still days you may well get sunstroke . . . And then . . . things are abroad.

And sure enough, descending, I had to step across the body
of the great snake that I have not yet seen this year. His head
was in one hedge and his tail in another. I suppose he knows
my step for he was moving very slowly and did not hurry
when I stepped carefully over him . . . I do not know what
that omen means. The great snake is the attendant on Aesculapius, so I may soon have to go to a doctor. On the other hand
he may be benevolent and his return may mean that I shall
not have to call in Demoulin for a long time.

And I would have sworn queer things were dodging down among the thin *fusains* beside me. You can clip the fusain like box. It must have been brought here by the first Cockney for it grows in every London back yard. But now I am back in my shade writing. The father of Aesculapius has not struck me with his darts . . . It is queer to think that Apollo, a golden and impetuous youth, should be the father of Aesculapius who has a long grey beard and sits for ever, contemplatively, with his hand over his moustachio.

And while I am about it I had better tell you how in Tarascon by the castle of the good king René I lost all my money . . . No, it went neither in gambling nor in liquor . . . *Afflavit Deus* . . . God blew and it was dissipated . . . But perhaps not God: the Destiny of Provence—Who gave five millions to M. Bonhoure and has ever since afflicted him with motor accidents . . . I see in today's paper—and if you look in the *Intran* for the 25th August you can see it too so that you may know that I am not inventing these things—I see then a photograph of M. Bonhoure looking at the underneath of his motor car that yesterday, as he was returning from Nîmes to Tarascon, must needs burst a tyre, turn over and burst into flames. And yet he must be fortunate, for relatively few people escape from automobiles that have caught fire . . . When I come to think about it, though, I was in a Buick not so long ago, and it caught fire and I got out of it all right. But it cannot have been the Destiny of Provence that either permitted the conflagration or looked after me, because that happened in Kentucky and they say neither white nor black magic can cross the sea.

Anyhow M. Bonhoure's car is burnt and considering how long it takes me to get to the story of my misfortune perhaps Destiny does not want that exploit of hers to be chronicled . . . It was like this. . . .

Mr Roosevelt had elected to shut down all the American banks at a moment when having worked too hard and too

long I was in Paris and in desperate need of a long holiday
. . . Well, no one in Paris had any money . . . We had to
give a wedding reception, for which we had issued the invita-
tions, on frs 60 *pour tout potage*. And the whole, largish number of Americans who came could not muster frs seventy-five
between them. It was amusing . . . but also a little tiring . . .
Or maybe I was too tired already. . . .

So when the dam burst and money came in—relatively large
sums of money—we all decided to make straight for Tarascon
. . . The problem was what to do with that money . . . It
was to provide me with a long, long holiday and afterwards
a long, long rest. So it was rather precious beyond most moneys.
But what then? . . . My American friends, anxious for my
prosperity, begged me not to put it into an American bank . . .
From Paris it looked as if all the banks in America and all
their branches elsewhere were popping off like thorns crackling
under a pot . . . And as for English banks, they, they said,
were all doomed because England was ruined and the pound
at about twenty and going lower.

So I turned it into francs . . . I would have turned it into
gold francs but that was *défendu*. Into *francs papier* it went.
There came then the question of what to do with it. I am
constitutionally incapable of not losing money. I would no
more trust myself with a large sum than I would consent to
carry a day old baby from Paris to New York . . . So my
advisers ordered me to hand it over for safekeeping to the most
honest, sober, industrious and unextravagant member of our
party. That I did with thankfulness and we set out.

Do you know what the mistral really is? . . . In Tarascon
where there are no hills between the plains and the Alps from
which the mistral comes. It is not a wind. It is force that
overwhelms a whole country, pushing, dragging, thundering,
panting—towards the Sahara. It will overset stone carts and
carry uprooted oaks half across a county. Under it the Mediterranean develops rollers like the Atlantic and half the soil

of a hundred acre field will by it be transported into the houses of the peasants to the south. . . .

Well, as soon as I had been shaved and perfumed with orange-flower water by M. Bonhoure, we set out through the roaring arcades of the market and were blown, like sails in the wind, down past the villa of Tartarin towards the castle . . . Just north of the Castle is a little patch of quiet before a former convent . . . Then it begins again . . . We staggered, leaning back, an extraordinarily as if drunken crowd, rolling from side to side. . . .

And leaning back on the wind as if on an upended couch I clutched my béret and roared with laughter . . . We were just under the great wall that keeps out the intolerably swift Rhone . . . Our treasurer's cap was flying in the air . . . Over, into the Rhone . . . What glorious fun . . . The mistral sure is the wine of life . . . Our treasurer's wallet was flying from under an armpit beyond reach of a clutching hand . . . Incredible humour; unparalleled buffoonery of a wind . . . The air was full of little, capricious squares, floating black against the light over the river . . . Like a swarm of bees: thick . . . Good fellows, bees. . . .

And then began a delirious, panicked search . . . For notes, for passports, for first citizenship papers that were halfway to Marseilles before it ended . . . An endless search . . . With still the feeling that one was rich . . . Very rich. With enough money in French notes to keep us in *Châteauneuf du Pape* for five years . . . And 1929 at that . . . But all the money is in the Rhone . . . It's nevertheless *my* money . . . Look, there's a thousand franc note . . . And a ten . . . And a first citizenship paper . . . And the blue and white patchbox that once belonged to Napoleon . . . Napoleon did his first service in the castle across the Rhone . . . Peep over the parapet at the Rhone . . . It is grey . . . It flows at a hundred miles an hour . . . My ducats . . . My daughter . . . Waiting at home over the Mediterranean, poor child . . . For ducats. . . .

I can no more . . . *Je ne peux plus* . . . What is that stone face with blind, relentless eyes? . . . That gives and takes away . . . *C'est le Destin* . . . We are people accursed . . . We shall never climb again up *this* slope . . . It was the riding that did it . . . Search through that patch of thistles under the wall again . . . We found a thousand. There *must* be others. . . .

No, not the Café de Paris . . . The coffee is twenty-five centimes dearer there than that at the café of M. Bonhoure . . . He wants me to buy a litre of his supreme oil of lavender from the Alps . . . I don't see why I shouldn't and have enough to make lavender water for two hundred years . . . Only five hun . . . No, but there's a reason . . . You see "75" on the saucer . . . Seventy-five centimes . . . It's a franc at the Café de Paris. . . .

I hadn't been going to do any writing for a year. For two. Perhaps not for ever if I could have laid that money out on a little bastide with an acre or so and a good, always flowing noria . . . But perhaps the remorseless Destiny of Provence desires thus to afflict the world with my books. . . .

The Great View from Italy into Provence

INDEX

A

Abbey Theatre players, 194-5
Abbey, Westminster, 23
Academe, 240
Academicians, Royal, 143-4, 146
Academy, Royal, Exhibition of British Art, 148, 224, 234
Adoration des Bergers by Campin, 328
Agnèse, Ste, 118
Aigues Mortes, 201
Aïoli, 278
Aix-en-Provence, 66, 96, 101, 159, 205, 207, 225, 235
Alaric, 113, 115, 135
Albi, 126, 128, 178
Albigenses, 80, 85, 102, 114, 122-34, 144, 149, 150, 159, 171, 174, 180, 202, 297, 299, 304, 306
Alboin, K. of Lombards, 115
Aletz, 176
Alexander, Sir George, 190-1, 196
Algiers, Dey of, 91
Aliscamps, 83-4, 86
Alphonse, I., K. of Aragon, 205
Alpilles (Alpines), 27, 54, 82, 118, 293
Alps, 128, 165, 166, 212-3, 258, 302
Alsace, 134
Amadeus VII, D. of Savoy, 205
Amalaric, 115
Amauri, Bishop of Cîteaux, 178
Amis and Amile, 143
Anabaptists, 127
Angers, 207

Anglais, Promenade des, 15, 155
Anglo-maniac, French, 316-20
Anglo-Saxondom, 16, 68, 170
Anglo-Saxons, 46, 62, 114, 324
Anjou, 69, 201
Anjou, Charles Ct., K. of Provence, 202-3
Annunciation by Brederlamm, 328
Antibes, 49, 186
Antipolis, 49, 186
Aquae Sextiae, Battle of, 96
Arabia, 117
Aragon, 176, 229-30
Arbaud, Joseph, 71-3
Archimedes, 307
Arianism, 126, 134
Aristophanes, 186
Arles, 14, 26, 31, 42, 54, 82-6, 101, 104, 111, 115, 124, 126, 128, 136, 159; Council of, 175, 176, 201, 212
Arms and the Man, 194
Arthur, King, 179, 284
Arundel, 288
Asquith Cabinet, 61
Astolf, K. of Lombards, 116-17
Athenaeum Club, 155
Athénée Ouvrier, Marseilles, 159
Athens, 17, 164, 186
Aubry des Trois Fontaines, 177-8
Aucassin and Nicolette, 15, 142, 167-9, 176, 185
Augustus, Emperor, 95, 97
Aurelius, Marcus, Emp., 19, 102-3
Authorized Version, 79
Auvergne, Peire d', 149

INDEX

INDEX

INDEX

INDEX

INDEX

INDEX

INDEX

INDEX

INDEX

INDEX